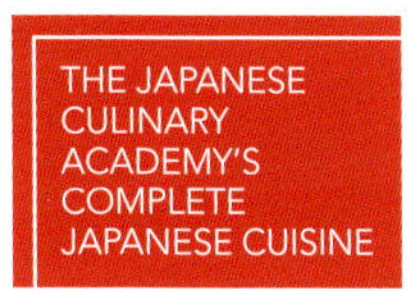

INTRODUCTION TO JAPANESE CUISINE

Nature, History and Culture

INTRODUCTION TO JAPANESE CUISINE

Nature, History and Culture

JAPANESE CULINARY ACADEMY

THE COVER AND CHAPTER TITLE PAGES present samples of paper dyed in distinctive colors by YOSHIOKA Sachio (1946–2019) was the fifth generation of a line of master dyers of Kyoto. Yoshioka was known for his technique of using the plant dyes used for colors passed down from the past to create beautiful original colors. The intense red of the cover, *hi*, associated with the color of a sacred flame; a vermillion red he calls *ake* evokes the glowing shades of the sun's orb (p. 8), the fresh green of spring pulses in *moegi* (p. 30), bright *murasaki* purple has been a symbol of nobility from ancient times (p. 56), *ruri* recalls the blue of lapis lazuli and deep seas (p. 84), the indescribable *nibi* is a gray color seen since the Heian period (p. 94), and finally *imayo*, a spirited pink that was fashionable in the Heian period (p. 136).

p. 2 *Rice, Hemp, and Cotton*, by Maruyama Okyo, 1791
Below: Back of sword guard. Inscribed on front: "Rice tassel and mouse openwork *tsuba*. By Kogitsune (Little Fox), resident of Echizen province."

NOTE: Japanese names in this book are given in traditional order, surname first.

Published by Japanese Culinary Academy
office@culinary-academy.jp
https://culinary-academy.jp/
#305 Eiwa Oike Bldg. 436 Sasayacho, Nakagyo-ku, Kyoto-shi, Kyoto 604-8187, Japan

Distributed in the United States and Canada by Kodansha USA Publishing, LLC.

Previously published by Shuhari Initiative Ltd.
2025 edition by Japanese Culinary Academy
Editorial supervision of both original and 2025 editions by the Japanese Culinary Academy

Published 2025
Printed in Japan

30 29 28 27 26 25 10 9 8 7 6 5 4 3 2 1

ISBN 978-4-911188-00-2

C O N T E N T S

PREFACE

MURATA Yoshihiro

Honorary Chairman, Japanese Culinary Academy

A little over 30 years ago, a group of ten Japanese chefs went to Paris and, in the dining room of a famous hotel, presented Japanese cuisine to a discriminating group that included members of the French nobility. They brought *all* their ingredients with them, from the kombu for dashi to the vegetables, the conger eel (*hamo*) and even a supply of soft water, and they did their utmost to prepare dishes no different from the very best they would have served in Japan. The meal was an overwhelming success and the chefs were interviewed on television. The event was hailed as marking the recognition of Japanese cuisine overseas.

It was a momentous achievement, and yet, at that time I was acutely aware of the limits of Japanese cuisine as we thought of it then. If all the ingredients had to be brought from Japan, how could we ever hope that Japanese cuisine would spread throughout the world?

Over the course of the past three decades, while running my own *ryotei* restaurant, I have been involved in the development and dissemination of Japanese cuisine. All the while my desire to introduce the world to its essential concepts and authentic techniques in a systematic and comprehensive manner has steadily increased. As the base for my activities I established a nonprofit organization called the Japanese Culinary Academy (JCA) in 2004. The JCA's main purpose is the advancement and spread of Japanese cuisine. The academy's membership extends beyond chefs to scholars in specialized fields such as the history of Japanese culture and the science of taste. We hold regular laboratory research sessions to further the scientific understanding of Japanese cuisine and we offer training and workshops to foster the development of Japanese food culture and sponsor a variety of activities about healthful foodways targeted at younger generations. We also offer training programs for chefs from overseas who want to learn Japanese cuisine. In these programs, they can approach Japanese food from many different angles; chefs visit workshops where professionals sharpen kitchen knives; they perform cooking demonstrations, learn directly from farmers about how to select the most appropriate vegetables, and are taught by fishermen how to spike fish.

Today there are more than 90,000 Japanese restaurants around the world, and only a few of them are run by Japanese. That does not count against them, of course; chefs do not have to be Japanese to cook the food properly. If Japanese cuisine is to truly spread across the world, then what really matters is the correct transmission of Japanese cooking skills, its positive impact on foodways and people's health, and hopefully also the use of basic ingredients from Japan like rice and fish.

This volume serves as the prologue to a multi-volume set, *The Japanese Culinary Academy's Complete Japanese Cuisine*, compiled mainly for professional cooks and chefs in Japan and around the world. With essays, photographs, and other materials introducing the Japanese natural environment and landscape, history, culture, and basic culinary techniques, this volume is intended to provide a unified understanding of and comprehensive introduction to the background and context within which the arts, techniques, and wisdom of Japanese cuisine have developed. True appreciation of a cuisine begins by gaining an understanding of such background. *The Complete Japanese Cuisine*, therefore, is not a how-to guide but rather sets forth the fundamentals and the scientific facts behind important traditions, showing how certain tastes and cooking methods developed—not just as a result of experience and intuition, but also for logical and scientific reasons. We hope that this information will be of use to cooks as they think about and incorporate this knowledge in developing their own original cuisine. In the same way that students of the tea ceremony have to learn the spirit of tea before they can build upon its traditions, those who learn about Japanese cuisine will be better able to devise their own principles for healthy and fine dining.

Since 2013, when *washoku*, "the traditional dietary cultures of the Japanese" was inscribed on the UNESCO list of Intangible Cultural Heritage of Humanity, international interest in Japanese cuisine and culture has risen to new heights. It is my sincere hope that this work will support the advancement and spread of Japanese cuisine and its contribution to the health and happiness of people everywhere. As a professional chef I hope, too, that it will help open new doors in Japanese cuisine for people of the century to come.

What Is Japanese Cuisine?

KUMAKURA Isao
Historian

[朱]
Ake

Japanese cuisine is sustained by the rich variety of ingredients available from fertile seas and land. Japanese people are attuned to nature and keenly aware of their reliance on its bounty. They express gratitude for the blessings of nature with the customary expressions "Itadakimasu"—I gratefully receive the blessings of this food—before eating and "Gochisosama"—I have partaken of the feast—after eating. Japanese cuisine is also a canvas for the beauty of nature. Distinct changes accompany the four seasons, and enjoyment of those changes provides the underlying motifs for Japanese arts, crafts and literature. In cuisine as well, reoccurring patterns and references, like the plum and cherry blossoms of spring, express attention to the beauty of the seasons.

One of the appealing qualities of Japanese food is that it is healthy. Relatively few ingredients contain animal fat, and those that do, like fish, are sources of largely unsaturated fats, which are good for the body. This cuisine is closely tied to traditions that cement ties in the family and community.

Japanese cuisine, which developed in tandem with a respect for nature, is centered around rice as a staple food. In the case of the fine kaiseki food served in restaurants, sake—alcohol made from rice—often takes the place of cooked rice, but for ordinary household meals rice and soup are the basic dishes, eaten together with side dishes and pickles. There are two main kinds of rice: so-called *uruchimai* or non-glutinous rice and *mochi-gome* or glutinous rice, and it is *uruchimai* that is used for making sake, vinegar, and miso, as well as the cooked rice eaten at meals. *Mochi-gome* is an indispensable food that is used for *mochi* and sweets, and for steaming with red adzuki beans to make the auspicious "red rice" (*sekihan*) for celebratory occasions.

The basic flavor of Japanese food is umami. Umami has been shown to be the "fifth taste," distinct from the four scientifically identified tastes of sweetness, sourness, saltiness, and bitterness. In order to accentuate the umami in ingredients, the Japanese succeeded some 500 years ago in mastering techniques for making dashi so that only the umami elements from kombu and dried bonito flakes are released. Around 200 to 300 years ago, a great many cookbooks were published, and most of them stressed the importance of using good dashi and recorded the methods for making it. This deep attachment to dashi led to Japanese scientist Ikeda Kikunae's 1908 discovery of monosodium glutamate (MSG), which is the umami element in kombu. Broth made from *katsuobushi* bonito flakes and kombu remains the basic flavoring for Japanese food, but it is difficult to make properly without using the soft water prevalent in Japan.

Water in Japan drains from mountain regions over comparatively short distances before flowing into the sea, so hard water resulting from seepage through rock is scarce and most water is soft and quite free of impurities. Water commands a very important position in Japanese cuisine, as evidenced by preparation techniques that use large quantities of water such as soaking to remove bitterness (*sarasu*) or rinsing to tighten fiber (*shimeru*). Foods like tofu and vegetables like daikon may contain more than 90 percent water, also demonstrating the extent to which Japanese food depends on abundant supplies of good, fresh water.

SPRING

春

あいなめ二種 えんどうスープ *Ainame Nishu Endo Soup*

Fat Greenling Two Ways in Pea Soup

Key to this dish featuring the fat greenling (*Hexagrammos otakii*) is the use of two cooking methods: parboiling and frying, allowing one to experience different textures from a single ingredient.

The vibrant green of the peas evokes spring. When food is served, appearance and aroma first capture our senses. Here, the green draws the eye irresistibly, the fresh fragrance of *kinome* leaves wafts from the bowl. With the very first bite one can appreciate the different textures of fat greenling. The accompanying *hoshiko* here are dried sea cucumber ovaries that add even greater diversity of texture and taste to the dish. RECIPE P. 184

造り 鯛鹿の子、烏賊、トロ
Tsukuri Tai-kanoko, Ika, Toro

Sashimi: *Kanoko* Sea Bream, Squid, and Fatty Tuna

A selection of spring fish, served as sashimi. Cuts are made in the sea bream's fatty skin to create a grid-like pattern known as *kanoko-giri* ("dappled fawn cut"). The squid is scored with vertical lines on the outside and diagonal ones on the inside, offering two different sensory experiences.

The serving plates are 400-year-old Chinese Tianqi porcelain *ko-sometsuke*, known as "leaf plates." Each has a different shape, these differences adding an extra dimension to be appreciated. Cherry blossom petals scattered round complete the vernal theme. RECIPE **p. 184**

Detail of a restaurant screen (*byobu*). The motifs on the screen are inspired by a grand cherry blossom viewing party thrown by the famous warrior leader Toyotomi Hideyoshi (1537–1598) at the height of his power.

Bamboo shoots whose tips have just broken through the soil are carefully separated from the root and unearthed.

Young bamboo shoots (*takenoko*) are indispensable for a spring menu. Once bamboo sprouts, it grows very rapidly, so the season for obtaining the young shoots is over within a few weeks, the short span increasing its cachet as one of the leading tastes of spring.

Soon after being cut from the root, the bamboo shoot produces a bitterness that only increases the longer it is left before cooking. Bamboo shoots are best parboiled immediately, right in the husk, although boiling too long will ruin the precious flavor and aroma for which it is prized. Pale colored, tender textured Kyoto grown *takenoko* are a particular spring delicacy. Farmers spread straw over the clay-rich soil and pile soil on top of the straw to nurture the bamboo plants that produce the shoots.

焼き筍 *Yaki Takenoko*

Baked Bamboo Shoots

Bamboo shoots fresh from the ground are parboiled to remove any bitterness, then placed unpeeled straight in the oven. Once cooked, the shoots are sprinkled with *kinome* Japanese pepper leaf buds to complete a spring treat that celebrates their delectable juiciness. RECIPE **p. 184**

SUMMER

夏

冷製 豆冬瓜すっぽんけんちん
Reisei Mame-togan Suppon Kenchin

Chilled Turtle *Kenchin* in Mini Winter Melon

A medley of ingredients such as sautéed daikon radish, carrot and wood ear mushroom mixed with tofu and then seasoned is known as *kenchin*. *Kenchin* encompasses a variety of dishes, *kenchin* broth being a well-known example. Steamed *Kenchin*-style dishes often consist of white fish stuffed with a *kenchin* mixture, however in this recipe, the fish is replaced with winter melon for a more summery feel. Mildly flavored and almost entirely water, winter melon is a summer favorite. The kudzu sauce on top creates a vision of icy coolness. RECIPE **p. 185**

夏の八寸 *Natsu no Hassun*

Summer Hassun

There are various ways to arrange food on ice, such as in split bamboo stalks or on small glass plates, and the dishes here are served on summer flora: lotus leaves, flower petals, Chinese lanterns. The contrast of green, pink and orange makes for a visually vibrant creation.

RECIPE **p. 185**

秋

AUTUMN

かます杉板焼き *Kamasu Sugiita-yaki*

Barracuda in Smoldering Cedar Shavings

Barracuda (*kamasu*), deliciously fat by autumn, are steeped in a miso *Yuan-ji* marinade that amplifies the flavor. Wrapping the ingredients in thin cedar shavings preserves their quality and also imparts a delectable cedar fragrance. The cedar shavings are lit when they come out of the oven and gently smoulder on a carpet of autumn leaves, smoke rising in a sight that recalls memories of autumns past. RECIPE **p. 187**

半月縁高 *Hangetsu Fuchidaka*

Half-moon *Fuchidaka*

A *fuchidaka* is a type of lacquered wooden dish with raised edges (*fuchi*). Originally stacked boxes, *fuchidaka* were used to hold the *omogashi* ("main sweets") served with thick *koicha* tea. These days, however, it is more common to use larger versions with lids to serve cooked foods other than confections. Removing the lid reveals a splendid array of treats, adding an extra level of anticipation to the meal. **RECIPE p. 187**

冬
WINTER

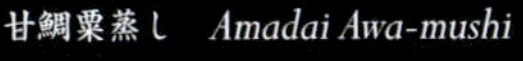

甘鯛粟蒸し *Amadai Awa-mushi*

Tilefish Steamed with Millet

Japanese prayers for bountiful crops traditionally focus on five kinds of grain: rice, wheat, foxtail millet (*awa*), Japanese barnyard millet (*hie*), and legumes. When steamed and pounded, *awa* becomes sticky like *mochi* (glutinous rice cakes). *Domyoji*, a flour made from glutinous rice, is then added to give it a softer texture. The resulting dough is used to wrap umami-rich ingredients such as tilefish and shiitake mushrooms, steamed, and topped with *an* sauce enriched with edible chrysanthemum greens. RECIPE P. 188

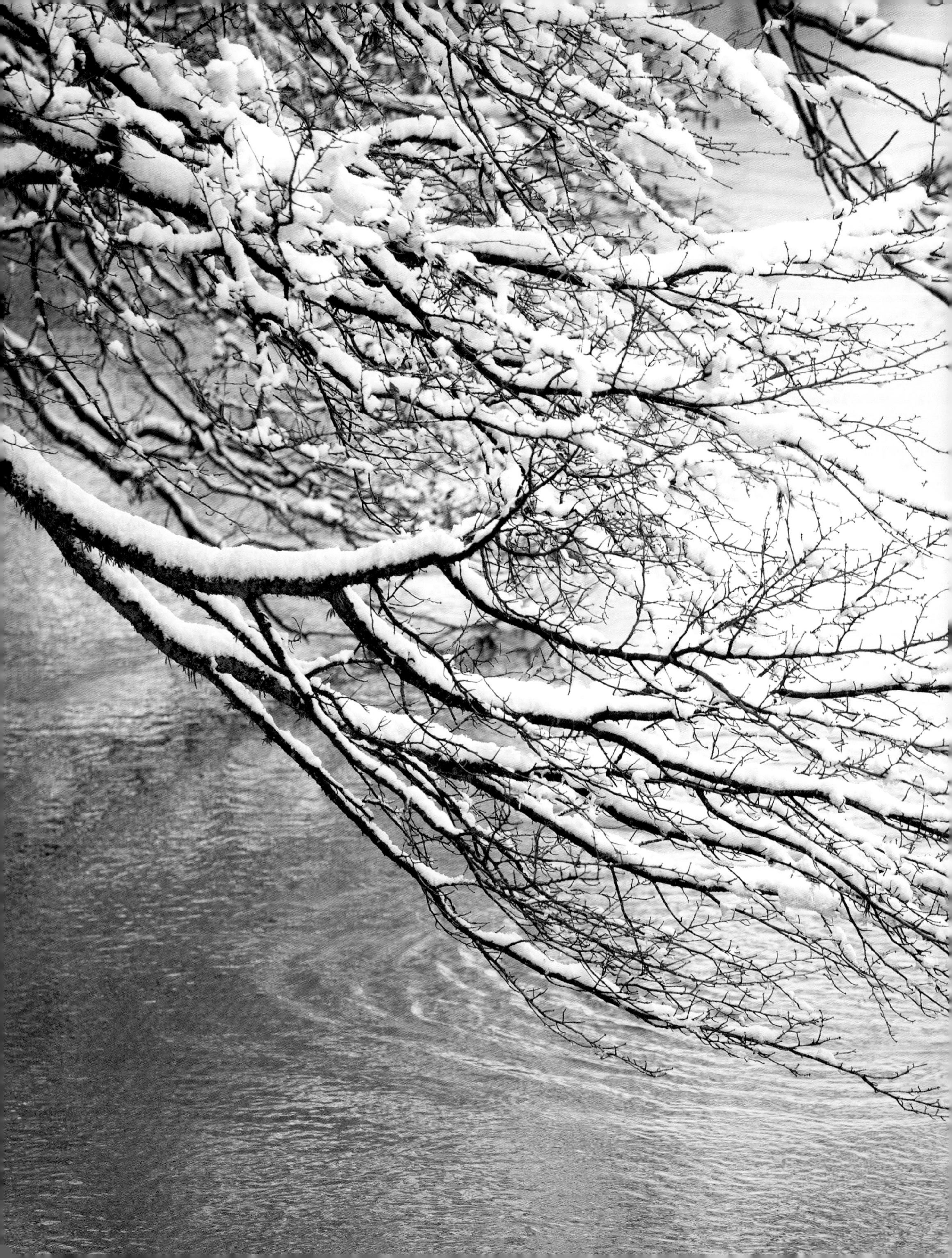

鴨真丈薄氷仕立て *Kamo Shinjo Usugori-jitate*

Duck Dumplings in Icy Pond

A delicate, almost transparent slice of turnip covers the surface of the soup, giving it the appearance of a thin layer of ice. While it looks icy, this "pond" surprises with its unexpected heat. Under the "ice," fragrant mugwort *kusamochi* rice cakes, daikon radish, carrot, and other ingredients cut into plum blossom shapes add color, heralding the imminent arrival of spring. RECIPE P. 189

Chapter 1

NATURE AND CLIMATE

A great variety of fresh food ingredients is available in Japan, with its regional diversity, changing seasons, and fertile soil. The moist climate led to the development of distinctive types of fermented seasonings like miso and soy sauce that have become essential seasonings for traditional dishes. This chapter introduces the characteristics of Japanese cuisine influenced by the natural environment and climate.

[萌黄]
Moegi

Food and the Natural Environment

The approximately 3,500 islands that make up the Japanese archipelago stretch from subarctic Hokkaido in the north to subtropical Okinawa in the south. These varied climates nurture a rich variety of plants. The convoluted coastline, extending for a total of about 36,000 kilometers, provides habitats for many species of seaweed, fish, and shellfish. Warm and cold-water currents meet in the seas that surround Japan both in the Sea of Japan and in the Pacific Ocean, creating ideal fishing grounds. As many as 4,000 species of saltwater and freshwater fish are found in the waters, rivers, and lakes, with roughly 300 species commonly sold at fish markets throughout the country.

Approximately 70 percent of Japan's total land area is mountainous. Most of the land is covered with forests and the average annual rainfall is 1,700 ml—more than double the global average. This damp climate nourishes the many species of wild and domesticated vegetables that form an important part of people's diets. One could say that the topography itself is the point of departure for Japanese cuisine.

Japan is located in the warm monsoon zone and has clearly differentiated seasons. Haiku, the well-known poetic form, expresses people's close relationship to the changing seasons. The most famous of all haiku masters, Matsuo Basho (1644–1694), once said that being "in tune with the four seasons" was the essence of the Japanese aesthetic. This sense of intimate connection with the seasons and the urge to capture their beauty are major themes in Japanese art. It is an important element of poetry and narrative literature, as well as kabuki, noh, the

tea ceremony, and ikebana. An appreciation of the seasons and the wish to share their beauty with one's guests are also integral to the culinary heritage.

The wet climate is key to Japan's rich tradition of fermented foods. The mixture of rice and *koji* mold known as *bara-koji* is unique to Japan. It is notable for its use in making sake and essential ingredients like miso and soy sauce. Sake is brewed using a method known as parallel fermentation (*heiko fuku-hakko*) (see p. 41). Miso is made in a number of types distinctive to particular regions, including the sweeter white miso made with a higher proportion of rice, red miso made using barley, and darker miso which consists primarily of soybeans. Soy sauce, too, comes in lighter (*usukuchi*) and darker (*koikuchi*) varieties that are used differently depending upon the region.

Important among fermented foods are the pickles known as *tsukemono*. Originally, people preserved vegetables by pickling them in salt, but today *tsukemono* are made in a wide variety of ways that include healthy options like *nukazuke* (in which vegetables are fermented in a rice-bran-based mixture) and *umezuke* (pickled plums). Another distinctive fermented food is *natto*. *Natto* is made by fermenting soybeans with *bacillus subtilis*. Its characteristic texture and smell may not appeal to all tastes, but *natto* has attracted a growing following in Western countries in recent years.

Agriculture and Gratitude to the Gods

Sowing seeds of "sacred rice" (*yudane*) in a special field at Ise Shrine. Grown with extra special care until it is harvest time in the autumn, the rice is presented as the offering of newly harvested rice to Amaterasu Omikami, the main deity of the shrine. The seed sowing is accompanied by a chorus singing a field-planting song (*mitauta*) passed down from ancient times.

Japanese agricultural festivals can be divided into two broad categories: those held in the spring to pray for successful crops and those celebrating the autumn harvest. Other important ceremonies take place between these two major periods, including rituals performed to rid the fields of harmful pests and ceremonies to protect crops from sun damage or heavy rain.

The first ceremonies of the year take place in Shinto shrines in the depths of winter, long before work in the fields begins, when people pray for a successful season by imitating the act of planting rice. Around April, when work in the paddies begins, it was once customary to celebrate with *dengaku*, dance and music performed on the ridges between the paddies. These ritual performances are thought to be part of the traditions that developed into today's noh drama. Wet-field rice farming is highly dependent on the weather and forces beyond human control can determine the success or failure of the year's crop. Such ceremonial observances can be seen as efforts to receive the protection of the Buddhist and Shinto deities. Agricultural festivals testify to both people's belief that spirits (*kami*) are present in all things as well as the awareness that people live within nature rather than outside it.

Sheaves of the first rice, harvested according to the Nuibosai rite, are laid into storage with care and gratitude until the Kannamesai harvest ritual is held. (see pp. 60–61)

Summer brings many insects and pests that pose a serious threat to farmers' crops. Ceremonies and dances known as *mushi-okuri* (literally, "sending off the insects") are performed to encourage pests to go elsewhere. The dances performed at O-bon around the fifteenth day of the seventh month of the lunar calendar were also originally part of a festival that accompanied these rituals. Summer is also a time of scorching temperatures. During unbroken periods of particularly intense heat, people might hold a festival to pray for rain. The Gion Festival (see p. 156) that takes place in Kyoto every July was originally such a rain festival.

Once autumn arrives, many kinds of ceremonies are held to celebrate the year's harvest. The Niinamesai is observed in the imperial palace on November 23rd when sake made with the year's new rice is offered to the gods to give thanks for a successful harvest. People make similar offerings of new rice and freshly brewed sake at shrines throughout the country. The Ae no Koto ceremony performed in Ishikawa prefecture in the Hokuriku region is a harvest ceremony that has been designated an Intangible Cultural Heritage by UNESCO. After the harvest, local people bring the god of the rice fields—though invisible to them—into their homes out of gratitude for the deity's protection of the community's crops during the preceding season. They offer the deity a hot bath and prepare a special banquet of offerings (the word *ae* means "banquet" or "feast"). Throughout the banquet, people treat the god as an honored (if invisible) guest. The god is housed throughout the winter and then returned to the fields in the spring in time for the planting of the new year's rice.

Agriculture, and particularly wet-field rice cultivation, is the foundation of Japanese cuisine, and similar ceremonies are observed all over the country. People make offerings of local produce, and then consume them with the gods in local celebrations on designated days of the traditional calendar.

The Blessings of Water

An abundant supply of fresh water is vital to Japanese cuisine. Thanks to the Asian monsoon climate, Japan's annual rainfall is plentiful and stable. Relatively early in history, people learned to harness this ready supply of fresh water to cultivate rice. Cascading from the steep mountain terrain that covers the islands, the water of rivers and streams runs rapidly, keeping it fresh and clean. Dutch civil engineer Johannis de Rijke, who helped the Meiji government modernize its riparian works in the late nineteenth century, famously described Japan's rivers as "more like waterfalls." With such rich resources, water was used freely throughout the country and it has played a key role in food preparation since early times.

As early as the Jomon period 10,000 years ago (ca. 10,000–300 B.C.), the inhabitants of Japan soaked (*sarasu*) acorns, nuts, and edible wild plants of the forest in running water for several days to remove unpleasant bitterness and toxins. Even today widely used sources of starch like *kudzu*, arrowroot powder, and *warabi* (bracken; fiddlehead fern) are produced by steeping plant roots in large amounts of water. Washing and rinsing is also an important part of making *konnyaku*, the *konnyaku*-potato gel used in a variety of simmered dishes.

The traditional technique of soaking or rinsing in water is also useful for processing ingredients other than vegetables. The flesh of cod and other fish meat can be shredded, soaked and rinsed in fresh water to remove unwanted flavors, then kneaded into a paste to make *kamaboko*, an everyday source of protein. The paste is formed into various shapes and then steamed. The quality of the water can make a big difference in the flavor of the finished product. Fresh water, of course, is commonly used in many areas of daily life to wash away impurities and toxins, hence the development of the spiritual sense of "purification" by water that is closely tied to the Japanese valorization of cleanliness.

Even today, many recipes and cooking techniques used in Japanese cuisine require large amounts of water. The cooked rice that is integral to most meals is steamed. Tofu, a frequent feature of the daily diet, consists of at least 90 percent water. It is often eaten just as it is, with the addition of a simple garnish or seasoning. Tea is prepared with hot water, and no additional flavors or scents are added. To make traditional dashi stock, which brings out the fundamental flavors of Japanese cuisine, hot water is used to extract umami and other subtle flavors from kombu and *katsuobushi* (bonito flakes). *Kanten* agar, a solidified polysaccharide extracted from seaweed that consists of more than 95 percent water, is often used in traditional confections and other dishes. In all of these cases, the quality of the water strongly affects the flavor.

The water present in most regions of Japan is relatively soft according to World Health Organization criteria, generally varying within the range of 30 to 60 milligrams of calcium carbonate equivalent per liter and with low levels of calcium and magnesium (in comparison, the hardness values of water for some of the leading brands of mineral water are as follows: Volvic 60, Evian 300, Contrex 1500). Many ingredients and techniques in Japanese cuisine rely on soft water's particular qualities. It readily penetrates kombu, helping to release umami. Attempts to

make good dashi with hard water will be less successful. Soft water is also ideal for brewing sake.

Confidence in an ample supply of fresh, pure water is reflected in the frequency with which ingredients are eaten raw in Japanese cuisine. Methods of preparation like sashimi, in which fish and shellfish are simply rinsed in fresh water before being sliced up and enjoyed raw, and *arai*, in which slices of freshwater fish like carp and *funa* (crucian carp) or saltwater fish like *tai* (sea bream) and *suzuki* (sea bass) are rinsed in ice water, require faith in and reverence for the natural purity of the water supply.

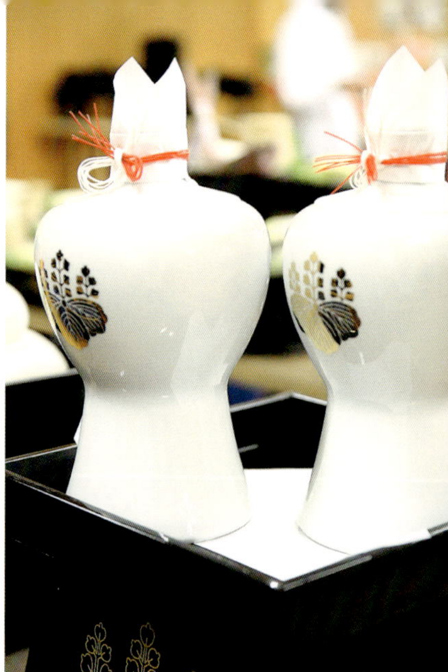

Purified sake (*omiki*) and special flasks (*omiki-dokuri*) for offerings of sake. Sake that has been offered to the gods is thought to be imbued with the spirit of the divine. By drinking *omiki*, one imbibes power of the gods.

Sake and Water

Water quality is crucial to sake brewing. Sake is made from very simple ingredients: rice, *koji*, yeast, and a lot of water. Because sake is not a distilled spirit, the main ingredient, water, has a major impact on the flavor of the finished product. In fact, many established brewing centers that have long been famous for their sake—Nada in Hyogo prefecture, Fushimi (Kyoto), Hiroshima, Suwa (Nagano), Aizu (Fukushima) and Akita—are located in places with ready access to water considered ideal for sake brewing.

The mineral content of water differs from region to region according to the nature of the soil. It is now understood that for sake brewing a rich mineral content is even more important than soft water. This mineral content stimulates the *koji* and yeast, encouraging their growth. Variation in the mineral composition of the water used is one factor that gives each sake its individual flavor.

People began to understand the importance of water in sake brewing during the Edo period. In 1840, the owner of several sake breweries in the Nada area noticed that the sake made in one of his breweries always tasted different from that made in another. After looking into various possible explanations, he became convinced that the difference had to do with the water being used and decided to conduct an experiment to prove it decisively. Brewery records from the time show that when the water the two breweries used was switched, the qualities of the sake produced changed accordingly, even though the brewing process in each brewery had remained the same. The water that produced the superior sake became known as "Miya-mizu" after the place where the brewery well was located, in the town of Nishinomiya. Miya-mizu became a byword for good sake water.

Beginning in the 1920s, a number of scientific surveys looked into the reasons why Miya-mizu produced such good sake. They found that the well was located at the confluence of three subterranean rivers. Very little rainwater got into this underground water system, which also had only minimal contact with seawater. Among the geological strata in the region was a layer formed from ancient shell mounds. Minerals from the shells must have been absorbed into the water and made it ideal for sake. An analysis of the water revealed higher levels of calcium, magnesium, phosphorus, and potassium than the average water in Japan, and extremely low levels of iron.

Compared to the relatively hard, mineral-rich water of Nada, the water found in Fushimi, another famous sake producing area, is soft, containing only 30 milligrams of calcium carbonate equivalent per liter. This mineral composition moderates the action of the yeast during fermentation. Perhaps because of this, while the sake produced in Nada has traditionally been seen as "masculine," sake from Fushimi has been regarded as milder and more "feminine" in character. Hiroshima, another area with soft water, also produces well-regarded sake with qualities similar to that found in Fushimi.

Today, scientific understandings of *koji* mold, yeast, and brewing methods have advanced to the point that water quality is no longer necessarily a decisive factor in making good sake. But expectations that sake from particular regions will possess a certain flavor profile continue to be important, and in that sense it is fair to say that water continues to define the individual characteristics of sake from different regions.

The Culture of Sake

Sake has been perceived as sacred since ancient times. It still plays a leading role in festivals and is central to *naorai*, the practice of partaking of food and drink that has been ritually offered to the gods. The sacred nature of sake is derived from the fact that its main ingredient, rice, is highly valued. Japanese marriage ceremonies generally take place in a Shinto shrine, and the ritual exchange of cups of sake between bride and groom before the altar of the *kami* is a traditional part of the ceremony still celebrated today. Sake is also often used as a celebratory gift and continues to play a role in toasts and formal gatherings.

The *Engishiki*, a tenth-century code of legal and customary procedures, contains a description of the brewing process, noting that steamed rice was mixed with *koji* mold and water to form a mixture called the *shikomi*. This was allowed to ferment and then, after being filtered, fresh rice and *koji* were added. This process of filtering and adding rice and *koji* was repeated a number of times.

The ingredients used in sake brewing remain unchanged today: steamed rice, water, *koji*, and yeast. Japan's abundant supplies of soft water, containing a moderate amount of minerals, contribute to the production of good sake. *Koji* mold is used to break down the starch in the rice and convert it into sugars. The *koji* used today is cultured from strains painstakingly selected from the many quality molds developed throughout the long history of brewing in Japan. During the brewing process, rice primed with *koji* is added to steamed rice and water and a carefully selected yeast is added to start the fermentation process. After fermentation is complete, the sake is carefully filtered and bottled and in most cases is consumed within a year. In addition to the continued use of naturally occurring yeasts present in the brewery that give each sake its unique characteristics, modern brewers use genetic analysis to develop effective and superior strains. Scientists have now obtained a full genetic analysis of the main strains of sake yeast.

The *toji*, or master brewer, monitors and manages the brewing process. It is no exaggeration to say that the *toji*'s vision and experience determine the characteristics of each brewery's sake. The individual skills and techniques of *toji* have been handed down from generation to generation at each brewery. Even today, when machines have taken over much of the work of controlling fermentation, the *toji* continues to be an important presence in every brewery, either as a full-time employee or as a skilled technician hired for the winter brewing season. A change of *toji* can result in major changes in a brewery's flavor profile.

The special varieties of rice used in sake brewing differ somewhat from the rice served at meals. Rice with a small depression in the starchy portion of the center of the grain is preferred for brewing. The outer layers of the rice contain proteins that can impart unwanted flavors. To avoid this, the rice is normally milled before use. According to Japanese law, the most highly refined sake, made with rice milled to remove at least 50 percent of the rice kernel, can be labeled *daiginjo*. Similarly, the term *ginjo* may be used for sake made with rice with at least 40 percent of the kernel removed. Sake whose alcohol content comes from the fermentation of rice alone (with no addition of distilled alcohol) is known as *junmai* (pure rice sake). Sake made from rice milled to at least 30 percent, to which distilled alcohol has been added in order to achieve a desired flavor, is known as *honjozo*.

The alcohol percentage of undiluted sake can be 21 percent or more, more than any other fermented beverage in the world. One distinctive characteristic of the sake brewing process (*heiko fuku-hakko*) is the unique fermentation method used, in which two distinct processes take place simultaneously. While the starch is converted into sugar by the *koji* mold, the sugars are fermented and turned into alcohol by the yeast. The *toji* needs to be highly skilled to control these processes and ensure that the end product comes out as planned. Of course, not every *toji*'s vision of the "best" sake is the same. The different tastes and visions of an individual *toji* lead to a wide variety of sakes, each with its own characteristics and personality.

The wide range of sake flavors arises from the diversity of brewing methods employed and the many different varieties of rice used. In recent years people have started to take advantage of this diversity and pair different types of sake with particular foods in a manner similar to that traditionally done with wine.

The deity of Matsunoo Grand Shrine in Kyoto is known as the god of sake brewing. With prayers for the prosperity of their business, breweries from all over Japan donate large casks of sake (seen in storage here) to the shrine. Adding water from the well on the grounds is said to ensure that the sake will never be cloudy, so many breweries add small portions obtained from the shrine as a good luck charm.

白鶴
白雪
瑞泉
住吉
神鷹
福寿
両関
龍力
旭日
樽平
櫻正宗
千代の園
白蘭
國盛
TAMAGAWA

Fermented Seasonings

Warm temperatures, abundant rainfall, and high humidity provide good conditions for the development of a wide variety of fermented foods in Asian cuisines. Many of the traditional fermented foodstuffs used in Japanese cuisine, including miso and soy sauce, originated in China and have evolved in distinctive ways and played a vital role in shaping contemporary food culture.

A traditional meal consists of rice or an other source of carbohydrate such as barley, a soup made with miso or other flavoring ingredients, pickles, and a number of small side dishes made with meat or seafood and vegetables. The seasonings traditionally used to flavor these dishes—the most important of which are soy sauce, miso, vinegar, sake, and mirin—are all fermented products. Even *honkarebushi*, a style of *katsuobushi* dating back over 300 years, can be considered a type of fermented food, as its flavor is enhanced by the deliberate growth of a specific kind of mold.

Both soy sauce and miso have a strong umami flavor that comes from amino and nucleic acids produced by microorganisms in the fermentation process. Miso is made by mixing steamed soybeans, rice or other grains, *koji* and salt. This mixture is then fermented to produce a paste that can be kept for a long time without spoiling. The extended maturation process produces the brown melanoidins that give the finished miso its complex flavors. There are various types of miso. Pale in color and lower in salt, white miso is made with more rice *koji* than other types. Although it does not keep as long as some other types of miso, it is prized for its distinct flavor.

Miso is categorized according to the ingredients from which it is made. *Hatcho* miso from Aichi prefecture and other types of *mame* miso (bean miso) are made by adding *koji* to steamed soybeans (before salt is added) and the mixture is left to ferment and mature. *Mugi* miso contains barley in addition to soybeans and is especially popular in the western parts of the country, including Kyushu and areas bordering the Inland Sea. *Kome* miso is made with rice; though this type is common throughout the country, it is particularly associated with Hokkaido and the Tohoku and Kanto regions.

Alongside miso, the most important fermented condiment in Japanese cuisine is soy sauce (shoyu). The origins of soy sauce and miso can both be found in *kokubishio*, a salted condiment made from fermented soybeans that was brought to Japan from Korea and China in ancient times. From this shared point of origin, miso and soy sauce have followed different paths as they evolved into their present forms. Today, Japanese soy sauce is divided into two categories: lighter *usukuchi* soy sauce and darker *koikuchi* soy sauce. The origins of today's soy sauce go back to the sixteenth century, when it was produced from the liquids left over in barrels used to mature miso paste. *Koikuchi* soy sauce, the most popular seasoning used in Japanese cooking today, is traced back to the early years of seventeenth century (Edo period), where a similar condiment was developed in places like Choshi and Noda in what is today Chiba prefecture.

A traditional soy sauce fermenting storehouse. The mash called *moromi* made of crushed, steamed soybeans and other ingredients mixed with a fermenting agent (*koji*) is placed in wooden vats and stored for around one year. As the fermentation progresses, foam collects over the liquid.

Usukuchi soy sauce can be identified by its lighter color and high salt content. It was created in the seventeenth century in Tatsuno (present-day Hyogo prefecture). In Kyoto, Osaka, and other areas in the Kansai region people tried as much as they could to keep soups and *nimono* (simmered dishes) lighter in color for aesthetic reasons. This called for lighter-colored soy sauce with sufficient saltiness. Today's *usukuchi* soy sauce is made by adding larger amounts of salted water to maintain the *moromi* (unrefined soy sauce) at a low temperature and limit melanoidin production. Sometimes *amazake*, a sweet and low-alcohol liquid made by adding *koji* to rice to break down the starch into sugar, is also added to make the flavor of *usukuchi* soy sauce milder.

Scenes of the salting-down of *suguki* turnips. Pickled turnips (*sugukizuke*) are traditionally produced in Kamigamo, Kyoto. After they are salted down to remove any bitterness, the turnips are packed tightly in between layers of salt in wooden buckets and pressure is applied to the lids using a beam to which weights are attached (see. pp. 48-49). After a few days, the buckets are moved to a temperature-controlled chamber (*muro*) for fermentation for one to two weeks. *Suguki* contains a variety of lactobacillus bacteria that catalyzes a natural fermentation process.

Fermentation and Food Preservation

In areas of Asia that are considerably hot and humid, spoilage has always been a serious problem. In order to preserve foods in an environment where the propagation of microorganisms easily causes spoilage, early inhabitants developed and refined a number of food preservation techniques such as drying, smoking, and salting. Deliberate fermentation was particularly well developed. This works by selecting benign microorganisms that do not adversely affect flavor and allowing them to propagate, keeping the food safe from infestation by other microorganisms. In tropical regions such as Southeast Asia, there is a constant risk that lactic acid fermentation will proceed out of control and spoil food, giving it a strong acidic flavor. In the cooler Japanese climate, however, conditions are better suited for the preservation of a wide variety of foods via fermentation.

Pickling in salt is the oldest method of preserving food. Since Japan is surrounded by the sea, people throughout the country have always preserved vegetables and other foods by soaking them in saltwater. The lactobacillus species that ferments plant-based foods can survive even in high-saline environments. This allows for the creation of fermented foods in which cooked rice bran or another type of grain is added to vegetables or fish that have already been pickled in salt. The combined ingredients naturally begin to undergo lactic acid fermentation. This tradition survives into the present in the form of the pungent *funazushi* (believed to be the forerunner of modern sushi) and the pickled vegetables that can be found in great abundance and variety throughout the country. Many vegetables, including daikon radish, turnip, eggplant, and leafy greens, are used to make pickles. By adding discernible umami and salty flavors to meals built around the traditional staple of rice, these pickles have played an important role in Japanese food culture.

Another preservation technique entails encouraging of microorganisms naturally present in the atmosphere or found on dried rice plant leaves to proliferate in order to prevent fermentation by bacteria that could cause spoilage. This technique is used in Southeast Asia to produce tempeh and other types of non-salted fermented foods made from soybeans. In Japan *natto*, a popular fermented soybean product well known for the sticky strands that stretch from one bean to another, is a food that is also produced in this way.

Fermentation not only preserves foods, but it also improves flavor. A mold is deliberately added during the final stage of making of *katsuobushi*. Use of this technique expanded to fermented condiments like miso, soy sauce, and mirin. Today, fermentation may be less important as a means of preservation but it continues to be highly valued for the complex umami flavors it imparts to food.

After a preliminary salting to remove any bitterness, *suguki* turnips are salted down in wooden buckets; pressure is applied to the lids using a beam hung with weights.

Foods in Season

Scene of cormorant fishing, using trained cormorants, the traditional method for fishing for *ayu* (sweetfish).

Festivals and special events held throughout the year play a role in heightening people's awareness of the four seasons. Living in harmony with nature has been central to Japanese culture since ancient times.

"Shun" is an important term in the context of food. Used chiefly with regard to fresh foods, *shun* refers to the time of year when particular types of seafood or vegetables are at their best in terms of flavor and nutritional value. Appreciation of such foods at their *shun* is one way of consciously appreciating the succession of the seasons. The peak of the season for a particular ingredient is preceded by a period called *hashiri*, or "coming into season," and followed by a time called *nagori*, when one savors one last time the flavors that will not be tasted for another year. The same ingredient can therefore be enjoyed in at least three different forms by paying attention to the subtle differences between *hashiri*, *shun*, and *nagori*. While with *hashiri* one looks forward to the arrival of the coming season, *nagori* is tinged with sorrow and mingled with an anticipation of enjoying the same foods once again the following year.

More than just a reminder of the changing seasons, the periods of *hashiri*, *shun*, and *nagori* offer distinct gustatory pleasures. Perhaps the best-known example of *hashiri* is that of *katsuo*, or bonito. This fish is enjoyed in two quite different ways during the two seasons when it is most widely available in Japan. *Hatsugatsuo* ("first bonito") refers to bonito caught from spring to early summer, when the fish is typically less fatty and is best enjoyed lightly seared, *tataki* style. *Modorigatsuo* ("returning bonito") back in Japanese waters in the autumn, has built up larger reserves of tasty fat and is ideal for serving as sashimi. The freshwater *ayu* (sweetfish) is particularly cherished during its *nagori* phase. Summer is the *shun* for *ayu*, but *ochiayu*, caught in the spawning season when the fish are often laden with eggs, is one of the pleasures of late autumn. As a general rule, vegetables are soft during their *hashiri* phase and delicious when eaten raw. Fully ripe *nagori* vegetables, on the other hand, often have a profoundly rich, sweet flavor. The same ingredients, therefore, vary in taste depending on the time of year.

The tradition of *deaimono*, in which specific seasonal ingredients are served together, is another typical way of enjoying the seasons and nature's bounty. Particularly famous is the combination of peak-season (*shun*) *matsutake* mushrooms and *nagori*-phase *hamo* (pike eel). *Matsutake* have a special aroma and a crunchy texture at their peak that harmonize perfectly with *hamo* at its succulent best—a pleasure that can be experienced only in the autumn.

Nowadays, although improved crop varieties and developments in refrigerated transportation technology mean that many ingredients are available year-round, people continue to appreciate seasonal foods. This enjoyment of nature and the passing seasons is one of the most distinctive aspects of Japanese cuisine and food culture.

鮎の塩焼き *Ayu Shio-yaki*

Salt-Grilled Sweetfish

A symbol of summer, sweetfish (*ayu*) represents all that is most delicious at this time of year. Grilling the fish at its freshest is the key to optimal flavor. An exquisite balance of umami, bitterness and texture comes to the fore when fresh *ayu* are cooked whole. *Ayu* at this time of year, when they are carrying the most fat on their bodies, are best simply salt-grilled. Roasting slowly over charcoal also gives the skin a wonderful fragrance and texture.

The basket here is inspired by those used to contain ayu caught by cormorants (above). Inside are charcoal embers and bamboo grass, which not only keep the fish warm, but give the impression that the fish has just been caught. **RECIPE P. 189**

鯛
牡

Edible Wild Plants and Japanese Food Culture

With so much of the country covered by mountains, gathering and eating edible wild plants, fruit, and nuts has a long history in Japan. Not only do people enjoy the taste of varieties only available seasonally, but they aim to boost their health and well-being by incorporating these nutritious wild plants into their diets. The tender spring shoots of the herb *yomogi* (a wild mugwort), for example, has been thought to be especially healthful because of its distinctive pungency. Crushed *yomogi* leaves, blanched and worked into pounded *mochi* cakes or boiled dumplings, are believed to ward off colds people are likely to otherwise catch as the seasons change. The custom of eating *nanakusa-gayu*, a porridge prepared with seven types of wild herbs on the seventh day of the New Year is still widely followed today. Traditionally it was believed that consuming these herbs early in the New Year would ensure vitality and help people to live long healthy lives. Often a family would eat the dish together in hopes that all household members could thereby avoid illness and misfortune in the coming year.

PREVIOUS PAGE
Painting of a sea bream (male)

BELOW
Sketches of vegetables (turnip and red daikon radish)

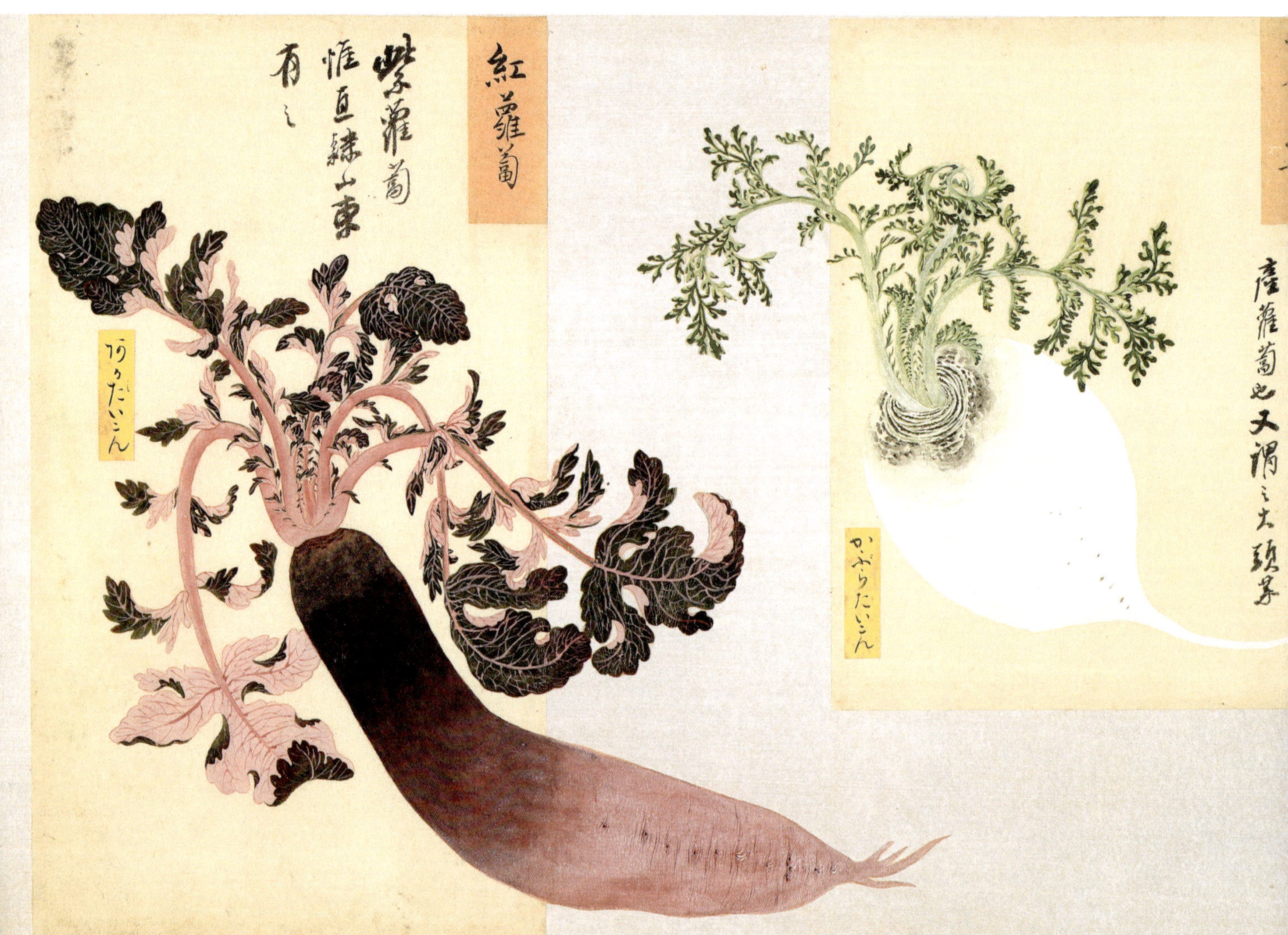

山菜土佐酢あえ *Sansai Tosazu ae*

Wild Vegetables in Tosazu Vinegar

A mix of wild spring greens called "mountain vegetables" including *udo, kogomi* and *fuki* is dressed in a soft Tosazu vinegar *gelée*. This Tosazu is milder and less sour than normal in order to highlight the distinctive fragrance, flavor and texture of each vegetable. A dish imbued with a breath of fresh vernal air and the vigor of spring growth. RECIPE P. 189

There are countless edible wild plants, but varieties enjoyed across the country include *fukinoto* (butterbur buds), which sprout from the ground as the snow melts and are thus regarded as harbingers of spring; the delicate little *tsukushi* (field horsetail) often found on riverbanks and along the ridges separating rice paddies; and the graceful *warabi* (fiddlehead fern). Deep fried as tempura, added to soups, or blanched to be served as cold greens (*ohitashi*), the astringent and earthy flavors of these plants are much appreciated.

Numerous species of mushroom can be found throughout Japan. Indeed, mushrooms have been a favorite ingredient in many types of cuisine since ancient times. Mushroom-gathering "hunts" were a favorite autumn pastime of courtiers as far back as the Heian period (794–1192). *Matsutake* gathering became popular among ordinary people approximately 300 years ago. Mushroom recipes developed during the Edo period (1603–1867) are still enjoyed today. Available wild plants and mushrooms that grow close to human habitation are integral to the Japanese approach to living in harmony with nature. Local traditional knowledge that teaches people what time of the year is best for enjoying each ingredient has been handed down through generations and continues to be valued today.

芹と合鴨胡麻だれがけ *Seri to Aigamo Gomadare-gake*

Roast Duck and Dropwort with Sesame Dressing

In Japanese cuisine chicken is commonly used, but quail and duck are also eaten. In this dish, duck meat is braised until tender and served it with dropwort, an excellent complement. The dressing is made from a special sesame base. The piquant mustard used in this dressing is superbly matched to the duck. RECIPE P. 189

Chapter 2

HISTORY AND DEVELOPMENT

The origin of Japanese cuisine is said to be offerings of food to the gods (*shinsen*). Prized foods were arranged with care on an altar and after prayer and rituals were over, they were used as ingredients for dishes partaken of as representing the blessings of the divine imparting energy for life. This chapter takes up the respect for the divine that is the basis of our lives today, the birth of kaiseki cuisine, and other developments and characteristics of Japanese food.

Murasaki

Eating with the Gods

The gods (*kami*) are customarily honored with offerings of food, called *shinsen*. Traditions of *shinsen* offerings reveal much about the dietary habits and food-related worship practices of people in antiquity. Offerings consist of local produce, mainly rice and rice products such as *mochi* (rice cakes) and sake, along with other grains, fruit and vegetables, fish, shellfish, and seaweed. Unlike Buddhism, Shinto neither proscribes fish and meat as unclean nor encourages that they be avoided. Offerings of meat are seen at some shrines, for in some areas boar, deer, and other game was part of the local diet.

Among the offerings may be special confections called *kara-kudamono* (lit., "Chinese sweets"). As the name suggests, this kind of offering developed after the introduction of Chinese culinary practices from the seventh century onward. *Kara-kudamono* were cakes made of rice-flour dough kneaded into traditional shapes and then deep-fried in oil; they may be considered one of the prototypes of Japanese *wagashi* sweets.

Shinsen offerings are first presented to the *kami* by being laid upon the altar, and after rituals have been performed, taken down and used to prepare a meal for those attending. Through this meal, called *naorai*, worshippers receive energy from the *kami*, establishing a link between humans and the gods. Although today *naorai* is often seen as signaling the return of worshippers to the mundane world following a ritual, in its original form the "partaking together" was a crucial part of the sacred proceedings themselves.

The sharing of food is a valued means of communication, and in Japan, it is

A *shinsen* offering of food to the gods prepared at a shrine includes a high mound of rice, a fresh sea bream, seasonal vegetables and a length kombu.

On the altar are laid out offerings of foods that are particular blessings for the people of that area to welcome the gods. In addition to rice, the staple of the diet, offerings also include sake and fresh seasonal foods from the sea and mountains.

considered to take place not only among humans, but also between humans and the deities that are thought to be part of their daily lives. That is why, even today, the preparation of a feast is a vital way to welcome the *kami*. The receiving of the "remainder" of the offerings is seen as confirmation of the human connection with the divine. Sake is thought to heighten the sense of communion; drinking sake after it has been presented to the *kami* (sake that has been offered to the gods is called *omiki*) is believed to bring union with the divine.

The Culture of Rice

The symbolic place of rice in the Japanese meal is signaled by the use of the word *gohan* to mean either "cooked rice" or alternatively "meal," depending on the context. White rice is the very basis of Japanese cuisine, and the culture that has developed around rice in Japan is extensive indeed.

Rice farming is thought to have entered Japan from the Asian mainland more than three millennia ago; the oldest archaeological evidence of a rice paddy site has been dated to about 2,500 years ago, and rice has been the principal crop since those ancient times. During the Edo period (1603–1867), taxes and samurai income, among other important economic quantities, were measured not in money but in quantities of rice.

When an offering is received, the priest chants a prayer (*norito*) to announce its delivery to the gods. The purpose of the offering is to express belief in the gods, celebration of the harvest, and gratitude.

Rice figures in every dimension of the Japanese diet. Some 8.5 million tons are produced in Japan annually and consumed directly as cooked rice or as *mochi* (rice cakes). It is also used to make sake, fermented seasonings such as miso and mirin, and snacks. Most rice in Japan belongs to the short-grained and sticky Japonica variety. While Japonica includes both paddy (wet) and upland (dry) varieties, wet cultivation has higher yield and is the overwhelming norm today. *Uruchimai* is the name given to the regular type of Japonica rice cooked for daily meals, while the chewy *mochi-gome*, variously referred to as "glutinous," "sticky," or "sweet" rice in English, is pounded into rice cakes or steamed with adzuki beans to make red rice (*sekihan*) for festive occasions.

Rice being the symbol of Japanese agriculture, countless festivals and worship practices associated with this crop are observed. The name of the deity of rice growing, called Inari, is is derived from *ine nari*, literally, "ripened rice." In the Imperial Palace, the most significant ritual of the year is the Niinamesai celebrating the rice harvest. Many manners and customs of everyday life, too, emphasize the value and important role of this grain that has traditionally been seen as the staff of life.

Respect for the Gods

Chopsticks have a very long history in China, where they were used as cooking implements long before the Common Era. They were introduced to Japan about 1,500 years ago, at which time they were used as eating utensils primarily by the aristocracy.

Everyday Japanese chopsticks are tapered at one end. Because chopsticks come into contact with the lips and absorb part of that individual's spirit, each household member will typically have a pair reserved for his or her personal use. For this reason, new chopsticks are always readied for guests or for ritual offerings (for the *kami*).

Chopsticks for use at New Year's or for other special occasions are tapered at both ends and sheathed in paper sleeves often bound by colorful cords called *mizuhiki*. The colors of the cords vary depending on the type of occasion: paired red and white or gold and silver are for auspicious events while black and white is for funerals. Given that the chopsticks are destined for a guest's mouth, they are encased in paper and tied with the *mizuhiki* to signal that they are new and untouched. Different knots, too, convey different meanings. For example, bow knots (in Japanese, *hana-musubi*) are chosen for celebrations that people look forward to repeating, such as births and milestone birthdays, because these forms can be easily done and undone. Hard-to-untie square or *musubi-kiri* knots are for weddings, hospital visits, and other occasions that hopefully the main participants will not have to experience again.

An example of *mizuhiki* (decorative cords) for the *iwaibashi*, round chopsticks used for festive occasions. For auspicious events, the decorative knots are generally made of silver and gold or red and white cord.

An example of the decorative knot on a *noshi* package. *Noshi* is actually the abbreviation of *noshi awabi*, which literally means "thinly stretched-out abalone." Abalone, which is believed to ensure long life, is served on auspi cious occasions. Today, a "noshi" is usually a sheet of paper printed with a stylized package design.

The mounded *mochi* offered to the gods on New Year's are called *kagami-mochi* ("mirror mochi"). In antiquity round bronze mirrors were thought to be the abode of the divine, and so the *mochi* is made in the shape of such mirrors.

Culinary Heritage and Celebrations in the Home

A number of festivals are celebrated within the home to mark the passage of time throughout the calendar year. Particularly important are the five dates known as *gosekku* (the Seven Herbs Festival on January 7th; the Peach Festival on March 3rd; the Iris Festival on May 5th; the Star Festival on July 7th; and the Chrysanthemum Festival on September 9th), and the first day of each new season. Under Western influence, Christmas is now celebrated in many Japanese homes without any particular connection to Christianity.

Alongside these annual events are special ceremonies that mark important points in a person's life course. Following the initial celebration of birth, a naming ceremony is held and parents often visit a shrine with their baby a month after the child is born to give thanks for a safe birth. About 100 days after birth the baby is given solid food for the first time in a ceremony known as *okuizome*, or "first meal." Red rice (*sekihan*, glutinous *mochi* rice with adzuki beans) is traditionally eaten on auspicious occasions. At the *okuizome* celebration, it is traditional to serve red rice along with a fish prepared with its head and tail intact. Using a pair of long chopsticks, the parents symbolically "feed" this to the child, in the hope that the tough fish bones will help the child to develop strong teeth.

Shichi-go-san is a festival celebrating children who have reached the ages of 3, 5, or 7. Parents dress their children in traditional formal attire and take them to a shrine to pray for their continued good health. Red rice and fish prepared whole are also served at the traditional family meal on these occasions.

Traditional family meals—sometimes involving the extended family—continue to mark the major events of childhood and beyond, including the child's first day at school, graduation ceremonies, and the "coming of age" ceremony the year a person turns 20, officially becoming an adult.

Perhaps the happiest event in anyone's life is marriage. Today, Western-style meals are served at most Japanese wedding receptions. A special kind of banquet cuisine called *honzen* (see p. 67) used to be served for traditional Japanese celebrations. This was characterized by an impressive succession of dishes served on individual trays. Other important rites of passage include celebrations marking important birthdays. Special meals are often prepared to celebrate propitious ages including 60, 70, 77, and 88. Auspicious foods are prepared to celebrate a long and healthy life.

Vegetarian *shojin* cuisine (see p. 70) is the norm at occasions of mourning. No fish or meat whatsoever is prepared for meals served immediately after a funeral or at Buddhist ceremonies held to mark the seventh and forty-ninth days after death. Later on, at ceremonies that commemorate the second year, twelfth year, and so on after a person's death, some fish and meat may be served in addition to *shojin* cuisine. Nevertheless, the food should convey a sense of mourning for the deceased.

Honzen Cuisine

Until the beginning of the twentieth century, people ate meals sitting on tatami mats with the food served on small individual tray tables. The tables, which came in many forms, were about thirty to forty centimeters square and either had no legs or were raised on either one or four legs. Each tray setting held rice, soup, and up to three side dishes; this arrangement, called *ichi-ju san-sai* ("one soup, three dishes," see p. 174), constituted the ordinary but quite respectable daily meal. To entertain a guest, a *ni no zen* ("second tray") was served with one more soup and two more dishes. This second tray was placed to the right of the main *honzen* tray with the *ichi-ju san-sai*—the meal now consisting of rice and a total of two soups and five dishes, or *ni-ju go-sai*. These trays formed the basic building blocks of *honzen* style of cuisine; if more dishes were desired, a *san no zen* ("third tray") could be added, and so on. The number of trays came to signify the sumptuousness of the meal, and feasts with up to seven settings for each guest became common practice between the sixteenth and seventeenth centuries.

No less extravagant than the number of courses was the presentation, which included ornate serving dishes alongside table decorations fashioned of artificial flowers of gold and silver. In pursuit of outward ostentation, however, the *honzen* style lost focus on the food itself. This failing eventually inspired the rise of kaiseki tea ceremony cuisine.

Honzen cuisine underwent gradual reform from the seventeenth century onward, persisting into the early post-World War II era as the main style for entertaining guests. A principal characteristic was the serving of more dishes than a person could eat, including certain foods that were according to custom not consumed then and there, but rather packed up at the end of the meal with other leftovers to be taken home by guests.

The *honzen* style survives in a more limited form today in the banquet cuisine prepared by Japanese *ryokan* inns for large groups as well as in the courses served during Japanese-style wedding receptions.

Shojin Cuisine

Shojin refers to abstinence from certain types of food, most commonly meat and fish, according to Buddhist precepts. Despite their shared basis in Buddhism, however, the specifics of *shojin* cuisine differ from one Buddhist sect to another, so it is incorrect to simply characterize it as "vegetarian" food. A more precise definition would be "cooking that supplies the minimum sustenance necessary for the pursuit of Buddhist training."

Japanese *shojin* cuisine, which developed from meals prepared for temple monks, initially not only forbade meat and fish but also emphasized austerity. The cuisine that we know as *shojin* today began to develop some eight centuries ago, when cooking methods grew more involved and spread from the temples to the populace more broadly. In due course, *shojin* cuisine lost its connection to religious taboos and came to be accepted more generally as an elaborate form for creating meals with vegetables.

One of *shojin* cuisine's contributions to Japanese food culture consists of various techniques for cooking foods in liquid. Up to that time foods had primarily been prepared by roasting, and less frequently drying, or they had been served raw. The metal pots required for stewing and simmering were much more difficult to come by than the implements required for dry heating. *Shojin* cuisine brought about the advent of foods cooked in broth and served warm. Grinding sesame seeds or beans in a mortar to obtain smoothly textured powders and pastes became popular as well.

As priestly diets and standards of living rose from the medieval era onward, once-humble *shojin* cooking grew increasingly elaborate. Inventive chefs gave birth to "mock" dishes that used vegetables to evoke the appearance or taste of fish and fowl, and that used dashi to bring out the umami flavors of the ingredients; one example now well known throughout Japan is *ganmodoki*, deep-fried tofu balls, whose name means "mock goosemeat."

The introduction of Zen Buddhism contributed greatly to the advancement of *shojin* cuisine. Zen monks brought the new Chinese culinary traditions into Japan, including soybean products like tofu and flour products like noodles, all of which dramatically expanded the range of *shojin* fare. The style of *shojin* meals was also established within the framework of Buddhist ceremonies. The meals prepared for ceremonies at Todaiji temple today pass down the Buddhist menus of four centuries ago.

An individual serving of a standard *shojin* cuisine meal, made entirely with vegetarian ingredients. Deep-fried tofu simmered in broth, *hijiki* seaweed simmered with *abura-age* tofu and soy sauce, blanched garden greens tossed with mustard and miso, pickled daikon, white miso soup made with daikon, for a full *ichi-ju san-sai* meal. Tofu is indispensable as a source of vegetable protein in *shojin* cuisine. The broth for soups and simmering, too, uses no fish or shellfish ingredients but is prepared with kombu, toasted soybeans, dried *kampyo* gourd, and dried shiitake.

Over time *shojin* cuisine spread beyond temple walls to become a familiar part of the Japanese diet. Techniques used in *shojin* cooking that fully draw out the delicate flavors of vegetables have had a significant impact on Japanese cuisine. No doubt the spiritual orientation found within Japanese dining culture, too, reflects something of the Zen attitude that the act of eating, no less than that of preparing or growing food, is a form of training in pursuit of Buddhist enlightenment.

Shojin Cuisine and Zen

Buddhism prohibits the killing of living things, including the slaughter of animals, and accordingly the meat of cattle, pigs, horses, fish and fowl, as well as wild animals was generally not eaten in Japan until the nineteenth century. Buddhist temples served vegetarian or *shojin* meals made only with cereal grains, vegetables and sea vegetables, mushrooms, and other plant-derived ingredients.

Shojin cuisine was originally quite simple and rudimentary. This changed, however, with the introduction of Zen Buddhism from China from the thirteenth century onward, when Japanese priests who had gone to China to study and Chinese priests who came to Japan as teachers brought the culture of the Southern Song dynasty (1127–1279) Zen clergy to Japan's shores. That culture included the refined food culture of the Zen priesthood.

Prior to this period, the use of stone mortars to grind grain was not well developed in Japan, so it was difficult to crush or grind wheat, beans, and tea. Once the technology of stone mortars was introduced, wheat could be ground, providing the flour for various kinds of noodles, soybeans could be crushed, facilitating the making of tofu and tofu skin (*yuba*), and tea leaves could be powdered to make *matcha* green tea. The making of the distinctively Japanese dashi broth also became well developed around that time. While bonito flakes were not an option because fish meat could not be used, kombu and dried shiitake mushrooms made it possible to make delicious vegetable-based broths for simmered foods and soups. With these developments, the vegetarian cooking that had once been very humble and plain was transformed into tasteful dishes that ordinary people wanted to eat.

Lay people became familiar with *shojin* cooking as *shojin* dishes were served at funerals or memorial services (*hoji*). This gave rise to professional cooks who specialized in *shojin* cuisine cooking for temple functions, funerals, and memorial services. They produced fine sesame tofu, wheat gluten (*fu*) based dishes, and other distinctive dishes. In the seventeenth century, the Obaku school of Zen Buddhism arrived from China's Fujian province, bringing with it the *shippoku*-style of cooking, which used large quantities of deep-fried ingredients. From the nineteenth century onward, *shojin* cuisine was consumed not only for memorial services but as a style of cooking people preferred, and various recipe books were published.

Shojin cuisine is known for being healthy not only because it does not involve the use of animal fat or protein, but also because its dishes contain protein derived from plant products. Moreover, its techniques for bringing out the inherent flavor of ingredients is celebrated. In this sense *shojin*-style dishes are really the embodiment of Japanese cuisine and one of its most important styles.

Hot water poured over a toasted *onigiri* rice ball makes a pleasant aromatic brew in place of the usual after-meal tea.

The water basin (*tsukubai*) located between the gate and the tea room in the tea ceremony garden. Guests rinse their hands and mouths here before entering the tea room. The basins are usually made of stone and set very low, so that one must stoop or squat (*tsukubau*; hence the name) to use it.

Chanoyu: Japan's Art of Hospitality

Tea is today enjoyed all over the world. The tea plant (*Camellia sinensis*) is thought to have originated in Southeast Asia, the area where the present-day borders of China, Laos, and Myanmar converge. The practice of drinking the beverage brewed from its leaves became a part of Han Chinese culture roughly two thousand years ago. It spread throughout China by the eighth century, extending to neighboring Korea and Japan and, in the seventeenth century, to Europe and beyond.

Although tea drinking first took place in Japan in the ninth century, the custom died out once and did not become established until powdered green tea was introduced from China in the late twelfth century. Tea utensils came to be prized among the upper classes, and appreciation of art and craft works, in particular those imported from China, was fashionable. Commoners, too, engaged in tea-tasting games, and tea became important not only as a drink but also as a means of enjoying life. The result was the development of practices related to tea utensils and their presentation, along with protocols for preparing and drinking tea and designs for tea houses and their gardens—the various components of *chanoyu*, or the tea ceremony, which developed to support appreciation for a lifestyle relating to tea.

In the sixteenth century, *chanoyu* developed further under the newly ascendant members of the warrior class and the affluent merchants from the port city of Sakai whom they patronized. The distinctive aesthetic that they shaped, called *wabi*, stressed the beauty of the simple and rustic. The tea ceremony can be characterized as a social gathering at which participants set aside the barriers of status and means, and establish rapport by spending a few hours in close company. Two to five guests may find themselves inside a room of less than 7.5 square meters, where they share a meal and sake, followed by tea. The host selects a scroll to hang in the tokonoma alcove specifically for the occasion and selects tea utensils according to the interests and preferences of his guests. The guests, in turn, seek to appreciate every detail of the host's ingenuity and care. This interaction, in which host and guests endeavor to mutually understand one another, is emblematic of Japanese hospitality and is quintessentially expressed in *chanoyu*.

The simple, minimally furnished tea room enjoins those who gather within to shed the trappings of worldly affairs and assume a spirit of humble reverence. The rinsing of hands with water at the *chozubachi* basin in the *roji* garden leading to the tea room is a gesture that signifies putting aside the "dust" of the outer world, both physically and spiritually, before crouching to pass through the *nijiriguchi*

A restaurant water basin depicted in a scroll painted by Kishida Ryusei (1891–1929).

The term "kaiseki" originally refers to food served during tea ceremony in accordance with set protocols. First a *zendashi* (left) of rice, soup and *mukozuke* (often sashimi) is served on a tray. This is followed by *nimono* (simmered/boiled dish), and *yakimono* (grilled foods) to make up the one soup and three dishes.

The *zendashi* is a serving of just two or three mouthfuls of soft cooked rice straight off the flame and not yet left to stand and absorb steam. Having rice ready at the start of the kaiseki meal signals to the guest that all preparations for the meal are going smoothly, a thoughtful touch by the host.

entrance into the space of the ceremony. The seventeenth-century Portuguese missionary João Rodrigues characterized the tea ceremony structure using the Japanese phrase "xichu no sankio"—a "hillside abode in the city," or a setting that, in the midst of the hustle and bustle of urban life, evokes the pure clean air of a mountain retreat removed from the dust of this world.

Chanoyu has had a tremendous influence not only on the cuisine of Japan but also its architecture, gardens, arts and crafts, not to mention its literature and philosophy.

Beauty in Tea Ceremony Cuisine

The purpose of the meal served prior to the tea ceremony is not to showcase the cuisine itself; the all-important consideration is that the food enhance the pleasure of the tea that will follow. Accordingly there is no need to provide an excess of dishes, or to serve sake in generous supply. At the end of the meal, guests are served some pickles and hot water, with which they rinse their rice bowl and other dishes to return them empty and clean; for this reason, the servings do not employ inedible decorations or other extraneous items. The menu and ingredients may be simple, but they will be flavorful, reflect a sense of the season, and touch upon themes the guests are deemed likely to appreciate. The serving vessels carefully chosen to achieve a desired effect may include vintage treasures several centuries old or delightful art pieces made by renowned craftsmen.

In entertaining his guests, it is vital that the host—no matter how exalted his social status or how venerable in age—show a willingness to personally carry and serve the food. The act of laboring with one's own hands to offer sustenance to guests is the highest gesture of hospitality.

Hassun

Hassun in a kaiseki setting is an appetizer course consumed by guest and host while enjoying sake. "Hassun" refers to the length (eight *sun*, approximately 24.2 cm) of one side of a square cedar serving tray, and has become the term used for both tray and the food on it. The basic pattern is one fish and one vegetable tidbit, with the fish placed at the top right of the tray, and the vegetables at bottom left.

RECIPE P. 190

Wagashi Sweets

One myth explaining the origins of *wagashi* Japanese sweets tells of a man named Tajimamori, who was ordered by Emperor Suinin to journey to Tokoyo, the Otherworld, to bring back the fruit *tokijiku no kagu no mi*, said to give everlasting life. By the time Tajimamori at last returned from his quest, however, the emperor had already died, and shortly after leaving an offering of the miraculous fruit before the emperor's grave Tajimamori passed away as well. This *tokijiku no kagu no mi*, reportedly the fruit of the *tachibana* citrus, is regarded as the first "sweet" in Japan. The story illustrates two key points about the nature of *wagashi*: first, that they embody people's wishes and prayers (for longevity, in the case of the Tajimamori myth), and second, that they originated with fruit.

A sweet that is an example of the first point is *minazuki*, which is named after the sixth lunar month, in early summer. Now enjoyed in June-July, this confection consists of a layer of adzuki beans atop a triangle of sweet white *uiro* rice dough whose color and shape recall a sliver of ice. Every year in the sixth month, the custom once was to bring out ice from where it had been stored through the winter and eat it while praying for healthy teeth (and, by extension, long life); eventually the confection came to be consumed instead of ice to prepare the body and mind against the onset of the summer heat. A favorite in November, meanwhile, is the *inoko-mochi* rice cake, which comes in many different forms, including those with stripes or specks to resemble the markings on boar piglets. The *i* in *inoko* means "boar," and because boars give birth to many offspring at a time, the confection symbolizes fecundity and family prosperity.

As to the second point, sugar cane was not grown in Japan and the main sweet foods were fruit. Dried persimmons and dried chestnuts remain popular sweets today. The introduction of imported sugar in the sixteenth century significantly broadened the range of available *wagashi*; malt syrup, made using enzymes from malted wheat to break down starches into sugars, was also adopted as a sweetener. By the late seventeenth century, hundreds of *wagashi* varieties were known, and many renowned confectioners had opened their doors, though chiefly in Kyoto. The origins of *wagashi* in fruit at least partly explains why these confections are often expected to express the seasons and the beauties of nature. Portraying seasonal flowers and scenes or emblematic allusions from verse and narrative literature, the colors and forms of *wagashi* constitute a treasure trove of designs.

The main ingredients of *wagashi* are the processed products of rice and rice flour, supplemented by other forms of starch including those derived from the *kudzu* arrowroot or *warabi* bracken. Adzuki beans are steamed and mashed into a paste called *an*, which as a filling determines the core flavor of *wagashi*; the paste may also be cooked with *kanten* agar to make *yokan* jelly. One notable feature of these and other ingredients of *wagashi*, including *kinako* soybean flour and wheat flour, is that they contain almost no fat, making *wagashi* healthier in this respect than Western sweets that rely heavily on dairy products.

Funoyaki, dry-baked wheat gluten (right). *Omogashi* (literally the "main sweets") consisting of *an* red bean paste wrapped in a crepe-like dough of wheat flour mixed with water. *Omogashi* are made to be served with thick *matcha* tea called *koicha* (below), and are generally unbaked sweets such as *kinton* (mashed sweet potato or beans with candied chestnuts) and *nerikiri* confections made with white beans. In kaiseki cuisine, *omogashi* and *koicha* are served after the meal.

Mukozuke (from placement on the "far side" [*muko*] of the tray) refers to both the dish and the food. Common dishes include seafood prepared *kobujime* style, or lightly salted, and are served at the start of a kaiseki meal, along with rice and soup. In October's "Nagori" tea ceremony, it is common to serve each guest the *mukozuke* using a different style of dish, in a custom known as *yosemuko*. In tea ceremony matching dishes are the norm, but deliberately offering food on dishes of different colors and shapes makes for a good conversation and deeper enjoyment.

Themes in Tea Ceremony Cuisine

Each tea ceremony occasion is organized around a theme, or *shuko*, set by the host. In terms of cuisine, the theme is executed with attention above all to the full enjoyment of seasonal flavors. This is not to say, however, that ingredients for the kaiseki meal need always be at the very height of their season. For example, early May, when the floor hearth for boiling water for tea in the cold months is covered and replaced by a portable brazier (*furo*), is a time when the fresh air of early summer is itself a wonderful treat; using vegetables and fish only just beginning to be available thus becomes a way of celebrating the coming season. In October, when the brazier is put away again, the focus of *chanoyu* gatherings turns to bidding farewell to the passing season, and the cuisine accordingly draws attention to ingredients nearing the end of their season. During this season, the *mukozuke* dishes used to serve food might not be presented in matching sets but rather from miscellaneous single pieces, one to each guest, to hint at a sense of lack or melancholy. While this practice, known as *yosemuko* ("mixed *mukozuke*"), is meant to express austere living, it also offers guests an opportunity to appreciate an array of different vessels.

Indeed, one of the greatest attractions of Japanese cuisine, kaiseki or otherwise, is the harmony between food and vessel. Guests enjoy savoring not only the meal, but also the choice of serving ware and the intentions of the host suggested therein.

Example of mixed *mukozuke* dishes: Raku ware chrysanthemum (left), Raku ware lily (center), a hexagonal dish (right).

Room in a *ryotei* restaurant in spring. The decorations and furnishings are changed in accordance with the seasons (see also pp. 152–153).

Distinctive Features of Kaiseki

In its original sense, kaiseki signifies food served in conjunction with the tea ceremony, though today it is also used more loosely to refer to similar cuisines served outside a formal *chanoyu* context. The kaiseki style originated in the sixteenth century and is thought to have achieved its classical form around the mid-eighteenth century.

The perfecting of kaiseki was a watershed event representing the establishment of one of the great pillars of Japanese cuisine. The *honzen* style (see pp. 66–67), which was prevalent before kaiseki, was characterized by many different dishes arrayed all at once on multiple tray tables. Kaiseki, which required only a single setting per person to hold courses as they were brought out one at a time, was an innovation, one might even say revolution, in Japanese culinary history. *Honzen* cuisine included many items that were in truth inedible because they had gone cold since being set out or were provided merely for the sake of decoration. By comparison, kaiseki courses were served warm with a great deal of attention paid to the proper timing of courses and appropriate portion sizes without wasteful frills. These characteristics constituted the reform of banquet cuisine.

As part of the tea ceremony, kaiseki is distinguished not only by its flavors and forms but also by its embodiment of the spirit of *wabi*. Kaiseki came into being to express the *wabi* aesthetic, and its innovation lay in the incorporation of communicative intent—of messages conveying a sense of the season or of celebration—into cuisine. Seasonality, for example, is evoked on the table not only through the ingredients but also through other details including the design of serving ware. These aspects of kaiseki have found their way into and greatly contributed to the flowering of Japanese culinary culture as a whole.

Spring Hassun

Appetizer tidbits (*hassun*) in a lively array of spring colors and shapes.

Shokado Bento Box

This serving box is divided into separate compartments, each containing dishes with distinct tastes and aromas to be enjoyed. A colorful array of grilled morsels, sashimi, sushi, and simmered tidbits (clockwise from top left) are arranged in the same box. Each restaurant's *bento*-style meals are unique, sometimes with the rice served separately in a bowl. RECIPE P. 190

In contrast to other portable or boxed meals (*bento*), the general image of the *Shokado bento* is that of a relatively deep box, divided into four compartments packed with rice and several different side dishes, and covered with a lid. There are countless types, depending on the shop and sashimi, grilled, simmered or other dishes included. When served in a *ryotei* restaurant, the rice is often served separately in a bowl. The compartments keep the flavors and aromas of the ingredients of different dishes from mingling, enhancing the enjoyment of each dish and the opportunities for presenting visually attractive arrangements. The lids on such boxes help retain the moisture of the ingredients and keep out dust, but have also been skillfully designed for convenience, allowing one to carry the boxes in stacks, for example.

The *Shokado bento* is named after a priest named Shokado Shojo (1584–1639) who lived at Iwashimizu Hachimangu in Kyoto. Taking inspiration from boxes divided into compartments with a cross bar used by farmers for their seeds, the priest is said to have used such a box for his smoking and painting implements. Smoking had become quite popular by the mid-seventeenth century and smoking sets (*tabako-bon*) were even provided during tea ceremonies.

About three-hundred years later, when Yuki Teiichi, founder of the Kitcho chain of traditional-style *ryotei* restaurants, visited the hut reconstructed on the site where Shokado once lived, he noticed in the corner of the room the famous "four-part" box the priest had used, and it gave him the idea of using a similar design for a container for serving food. He developed an original design, with slightly smaller and deeper dimensions, and used it for serving the light meal (*tenshin*) in the tea ceremony. The form we see today is much the same, with some further innovations.

One of Yuki's innovations was to insert serving vessels into the compartments of the *bento* box. It was a brilliant idea that made it possible to serve delicate or soft ingredients or dishes containing liquids, raising the *Shokado bento* to a new level and allowing it to be used to serve an even wider variety of foods—dishes that were warm, chilled, or contained liquids. The *Shokado bento*, providing for the inclusion of a variety of dishes in one container, gave birth to a new style of cuisine that transformed the ordinary boxed lunch into what has been called "kaiseki in miniature."

Chapter 3

ARTISTIC AWARENESS

Two traditions of beauty course through Japanese history—one lineage is bold, intense, and wild, while the other projects gentleness and elegance. Prizing beauty in the presentation of food, Japanese cuisine stresses visually attractive arrangements with color and a sense of the seasons. Close attention is given to coordinating the shape and coloring of the vessels as well as the decorations of the room where the dishes are served.

The Two Lineages of Japanese Aesthetics

The Japanese sense of beauty is said to have two lineages. The first is full of intense energy, bold and wild. This primeval beauty is captured in the flame-decorated pottery produced 5,000 years ago during the Jomon period. We can identify this quality in many works and movements over the centuries, for example, in the heroic culture that burst forth during the sixteenth-century Sengoku period when struggles among local warlords led to the breakdown of the existing order.

Society has been more or less stable throughout Japanese history, however, and the imperial line has continued without overthrow of the sovereignty of the court by armed force for more than 1,500 years. The Japanese spirit of harmony (*wa*) emerged from indigenous animistic beliefs and was later buttressed by the magnanimous teachings of Mahayana Buddhism. The spirit of an agrarian people respectful of nature and aspiring to harmony with nature is thought to have developed in the Yayoi period starting around 1,000 B.C. when wet-rice agriculture became prevalent. The vigorous, boldly creative beauty of Jomon pottery gave way to gentler, more restrained forms and motifs in earthenware with the reddish, low-fired pottery of the Yayoi period and later the bluish, high-fired Sue ware.

The lineage of gentle and moderate beauty developed immeasurably during the Heian period (ninth to twelfth centuries). Waka poetry flourished among the aristocrats of the imperial court: Murasaki Shikibu wrote her famous multi-volume tale of amorous liaisons, *The Tale of Genji* and the stylized genre of decorative painting known as *yamato-e*, exemplified by the paintings in the *Genji monogatari* handscrolls, was born. Cultural pursuits like calligraphy and flower arranging enriched the quality of daily life and distinctive styles of textiles and architecture were established. Indeed, it was in the Heian era that the most basic elements of the Japanese aesthetic evolved.

Rimpa

In the Edo period, beginning in the early seventeenth century, a new Yayoi-type culture developed that drew on the sixteenth-century resurgence of Jomon-like qualities. In the field of visual culture, there was a creative revival of *yamato-e* centering on the Rimpa school of painting. This school, which traced its beginnings to Hon'ami Koetsu (1558–1637) and Tawaraya Sotatsu (a Koetsu contemporary; dates unknown), was founded by Ogata Korin (1658–1716). One of the successors to Ogata Korin's style of painting was Sakai Hoitsu (1761–1828). Transcending realism, Edo-period Rimpa painting, founded by Hoitsu, was stylized and decorative, featuring elegant and refined lines as well as lavish use of color; birds, flowers, and scenes from nature were their usual subjects. The influence of this Rimpa-style painting permeated all aspects of Japanese culture—textiles, lacquerware, ceramics, architecture, gardens—including cuisine.

Chefs take special pains in arranging the presentation of their dishes. It is often said that Japanese cuisine can be "eaten with the eyes," and the aesthetics of decoration and color take their inspiration from Rimpa-school art. Some of the most famous serving dishes are ceramics made by painter Ogata Korin collaborating with his younger brother and ceramic artist Ogata Kenzan. The motifs used in the design of plates and bowls are often Rimpa in inspiration, which demonstrates its enormous influence.

隠れ梅 *Kakure Ume*

Hidden Plum

A dish inspired by the last snows on plum blossoms in early spring, when days are alternately balmy and cool. A cream of sea bream white milt (*shirako*), adorns a pickled *ume* plum soft from simmering, a tantalizing glimpse visible beneath what is made to look like a blanket of light snow. The peach blossom garnish hints at the change of seasons. RECIPE P. 192

Ogata Korin's "Red and White Plum Blossoms" Screens.

Yugen

The highly refined performing art known as noh drama came into being during the fourteenth and fifteenth centuries through the efforts of a talented father and son, Kan'ami and Zeami. Centering on songs and dances, the noh plays developed under the influence of Zen Buddhism and *suibokuga* ink painting. A distinguished actor, Zeami is also known for his outstanding theoretical treatises on the subject. Zeami wrote many plays, including those known as "yugen noh," in which the main character is a ghost or spirit. In the typical plot for this type of play a traveling priest meets an old man and listens to the story of his woes. After returning to his inn for the night, the priest has a dream in which the old man appears as the spirit of a person who has died. In the dream, the spirit takes the guise of the old man when he was young, performing a dance while recounting the past troubles and sins that prevent his peaceful passage to the Pure Land of Buddha. After hearing the story, the traveling priest chants sutras to calm the spirit, which is then eventually able to enter the Pure Land. The intertwining of past and present, dream and reality explores the essential nature of humanity.

Zeami explained noh aesthetics using the word *yugen*. "Yugen" is written with the characters *yu*, meaning "fleeting" or "subtle," and *gen*, meaning "profound." The word was introduced from China and was used in the appraisal of waka poetry in the thirteenth century to describe a good, profound poem. It also acquired the meaning of "gentle and enchanting," and when Zeami first began to use it to explain the aesthetic of noh drama, he described it as a soft, feminine quality. Later he used *yugen* in the sense of a simple and refined beauty that is attained over the passage of time.

The quality of beauty represented by *yugen* is refinement and elegance. It is not expressed clearly and directly, but subtly and indirectly. Moreover, *yugen* refers not to the expression itself but to the sense of beauty felt as a result of the lingering fragrance or trace of that expression after it has ended.

Japanese cuisine is said to be extraordinarily sophisticated when it comes to aesthetic expression, not only because the arrangement of shapes and colors makes it beautiful or due to the tasteful choice of serving utensils, but also because it suggests the aesthetic of *yugen* through symbolic techniques. The importance attached to the sensations that linger after food has been eaten exemplifies aesthetic traditions prizing suggestion and lingering resonances.

Wabi and *Sabi*

The aesthetic concepts of *wabi* and *sabi* emerged in the sixteenth century. "Sabi" is closely connected both with the rusting (*sabiru*) and deterioration of iron and the pathos felt at the sight of something worn, ruined, or desolate. *Sabi* is a term that has been historically used in literature to express the beauty of something that has passed its prime and is in the process of decline, as well as the fulfillment that can be found in *sabishisa*, the pathos of being alone. "Wabi" comes from the word "wabishii" which is used to express the disconsolate or miserable feeling of unfulfilled or unrequited sentiments. *Wabishii* originally expressed how a person felt when feelings of love were not returned, but it gradually came to connote the condition of poverty or economic want. Poverty is not a desirable condition, but the idea developed that contentment could better be achieved by a simple life than one of material wealth, and this aesthetic was described by the word "wabi." At first *wabi* was used for a style of tea ceremony at which the wealthy would put aside the luxuries of their lives for the day to hold a deliberately austere party in a rustic, humble structure. In due course, people who might be genuinely poor but were known for their spiritually uplifting and artistically tasteful tea gatherings came to be highly respected, and the tea gatherings (*chakai*) held according to these principles were called *wabicha*.

In the seventeenth century, *sabi* took its place among Japan's aesthetic concepts as the great poet Matsuo Basho wrote haikai poetry, the abbreviated form of verse characterized by a sense of tranquility and refined simplicity. What is distinctive about the aesthetics of *wabi* and *sabi* is that they not only capture certain ideas in art and aesthetics but they are also deeply connected to the very way of life that they describe. It may even be better to consider them less as aesthetic terms than as ways of viewing humanity.

The influence of this perspective is also evident in Japanese cuisine. A splendid and luxurious feast is complete, leaving nothing more to be desired. Yet a different kind of repast is possible, one that falls just short of enough, leaving something to be desired. Without relying on particularly unusual ingredients, the host can prepare a meal that will be deeply appreciated, using plants that grow wild in the hills and fields or ordinary ingredients at their freshest. Japanese cuisine does indeed incorporate the *wabi* and *sabi* aesthetic.

Hasegawa Tohaku's "Pine Trees" Folding Screen.

かます味噌柚庵焼
Kamasu Miso Yuan-yaki

Grilled Barracuda with Miso *Yuan-yaki* Baste

The refreshing fragrance of *yuzu* and rich earthiness of miso highlight the subtle umami of barracuda in this simple yet sublime grilled dish. RECIPE P. 187

Fukiyose

A tremendous variety of designs symbolizing the seasons feature in Japanese dishes and confections. Around November, when the foliage changes color, gardens are filled with red, orange, and yellow. Chestnuts and gingko nuts begin to fall to the ground. The medley of bright-colored leaves and nature's other autumn bounty piled up as one cleans a garden has become a motif known as "fukiyose" ("blown together by the wind") used in food presentation and the design of sweets. Serving dishes with a dustpan shape may serve as the backdrop for such colorful arrangements of foods. When the contents are sweets, they can be created in various shapes and piled on a serving dish as if "windblown." The delicate, colorful design hints at the pathos we feel as autumn deepens.

Many different motifs can be found in the dishes served and sweets created in accordance with the annual events held for each season—peach and cherry blossoms for spring, wisteria and iris in early summer, as well as for Children's Day in May and the Tanabata Festival in July. The designs are deliberately abstract, however, as they are intended as symbols—indirect expressions of meaning.

A plate of dry sweets (*higashi*) served in the *fukiyose* ("wind blown") style evokes the beauty of colorful autumn leaves swept by the wind.

Sakai Hoitsu (1761–1828). White satin *kosode* kimono with painted pattern of pink plum blossoms (detail).

Neji-Ume
PLUM

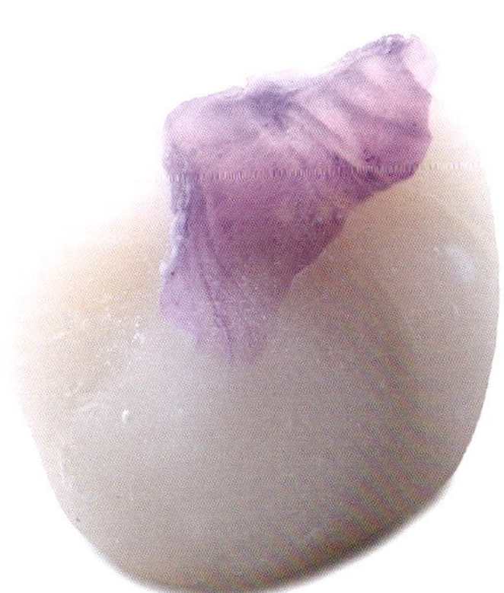

Hana-Ayame
IRIS

Wagashi can be tremendous masterpieces of design inspired by plants and a refined sense of the seasons. "Neji-Ume"(above) distills the wintry beauty of the blossoming plum tree, "Hana-Ayame" (below) abbreviates the soft lavender of the petals of the wild iris (*ayame*).

Watanabe Shiko (1683–1755). "Rabbit-ear Iris" folding screen (detail).

Chapter 4

THE ESSENTIALS

Japanese cuisine brings out the natural flavors of ingredients. Though often understated and subtle, it calls for expert understanding of specific ingredients and techniques. This chapter introduces the essentials, including dashi, umami, and the five basic methods (*goho*) of food preparation.

Nibi

Dashi and Umami

Dashi stock and the taste of umami are fundamental. The most common type of dashi is made with kombu and *katsuobushi* flakes, but a number of types are used, such as that made only with kombu and using no fish or animal ingredients. One major feature of dashi is the use of its umami to bring out the flavors of ingredients to best advantage. For its techniques of bringing out the inherent flavor of foods by the skillful augmenting of umami—thereby reducing the use of salt and animal fat—Japanese cuisine has won attention all around the world.

Goho: The Five Basic Cooking Techniques

The essence of Japanese cuisine is said to consist of the "five flavors," the "five colors," and the "five techniques." For this cuisine that stresses the freshness of ingredients and harmony with the seasons and nature, these sum up the key principles.

The balance to be obtained between the inherent savory umami of ingredients and the other five traditional tastes—sour, bitter, sweet, spicy hot, and salty is basic. The five colors are white, black, yellow, red, and blue/green. These colors are kept in mind when serving dishes, considering the presentation of the food in terms of the serving vessel and flowers or other decorations used alongside. The five techniques, meanwhile, are cutting (especially significant for foods eaten raw), simmering, grilling, steaming, and deep-frying.

Dashi

Stock made with kombu and *katsuobushi* flakes is basic and the mainstay of many dishes. When the two ingredients are combined, a synergy arises between the glutamic acid of the kombu and the inosinic acid of the *katsuobushi* that results in an ideal umami taste. Research has shown that the greatest amount of umami can be extracted from kombu by heating it in water on a low 60°C heat for one hour. The role of dashi is to bring out the inherent flavor of ingredients without impairing the distinctiveness of the dish.

The flavor of dashi differs not only depending on the type of kombu but also the type of *katsuobushi* flakes used. The *karebushi* flakes (see p. 99) yield a stronger flavored stock than *arabushi*. People of the Kansai area, who prefer lighter, more refined tastes, tend to use *arabushi*, while the stronger-tasting *karebushi* flake stock is more popular in the Kanto area. Flakes made from fillets of bonito (*katsuo*) is the most common, but tuna (*maguro*), mackerel (*saba*), and sardine (*iwashi*) flakes are also used. *Niboshi*, which are small, dried fish such as *iwashi*, are also used to make stock. The most common type used for stock are Japanese anchovies (*katakuchi iwashi*), which contain fat and make a rich-tasting stock. *Niboshi* are not usually used alone for stock, but generally added to further enhance the richness of flavor in a kombu and katsuobushi stock.

Dashi has been a familiar element of Japanese cooking for centuries, as we can tell from works compiled in the Muromachi period (1336–1573) detailing how to make kombu stock. Indeed, stock has a long tradition in various parts of the world—the bouillon and *fond* of France, the *tang* of China, and so forth—although the ingredients and the way stock is used in cooking may differ from one place to another. With the healthy aspects of Japanese food gaining the limelight in recent years, chefs around the world who have learned about the techniques of making Japanese stock have begun to develop original recipes utilizing bouillon and umami-rich ingredients in place of butter and cream. Mushrooms, tomatoes, chicken and other ingredients that make good stock are available around the world and research led by chefs is progressing in the uses of umami-rich ingredients. The potential for new types of stock seems to be infinite.

Kombu and *Katsuobushi*

Kombu seaweed and *katsuobushi* (dried bonito) are indispensable to good dashi. The types of kombu most commonly used to make broth are Rishiri (*Saccharina ochotensis*; right page), Rausu (*Saccharina diabolica*), Hidaka (*Saccharina angustata*), and Makombu (*Saccharina japonica*). Rishiri kombu makes a clear, mild broth ideal for refined kaiseki soups. Hidaka kombu, meanwhile, is used for dashi, but because it is soft and thick it is also suitable for kombu rolls and simmered dishes.

Katsuobushi is processed by drying and smoking, and may be found as *karebushi*, covered with mold, or *arabushi*, without mold. The mold causes the breakdown of proteins in the fish and the formation of amino acids that enhance umami. *Arabushi* produces a relatively clear soup, while *karebushi* has a deeper aroma and a richer flavor.

Rishiri kombu (right page, right hand), which yields a clear, lucid dashi and *karebushi*, known for its deep, umami-rich flavor (lefthand).

甘鯛すまし仕立て
Amadai Sumashi-jitate

Tilefish in Clear Broth

The flavor of *nimono* is determined by the quaity of the broth (*suiji*) made by seasoning dashi with soy sauce, salt, and other ingredients. *Sumashi-jitate* is the most basic method of preparation, and uses ichiban dashi. In this recipe, dried sea cucumber ovaries plus rapeseed blossom, a spring vegetable, are added to tilefish grilled to a fragrant golden brown, the tang of *yuzu* providing the final touch. RECIPE P. 192

おこぜ丸仕立て *Okoze Maru-jitate*

Devil Stinger in "Turtle Style" Broth

Maru-jitate broth is also known as "turtle style" broth and refers to a type of dish in which an ingredient with a distinctive flavor—like turtle—is boiled in a considerable quantity of sake to make dashi, then seasoned with soy sauce and other ingredients. The technique eliminates overly strong flavors and odors, and also takes advantage of the umami produced by gelatinous ingredients. In addition to turtle, devil stinger (*okoze*), flathead, or chicken may also be used. RECIPE P. 192

鰻潮仕立て *Unagi Ushio-jitate*

Eel in Salt Broth

This dish is based on the technique used to make sea bream salt broth. The art of cooking sea bream this way has to do with striking the perfect balance between obtaining broth from the fish and cooking it only so long that one can still eat the flesh. The fish must have bones, and some gelatinous component. For sea bream, prep to remove any odor before cooking in kombu stock, skimming as needed, and about 10 minutes after it boils the result will be a clear, tasty soup.

Preparing stock from eel is unusual, and here the stock is made in essentially the same manner as salt broth from sea bream, paired with unseasoned grilled eel. The grilled aroma transfers to the stock, adding extra body to its flavor. Foods such as turtle and chicken can be served in a salt broth in a similar manner. Think about how to substitute different ingredients and many variations will come to mind.

RECIPE P. 192

Shojin dashi

Vegetarian dashi, made mainly from kombu, but also from dried shiitake, soybeans, dried *kampyo* gourd peel, and the dried peels of other vegetables, has been used since olden times as a *shojin* broth that does not use animal or seafood products. Water in which dried shiitake mushrooms have been soaked becomes fragrant and rich with umami, but in order to keep its taste from becoming overpowering, attention must be paid to balancing its flavor. Toasted soybeans add a delicate and light aroma.

Since *shojin* dashi does not use animal-source ingredients, its taste may be weak, and a skillful combination of ingredients can obtain a deeper flavor. The umami of shiitake is said to be increased 10 times by drying. Part of the spirit of *shojin* cuisine is taking time and trouble to dry, roast, or otherwise prepare ingredients.

Soybeans, dried shiitake mushrooms, *kampyo* gourd peel—ingredients for *shojin* dashi.

飛龍頭椀 *Hiryuzu-wan*

Hiryuzu Tofu Dumplings

Hiryuzu dumplings are made by adding vegetables and other plant-based ingredients to a dough of tofu and *yamato* imo, a type of tuber, which is then formed into balls and fried. The word *hiryuzu* is said to be adapted from *filhos*, a fried Portuguese confection, and the dumplings are also known as *ganmodoki*. *Hiryuzu* are filling, and in *shojin* cooking often serve as a meat substitute. The inclusion of carrot, *kikurage* (a mushroom known as wood ear: *Auricularia auricula-judae),* lily bulbs and gingko nuts make for a complex taste and texture experience. Accompanied by edible wild bracken fern and topped with grilled butterbur sprouts, this dish is a symphony of spring fragrances and flavors.

RECIPE P. 193

What Is Umami?

Umami is one of the five basic tastes. Following sweet, sour, salty, and bitter, it was the last of the five to be identified. A basic taste is one for which the tongue has unique receptors and one that cannot be obtained by combining other tastes. Umami fulfills both of these criteria. Often described as "savory," umami is associated with foodstuffs as diverse as kombu kelp, aged cheese, and ripe tomatoes.

Umami is found in amino acids like monosodium glutamate and nucleic acids like inosinic acid and guanylic acid. Extensive research has shown that umami is a taste naturally enjoyed by humans and other animals. In fact, glutamate is present in human breast milk and research has shown that newborn babies react positively to the flavor of umami.

The Japanese kelp known as kombu contains particularly high concentrations of glutamate, and it is possible to obtain a solution with a highly pure and concentrated umami flavor simply by steeping kelp in hot or cold water. Because kombu-based stock is commonly used throughout Japan to prepare a variety of dishes, Japanese people are regularly exposed to foods rich in umami. This cultural context is part of the reason why the basic taste of umami was first discovered by the Japanese biochemist Ikeda Kikunae, who identified it 100 years ago. Crystals of monosodium glutamate have been sold in Japan as umami flavorings since Ikeda's discovery.

When the umami flavor in kombu combines with nucleic acids found in foods like bonito flakes or shiitake mushrooms, the concentration of umami increases dramatically. This is known as "umami synergy." Kinoshita Shukuo was the first to identify the umami synergy effect produced by glutamic acid and inosinic acid (by combining kombu and bonito flakes), while Kuninaka Akira identified the umami synergy resulting from the combination of glutamic acid and guanylic acid, as occurs when using kelp and shiitake mushrooms together. These discoveries allowed for the development of new ways of producing the rich umami flavor found in traditional Japanese dashi stock.

Ingredients like kombu that contain high natural concentrations of pure umami are not widely used outside of Japanese cuisine. Because of this, it took

蛤真蒸 *Hamaguri Shinjo*

Hamaguri Clam Dumpling

Hamaguri clams come into season in the spring. These clams are rich in glutamate and other umami components and taste distinctly sweet. Most of their umami flavor is found in their juices, so items such as soups and steamed dishes in which their juices are dissolved are the best way to savor this shellfish's exquisite flavor. To capitalize on the synergistic effect of the umami ingredients glutamate and inosinate, serve in a blend of *hamaguri* juice and ichiban dashi,.

Zinbaso is a variety of brown seaweed of which mainly young shoots are eaten. Low in calories and high in minerals, particularly when in bud, its tender mouthfeel is in a class of its own.

RECIPE P. 193

time for cooks and consumers around the world to become aware of umami. Now that umami is better understood, it is recognized that many ingredients familiar elsewhere, including raw tomatoes, vegetables, and mushrooms, also contain glutamate, albeit in lower amounts than kombu. Since many types of seafood and meat contain inosinic acid, combining them with glutamate-containing ingredients releases a strong umami flavor via umami synergy. In fact, many kinds of soup are made around the world by boiling meat, bones, and vegetables, and almost all of them are built around the taste of umami.

Fermentation also produces amino acids and nucleic acids with a strong umami flavor. Fermented products made with grain and fish contain high concentrations of umami, and foods with a strong umami flavor produced by fermentation have existed since ancient times in many world cuisines. This tradition is particularly strong in Asia, where examples include miso, soy sauce, and fish sauces like *nuoc mam* and *nam pla*.

Matsutake mushroom *hitashi*: *matsutake* mushroom, kikuna and *katsuobushi*.

八寸 黒桶秋草飾り

Hassun Kuro-oke Akikusa-kazari

Hassun in a Black Barrel with Autumn Wildflowers

The sensation that something is "delicious" is experienced along dimensions that include the five basic tastes, aroma, texture, and surroundings. Consuming umami results in the release of beta-endorphins, endorphin being an abbreviation for "endogenous morphine," in other words a drug produced in the brain, imparting a feeling that something is "delicious."

Japanese people have been consuming umami-rich foods such as miso and dashi for centuries, so they are attuned to umami, but everyday umami foods incorporating local ingredients can be found the world over. Combining western and Japanese ingredients such as tomatoes and *katsuobushi*, meat and kombu, opens up endless new possibilities for savoring umami.

This medley of foods maximizing umami synergy can be described as "umami hassun." Each component utilizes this synergistic effect to draw out rich umami flavor: inosinate and glutamate in the salt-grilled *kobujime* style beef, guanylate and inosinate in the *matsutake* mushroom *hitashi* and *katsuobushi*, inosinate and glutamate in the prawns and sea urchin.

Adorned with autumn flora, this is a delight for the eyes as well as the palate. RECIPE P. 193

五法

The Five Techniques

Kiru [CUTTING]

No other cuisine emphasizes cutting techniques quite to the extent that Japanese cuisine does. The importance of knife skills stems, no doubt, from the many dishes—among which sashimi is but one—that are prepared from raw ingredients. Slicing raw fish demands seasoned practice, but more than ten ways of cutting vegetables are used for everyday cooking, and far more if the techniques for creating decorative trimmings to enhance the beauty and seasonal character of dishes are included. Using ingenious, specialized cutting techniques for each ingredient in a simmered dish ensures that all ingredients can come out perfectly cooked, producing dishes that are pleasing to the eye as well as the palate.

Japanese Knives

庖丁

There are several dozen kinds of traditional Japanese knives, each with a distinct purpose. The *deba* knife, with its pointed tip and thick blade, is for efficiently cleaning and filleting fish, cutting through tough joints, and cleaving bones. In order to cleanly slice the soft flesh of raw fish and shellfish, sashimi knives are slim along their length. In the Kansai area, the sashimi knife is called the *yanagiba* because it is shaped like a willow (*yanagi*) leaf and has a pointed tip, while the Kanto-style sashimi knife, known as *takobiki* for its utility in cutting the curled legs of octopus (*tako*), is of equal width from hilt to tip. The *usuba* knife has a broad, thin blade handy for cutting vegetables; its sharp edge allows for finely dicing and chopping vegetables as well as *katsuramuki* rotary peeling using the center

of the blade. In the Kansai area, the tip is rounded off in a shape resembling a sickle, hence its other name, *kamagata*. In the Kanto area, the squared off *usuba* is the norm.

While these are the most common knives, there are also more specialized knives like the *sushikiri*, used to slice rolled or pressed sushi; the *honekiri*, used to cut through the fine bones of *hamo* (conger eel); the *unagisaki*, used to fillet eel (there are different kinds such as Kanto-style, Osaka-style, and Kyoto-style, because the way an eel is filleted differs by region) the *barankiri*, used to cut the *haran* (Aspidistra) leaves used as separators when combining dishes in one vessel and the *kurimuki*, for removing the hard shells from chestnuts.

ふぐ菊花造り　*Fugu Kikka-zukuri*

"Chrysanthemum" of *Fugu* Sashimi

Fugu (blowfish) is a high-protein, low-fat, premium fish rich in umami that comes into season in mid-winter. Since the liver contains a deadly toxin, a specialist's license is required to handle the fish.

The flesh of *fugu* is chewy, so it is sliced thinly using a specially designed knife to make it easier to enjoy its delicate flavor. Chefs in the Kanto and Kansai regions have different ideas regarding the ideal thickness of *fugu* sashimi: in Kanto the fish is sliced thin enough that the pattern on the plate underneath is visible, while in Kansai, *fugu* slices are a little thicker, the emphasis being on flavor. Different knives are used in each region.

Fugu sashimi is accompanied by citrus fruit such as bitter orange, *yuzu* or *sudachi*. There is also a custom of serving pickled eggplant, traditionally thought to possess antidotal properties.

五色和え　*Goshiki-ae*

Five-Color Salad

Goshiki-ae is a medley of foods of five colors (*goshiki*) such as green, white, brown, yellow and red. There are myriad combinations of ingredients, and the result is a dish not only visually appealing, but nutritionally balanced as well.

This *goshiki-ae* salad is a refreshing vinegared five color combination of crab, cucumber, *Kintoki* carrot, daikon and *nori*, colorful to the eye and pleasing to the palate. RECIPE P. 194

Niru [COOKING IN LIQUID]

Simmering (*niru*) one or more ingredients in dashi with soy sauce, mirin, or other seasonings until most of the liquid has been boiled away is one important method of cooking. Another is cooking until the liquid is completely gone (*taku*) as is the case when cooking rice. In the Kansai area, the two words tend to be used more or less synonymously.

There are a number of types of pot cooking distinguished by the seasonings used and cooking methods, including *umani* (sweet-seasoned with mirin and simmered to a glossy finish), *nishime* ("waterless" simmering of ingredients in their own juices), and *miso-ni* (simmering in a mixture of miso, mirin, soy sauce and other seasonings). Sometimes ingredients are simmered separately and then combined (*takiawase*), a technique that demands seasoned knowledge of timing and selection of ingredients.

Prominent among simmered foods is the *nimonowan* (simmered dish) course of kaiseki cuisine. This dish showcases seasonality in the choice of a main ingredient (*wandane*) that is simmered in a basic broth known as *sui-ji* and presented with a standard garnish (*aomi*) and aromatic element (*kaori*). When one removes the lid of the *nimonowan* bowl, one finds the highly perfected essence of Japanese cuisine.

煮しめ *Nishime*

Simmered Vegetable Stew

The perfect way to prepare root vegetables like burdock root (*gobo*) and lotus root, *nishime* is also ideal for foodstuffs such as kombu and *konnyaku* (devil's tongue). The ingredients are simmered until they completely absorb the flavors, then they are removed from the stock to be served.

RECIPE P. 194

冬瓜まんじゅう *Togan Manju*

Winter Melon Dumplings

Despite its name, winter melon is a summer vegetable. Over 90 percent water, it is effective in reducing inflammation. Rubbing baking soda and salt onto the skin of winter melon and boiling it gives it an attractive green finish. And when a fine crosshatched pattern is carved onto its surface and the melon is squeezed in a cloth, it forms a neat parcel that retains its shape. Stuffed with wood ear mushroom and lily bulb, in this dish it is served with horsehair crab, in a chilled combination that looks as refreshing as it tastes and is a superb summer treat.

RECIPE P. 195

鯛かぶら *Tai Kabura*

Stewed Sea Bream and Turnip

Sea bream and turnip ranks as one of the top winter food pairings. Swapping a portion of the stocks while separately simmering the ingredients enables the umami of each to penetrate the other, making both even tastier. **RECIPE P. 195**

伊勢海老具足煮
Ise ebi Gusoku-ni

Ise Lobster Cooked in the Shell

Boiling lobster, prawns and crab in the shell is known in Japanese as *gusoku-ni*, because this makes them look like the *gusoku* (shinguards) worn by samurai in battle. This dish is also similar to bouillabaisse, the lobster soup in which the shells can be oven-roasted for a more intense flavor. To finish, the lobster is very briefly simmered once more to maximize its fragrant seafood umami. RECIPE P. 195

筍と若布炊き合わせ
Takenoko to Wakame Takiawase

Simmered Bamboo Shoot and *Wakame*

Bamboo shoot with *wakame* seaweed is a classic spring combination that makes sense not only as a tasty blend of foods from mountain and sea, but also at a more scientific level. Combining bamboo shoot, which contains glutamate, and *wakame*, a source of inosinate, stimulates the appetite. Coating the bamboo shoot—already cooked in kombu stock—with a thin layer of *katsuobushi* amplifies the synergistic effect of the umami even further. The ingredients are cooked in a manner that draws out their best qualities in stages: one first senses the umami, then tastes the sweetness and flavor of the bamboo shoot core. Grilling the broad beans amplifies their fragrant aroma and adds a hint of bitterness.

The dish is served in a bowl with an auspicious *unkin* pattern depicting cherry blossoms and maple, the intertwined flowers and leaves a reference to the way spring and autumn always come around, just as a long life continues. RECIPE P. 195

冬野菜炊き合わせ *Fuyuyasai Takiawase*

Simmered Winter Vegetables

Cooking vegetables in stock made from the same vegetables—for example cooking turnips in dashi made from turnips—is a similar technique to that of *court-bouillon*. Each ingredient may be simmered with only light seasoning, but cooking in vegetable dashi is what makes this vegetable-only dish so flavorsome.

RECIPE P. 196

煮物椀 清汁仕立て *Nimonowan Sumashi-jitate*

Simmered Bowl of Clear Broth

Sumashi-jitate is a cooking technique that involves adding salt to ichiban dashi for flavor, then imparting extra aroma and flavor with soy sauce. It relies on the use of delicious dashi. Numerous variations are possible using different ingredients. RECIPE P. 196

鳴門鱧葛叩き *Naruto Hamo Kudzu-tataki*

Naruto Conger Eel in *Kudzu* Coating

Featuring conger eel rolled into a spiral shape inspired by the whirlpools of the Naruto Strait, the striking appearance of this dish equals its exquisite taste. A ring of *yuzu* peel is placed on top to emphasize the spiral pattern. The accompanying bamboo fungus (*kinugasatake*) is stuffed with burdock root (*gobo*) to form a distinctive cross-section. Served with a clear soup with a subtle flavor.

RECIPE P. 196

Yaku [COOKING WITH DIRECT HEAT]

Yakimono is a broad category that includes all manners of cooking by exposing ingredients directly (or semi-directly) to heat—grilling over an open fire, frying in a pan, or roasting in an oven. It is the simplest and probably the oldest form of cooking. Whether the flavor of the ingredients can be savored to best advantage or not depends on the cook's skill in utilizing the heat source. The main types of *yakimono* are open fire (*jikabi*) grilling—whether charcoal or gas. Grilling removes bitterness and excess moisture and brings out the inherent flavors of ingredients.

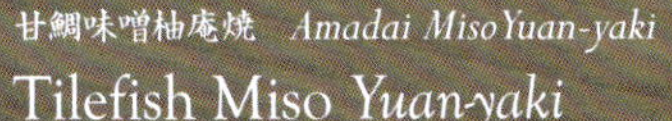

甘鯛味噌柚庵焼　*Amadai Miso Yuan-yaki*

Tilefish Miso *Yuan-yaki*

Yuan-yaki is a cooking technique in which fish is marinated in a "Yuan" base containing sake, soy sauce, and slices of *yuzu* before cooking. In miso *Yuan-yaki* white miso is added to the marinade for a richer flavor. Commonly used for white fish such as tilefish, bream and Spanish mackerel, in winter it is also used for butterfish. The marinade also serves as a good complement for oily fish and chicken. RECIPE P. 197

諸子つけ焼き *Moroko Tsuke-yaki*

Biwa Gudgeon Grilled with Soy-based Sauce

Biwa gudgeon (*moroko*) is a freshwater fish found most famously in Lake Biwa and prized for its delicate, "non-fishy" flavor. Roe-carrying specimens, caught in March and April, are especially sought after.

In this recipe gudgeon are partially grilled, then cooked over charcoal. These are in fact tricky fish to cook: when the head is not thoroughly cooked it is chewy, so the fish are grilled upright to ensure that their fat runs down, for a crispy finish. RECIPE P. 197

賀茂茄子 枝豆味噌田楽 *Kamo nasu Edamame Miso Dengaku*

Kamo Eggplant in Edamame *Dengaku* Miso Glaze

Dengaku miso dishes can be adapted to the season: butterbur shoots in early spring, *kinome* leaves from spring into early summer, and so on. Here Kamo eggplant, a summer ingredient, is served with a puree of edamame—another summer ingredient—mixed with white miso, in a delectable combination of complementary seasonal specialties.

RECIPE P. 197

落葉焼き *Ochiba-yaki*

Grilled Autumn Leaf Medley

Grilled combination of tilefish, prawns, chestnuts and gingko nuts arranged with fallen leaves, chestnut leaves, and the like in a dish inspired by the autumn landscape. Grilling cedar shavings soaked in sesame oil over charcoal contributes a tantalizing aroma, and keeps the dish warm, while the smoke adds a performative element. RECIPE P. 197

Musu [STEAMING]

Placing ingredients in a tightly lidded pot and cooking them in steam preserves their subtle flavors and nutrients and keeps them tender and moist while avoiding the risk of scorching present when cooking with direct heat. It is a method especially well-suited for preparing white fish and plain-tasting vegetables. Steamed turnips (*kabura-mushi*), steaming in sake (*saka-mushi*), and steamed fish hot pot (*chiri-mushi*) are some well-known steamed dishes that convey a sense of seasonality.

菜の花蒸し雲丹あん　*Nanohana-mushi Uni-an*

Steamed Field Mustard in Sea Urchin Sauce

Steamed rapeseed blossom (*nanohana*) is often topped with the sieved yolk of boiled or scrambled egg to resemble the yellow rape flower. In this recipe, the yellow color is produced by dashi containing sea urchin instead. The rapeseed blossom is stuffed with various ingredients including woodear mushroom, soy pulp and lily bulb, and finished with a rich umami broth containing sea urchin. The vibrant yellow and verdant green of this dish herald the arrival of spring. RECIPE P. 198

若草蒸し *Wakakusa-mushi*

Spanish Mackerel Steamed with Spring Herbs

Spanish mackerel (*sawara*) is a fish associated primarily with spring, hence its other name: the "herald of spring." Its tender white flesh and subtle taste make it a sought after indulgence at this time of year. *Sawara* is the main ingredient in this steamed dish that also includes other spring temptations such as rape blossom and horsetail. The green of the rape blossom represents early spring, when the snow melts and new sprouts emerge. **RECIPE P. 198**

丹波蒸し *Tamba-mushi*

Tamba-mushi

The Tamba region, comprised of parts of central Kyoto prefecture and central Hyogo prefecture, produces brands of beef, vegetables and other agricultural and food products renowned throughout Japan. This steamed dish, full of Tamba specialties like chestnuts, *matsutake* mushrooms, and adzuki beans, is suffused with a sense of the Tamba autumn.

A dough made from sieved chestnuts and eggs is steamed, and chestnuts simmered in dashi are placed on top. Tamba chestnuts are huge (reputedly the largest in Japan), tender, and also intensely sweet and fragrant, making them a popular variety for gifts. A true indulgence, this dish is crammed with seasonal treats that include *matsutake*, barracuda, and lily bulbs. It is visually stunning as well, thanks to the vibrant yellow of the chestnut dough. RECIPE P. 198

Ageru [DEEP-FRYING]

Tempura is the most common dish prepared by deep-frying (*ageru*) ingredients at a high temperature in a large amount of oil. The batter (*koromo*) into which the ingredients are dipped before they are deep-fried traps their subtle umami during high-temperature, rapid cooking. The allure of tempura is in the combination of textures—the crisp coating contrasts with the tender, moist ingredient within. All sorts of variations are possible by applying seasonings to the ingredients or changing the *koromo*.

秋の吹き寄せ盛り *Aki no Fukiyose-mori*

Autumn *Fukiyose* Medley

The word *fukiyose* (see p. 92) refers to the leaves of different trees blown by the wind to settle in one place, and it is used for dishes featuring several varieties of simmered and fried foods, carefully arranged together, or for combinations of dry confections in the shape of pine needles, maple leaves and so on. In this *fukiyose* medley, ingredients such as gingko nuts and "pinecones" are arranged to reflect autumn leaves or landscapes.

Tilefish is a prized fish, low in fat and with melt-in-the-mouth white flesh, that comes into season during the cool period from late autumn to early spring. Lightly salted, the tilefish is sweet and richly flavorful in a way that easily rivals the mellow aroma and flavor of ingredients like *matsutake* and log-grown *maitake* mushrooms. RECIPE P. 199

目板鰈唐揚　*Meitagarei Kara-age*

Deep-Fried Finespotted Flounder

Finespotted flounder (*meitagarei*) is a small turbot delicious salt-grilled, stewed, or deep-fried. In this dish the fish is dried before frying. Drying accelerates the maturation process, boosting the umami content, and removes moisture for firmer flesh. RECIPE P. 199

アイナメあられ粉揚げ桜餡
Ainame Arareko-age Sakura-an

Fried Greenling in Cracker Crumbs with Cherry Blossom Sauce

The highly valued fish *ainame* (fat greenling, *Hexagrammos otakii*), also known as *aburame,* is a white fish that has a good covering of fat and comes into season in late spring and early summer. It is prepared in many different ways—grilled, fried, or as sashimi—that give full play to its delectable flavor and texture.

The flour used to dredge the *ainame* consists of finely-crushed rice crackers. The crackers are made by drying cooked glutinous rice cakes (*mochi*), baking, then crushing them finely into "arare" crackers, resulting in crackers with a delicious aroma.

The pale pink *an* (sauce) is made by blending steamed cherry blossoms and lily bulb *an*. The color and fragrance of the blossom gives this dish the true feel of spring. RECIPE P. 200

若鮎南蛮漬け 木の芽おろし
Wakaayu Nanban-zuke Kinome-oroshi

Young Sweetfish "Nanban-zuke" Style Served with Grated *Sansho* Pepper Leaves

Nanban-zuke is a style of cooking in which fish or other foods are fried and then marinated in vinegar. On this occasion we used several young sweetfish (*ayu*), an early summer treat, grilling the fish over charcoal before frying to bring out their aroma. When thoroughly grilled, they retain their delicious fragrance even after frying. Grilling and then frying heats the fish through twice, leaving even the bones tender. The fish's mouth is opened for grilling, which helps the heat to penetrate, and ensures a crisp texture. The vibrant green, fragrant leaves of the *sansho* pepper tree are beaten and mixed with grated daikon radish to highlight the fish's flavor and aroma. RECIPE P. 200

Chapter 5

DISHES FOR SEASONAL FESTIVITIES

Japanese food culture has evolved in close relation to traditional rituals and festivities of the four seasons. Such events bring families or communities closer together through the sharing of seasonal foods and reaffirmation of traditions. Here we look at the meaning and spirit of these events and celebrations that mark the changing seasons and the rites of passage in people's lives.

[今様]

Imayo

The names for the months of the lunar calendar year evoke a sense of the cycle and events of the seasons. The list here gives the brief meaning of these traditional names. *Mutsuki*, for example, evokes the gatherings of family and relatives customary at the New Year; *Kisaragi* is a month of the still-bitter cold of winter, *Yayoi* brings the advent of warm weather, and so on. Japan shifted to the solar calendar in 1873, but these names are sometimes used in the arts, literature, and observance of customs and rituals.

睦月	*Mutsuki*	Month of family gatherings (1st month)
如月	*Kisaragi*	Month of adding an extra layer of clothing (2nd month)
弥生	*Yayoi*	Month of rebirth (3rd month)
卯月	*Uzuki*	Month of the deutzia flower, *u-no-hana* (4th month)
皐月	*Satsuki*	Month for planting rice seedlings (5th month)
水無月	*Minazuki*	Month of drawing water into paddy fields (6th month)
文月	*Fumizuki*	Month of rice ripening (7th month)
葉月	*Hazuki*	Month of falling leaves (8th month)
長月	*Nagatsuki*	Month of long nights (9th month)
神無月	*Kannazuki*	Month of the gods (10th month)
霜月	*Shimotsuki*	Month of frost (11th month)
師走	*Shiwasu*	Month of busyness even for priests (12th month)

正月 The New Year's Celebration (*Shogatsu*)

The most important traditional annual event in Japan is the celebration of New Year's. People look forward to the opportunity to make a new start both mentally and physically, and they believe the deity of the New Year—Toshigami—will bring them happiness. To make sure the New Year deity finds its way into the home, a pair of pine branches is traditionally attached to the gate. Being an evergreen, the pine is thought to be an auspicious tree sure to provide a comfortable abode for the deity whenever it visits.

Toshigami bestows upon a home an energy called *ki* that replenishes the minds and bodies of all who live there. The image of this *ki* is of a round ball, so to represent it for the New Year discus-shaped cakes of pounded glutinous white rice (*mochi*) called *kagami-mochi* (lit., mirror *mochi*) are made to decorate the household altar to the gods (*kamidana*) with a stack of two *kagami-mochi* festooned with a bright orange *daidai* citrus fruit. (see p. 64)

Having put in place such decorations to welcome the deity, it is customary for the family to gather on New Year's morning for a special meal of festive foods. One of the main dishes is *zoni*, a soup made in different ways and with different ingredients from one part of the country to another, but invariably containing *mochi*. The other festive foods, together called *osechi ryori*, consist of a variety of delicacies prepared to symbolize happiness throughout the year and attractively served in square lacquered boxes called *o-ju*.

正月の八寸 *Shogatsu no Hassun*

New Year *Hassun*

When preparing *hassun* for New Year, it is important to visually convey the jubilant feel of the holiday. At this time of year, kaiseki *hassun* are crammed with traditionally auspicious foods such as dried sardines, a celebratory snack to accompany drinks; herring roe on kombu, representing prosperity for one's descendants; prawns, symbol of longevity; and arrowhead bulb (*kuwai*), deemed auspicious due to its large shoot.

RECIPE P. 200

The standard pair of *kadomatsu* festoons flank the gate of a house at New Year's.

Nirami-dai; glaring sea bream

One of the dishes prepared for the New Year in Kyoto is called *nirami-dai* (lit., glaring sea bream). A large sea bream is scaled, salted, and grilled whole and placed on display (to "gaze at"—*niramu*—only) alongside the boxes of festive foods served in stacked boxes (*o-ju*) at New Year's. For the first three days of the New Year the dish is left untouched, and then on the fourth day it is eaten. By then the meat of the fish has become firm and tasty and when it is simmered with tofu and other plain-tasting ingredients, they as well as the meat are delicious. While a somewhat unusual custom, *nirami-dai* passes down the wisdom of the past for enjoying this fish associated with festive occasions.

The Beginning of Spring *(Setsubun)*

The changing of the seasons is the focus of special attention and traditional observances. One of these is the first day of spring (Risshun) according to the traditional lunar calendar. The date falls at a time when it is actually still very cold in Japan, so its celebration is an expression of eager anticipation of spring even as cold weather continues.

Since Risshun marks the beginning of the year, a ritual called Setsubun (lit., "division of the seasons") is held the day before Risshun to usher in the new year. Many different beliefs surround ways for driving away ill fortune and ushering in good fortune and happiness. Misfortune is thought to come in the form of evil spirits called *oni*, and to keep them away garlands of thorny holly or strong-smelling sardine heads may be placed at the entrance. On the evening of Setsubun, hard, roasted soybeans are tossed from inside the rooms toward the outside, symbolically pelting the unwelcome *oni* and driving them away. Then, in accordance with custom, each person eats the number of the roasted beans corresponding to his or her age, thereby warding off illness and misfortune for the entirety of the coming year.

A new dish has been recently added to the more long-established foods of Setsubun: *ehomaki* rolled sushi. The custom originated in the Kansai region near Kyoto and Osaka, but has lately spread throughout the country. The name means "direction-of-blessings sushi roll," and it is to be eaten silently, facing the direction from which happiness for that year will come.

On the lid of the dish is the label *Risshun Daikichi,* meaning good fortune on the first day of spring, an expression it is said will disperse demons, and allow you to pass the year safely.

節分の八寸 *Setsubun no Hassun*

Hassun for Setsubun

At the festival of Setsubun, on the day before the official start of spring, the ritual cleansing of evil spirits is performed ahead of the new season. As well as this purification, this *hassun* signifies joy at the onset of spring. The plate used is *horaku* (bisque pottery), inspired by *horaku-otoshi*, a demon-exorcising ritual performed at Kyoto's Mibudera temple.

Rites to drive out "demons" as symbols of evil spirits are an essential element of Setsubun celebrations. Here a dish with a demon's face on it is used, a prawn prepared to resemble the golden staff (*kanabo*) purportedly carried by demons, and a square box carved from daikon radish to resemble that used for the ritual scattering of beans.

Arrowhead (*kuwai*) bulb, carved into the shape of a votive picture, expresses the joy of the new spring, while the chubby-faced "otafuku" sushi is another talisman deemed to bring good fortune. RECIPE P. 201

桃の節句 The Peach Blossom Festival —Dolls' Day (*Momo no Sekku*)

The series of annual events celebrated in Japan known as the *gosekku* (lit., "five divisions") were adopted from China but evolved in distinctive ways as part of Japanese culture. These special days are the Seven Herbs Festival on January 7th; the Peach Blossom Festival on March 3rd; the Iris Festival on May 5th; the Star Festival on July 7th; and the Chrysanthemum Festival on September 9th.

These events mark auspicious days but also opportunities to drive away ill fortune and trouble, so their celebration has acquired distinctive rituals. March 3rd, which is called the Shangsi festival in China, has come to be celebrated in Japan as "Dolls' Day" and is dedicated to the healthy growth of girls. This day is most significant because it provides an opportunity to remove and eliminate the ill-luck that may cling to our bodies and bring us trouble or misfortune. Long ago, people made effigies of themselves and cast them into a river to carry the ill luck away downstream. Later when the craft of doll-making had developed and fine and beautiful dolls were being made, dolls were not thrown into a river but kept in the home instead. The lovely images of the dolls mirror the charms of the little girls in the household, and are also associated with peach blossoms, which are used as decorations because they are blooming at just this time, giving the day its other name: the Peach Blossom Festival.

The food and drink most strongly associated with the Peach Blossom Festival include *hishi-mochi*, which are three-colored, diamond-shaped *mochi* cakes, and *shiro-zake*, or sweet white sake. Another is *kusa-mochi*, sweets made by pounding pungent-smelling *yomogi* (mugwort) leaves with glutinous rice. The highly aromatic cakes are believed to drive away evil. In early March, moreover, spring is finally on its way, and ingredients that herald the coming of spring like *hamaguri* clams and *tsukushi* (field horsetail) shoots are seasonal favorites.

姫ちらし *Hime Chirashi*

Scattered Spring Sushi Fit for a Princess

This variation on *chirashi-zushi* ("scattered sushi") contains over ten different ingredients, however both those mixed into the rice and those on top have their own individual flavors, and care is taken not to mix those flavors. Accompanied by wild vegetables, flower petal ginger and *kinome* leaf, this dish sings of the vibrant beauty of spring. RECIPE P. 202

The emperor and empress dolls put on display for Doll's Day (Momo no Sekku).

Cherry Blossom Viewing (*Hanami*)

Cherry blossoms are probably Japan's favorite flower. The timing of their much-anticipated blossoming changes from year to year depending on the weather, so predictions of when the flowers will first open and when they will reach their peak are important topics of conversation. Once the flowers are in full bloom, people hold parties under the trees, enjoying food and drink, singing and dancing. Why do people hold parties under cherry blossoms and not the blossoms of other trees? Ultimately, the reason is that the cherry tree is believed to be a favored abode of the gods.

The cherry blossom season coincides with the beginning of the wet paddy rice growing cycle. The ancients believed that their blooming was a sign that the gods of the fields, who had retired into the mountains for the winter, had returned to their fields and villages. So the blossoms represented the appearance of the field deities who would ensure a healthy growing season in the fields and paddies. When the cherry blossoms bloomed, people would make offerings of food and drink to please their divine visitors, and, while eating and drinking "with the gods," would offer entertainment in the form of song and dance. Those celebrations were the original form of *hanami*, or cherry blossom viewing. Of course, that original meaning has gradually been forgotten and *hanami* is now thought of simply as a spring ritual.

Following in that old tradition, feasting during the cherry blossom season was generally held out of doors and the food served in portable containers (*bento*). Some 400 years ago during the Edo period, elaborate cherry blossom viewing picnic sets were made, equipped with everything needed for drinking sake and serving a lavish meal. Cooks devised countless brightly colored morsels for an enjoyable outing under the blossoms.

花見重　*Hanami-ju*

Flower-viewing *Bento* Stack

During the Edo period, containers (right page) were designed to hold flower viewing (*hanami*) food and alcohol, for use at social gatherings under cherry trees in full bloom.

This flower-viewing *bento* stack contains a selection of over 20 delectable treats. *Bento* box contents center on snacks for consumption with party drinks, as well as foods easy to eat with the hands, such as sushi sticks. RECIPE P. **203**

Containers designed for *hanami*.

端午の節句 The Iris Festival—Children's Day (*Tango no Sekku*)

The seasonal festival *Tango no Sekku* was traditionally for boys, but it is now celebrated for all children. Its name comes from the fact that the date was traditionally the "first (*Tan*)" "Horse (*Go*)" day of the "Horse" month (the fifth month); later it was set to fall on the fifth day of the fifth month. Customs for driving away ill fortune and illness on this day include taking a bath in which strong-smelling iris leaves have been soaked, and throwing a bundle of iris leaves onto the roof of the house to protect the house from misfortune. The Japanese word for iris, the plant that represents this festival, is *shobu*, which is a homonym for another word that means "reverence for the code of samurai." As this suggests, the Iris Festival was most readily observed by samurai families. The typical decorations set up for this day feature dolls dressed in warrior garb, helmets of the type used by medieval warriors, and replicas of the bow-and-arrow sets used by the samurai of old. In Kyoto, the horse races held at the Kamo Shrine on this day recall the samurai love of competing with fine horses.

Another hallmark of Children's Day are "carp streamers," a relatively recent adoption with roots in the nineteenth century. Made of strong paper, they represent the family's prayers for their boys' success, that they may journey through the currents of life as vigorously as carp. The streamers may be large ones tied to tall poles hoisted in household gardens or miniature streamers hung from an apartment veranda. Sometimes they are strung on wires across rivers; in certain places hundreds of carp streamers

ちまき寿司 *Chimaki-zushi*

Sushi Wrapped in Bamboo Leaves

The Children's Festival on the fifth of May, dedicated to the healthy growth of children, is celebrated with two auspicious foods: *kashiwa-mochi* rice cakes and *chimaki-zushi*. The form and fillings of *chimaki* vary from region to region. In this version, *kinome* leaf buds—the signature fragrance of early summer—are mixed into the sushi rice, which is then topped with vinegared sea bream, wrapped in bamboo leaves, and bound with multiple gold and silver *mizuhiki* cords, a symbol of celebration. RECIPE P. 206

can be seen vigorously "swimming" in the wind, the sight brightening the landscape of late April and early May.

Festive foods for Children's Day include two kinds of wrapped *mochi*, *kashiwa-mochi*, *chimaki-mochi* and *chimaki-zushi*. Wrapping foods in leaves is a custom with a long history. *Kashiwa-mochi* is a sweet made of adzuki bean paste wrapped with pounded glutinous rice (*mochi*) and wrapped in an oak leaf before steaming. The oak tree (*kashiwa*) is a symbol of the continuation of the family line that also wards off evil and brings good luck. *Chimaki*, made with glutinous rice and adzuki bean powder and wrapped in *sasa* bamboo leaves, are a type of steamed sweet that was imported from China in ancient times.

Chimaki bound with multiple gold and silver *mizuhiki* cords.

Summer furnishings (*shitsurai*) of a *ryotei* restaurant room. Replacement of shoji with reed blinds for good ventilation and use of materials designed to look and feel cool are customary arrangements for relieving the heat of summer.

七夕

The Star Festival (*Tanabata*)

The origin of Tanabata is an old Chinese legend called Qixi. Vega, the brightest star in the constellation Lyra, is known in Asia as the "Weaving Girl" (*Orihime*) star while Altair in the constellation Aquila is called the "Cowherd" (*Hikoboshi*). The weaver and the cowherd married, but enjoyed each other's presence so much that they neglected their work, angering the king, who separated them across the Milky Way. Legend has it that only on the seventh day of the seventh month are they allowed to be together, and this day is celebrated as Tanabata.

When Tanabata was first celebrated in Japan, people prayed to the Weaving Girl star for weaving skills, as weaving was an important household industry. Over time Tanabata evolved into a festival for offering prayers of various kinds by writing them on strips of paper (*tanzaku*) and tying them to the branches of a bamboo stalk. In the past it was customary to cast the prayer-bedecked stalks into a river or the ocean to simultaneously drive away misfortune and have the prayers answered, but today displaying the decorated bamboo stalks is the main activity of the festival. In some cities, shopping arcades install Tanabata decorations featuring large-sized prayer cards, giant colored streamers, and many stalks of bamboo. Local communities look forward to this summertime event.

At Tanabata, decorations made from five strings of different colors are fashioned to symbolize the theme of weaving. People also exchange gifts of *somen*, the very thin wheat noodles reminiscent of threads on a loom.

Back cover of "Ama," noh song book *Koetsu utai-bon*.

七夕向 *Tanabata Mukae*

Tanabata Temptation

Around the star festival of Tanabata, to obtain nourishment for the coming summer it is common practice in Kyoto and other parts of the Kansai region to consume octopus on the day known as *hangesho*, eleven days after the summer solstice, and traditionally deemed the last day to sow seed for good harvests. Here the octopus is replaced by abalone, with its more intriguing texture, in an assembly of simmered abalone with Tosazu jelly accompanied by taro stalk sesame cream, a dish inspired by the Tanabata Weaver and Cowherd story that showcases exquisite contrasts in taste and ingredients, namely between tart and full-bodied, and between products of "mountain and sea."

The bamboo grass decorations of Tanabata add a delightful visual dimension to the dish. **RECIPE P. 206**

七夕祭

Gion Festivals

Gion festivals are a type of summer festivals celebrated in different parts of Japan, but by far the most famous is that held by the Yasaka Shrine in Kyoto. Kyoto's Gion Festival has been inscribed on UNESCO's list of Intangible Cultural Heritage sites, and any mention of *gion* festivals will evoke Kyoto's for most people.

Some 1,150 years ago, an epidemic struck the city of Kyoto, and at the time, it was thought that epidemics and disasters were caused by the vengeful spirits of people who had died unhappy deaths. Rituals, called *goryo-e*, were performed to transform such vengeful spirits (*goryo*) into deities that would use their powers not to do harm but rather to protect local residents. The rituals entreated the spirits to protect people from sickness and disaster and defend them from harm, and the *gion* festival is one such festival. A summertime festival, it focuses on prayers to be spared from disease and drought.

The highlight of the Kyoto Gion Festival is the parade of more than 30 floats (*dashi*). Some are very large, mounted with a tall pole representing a halberd (*hoko*) that is decorated with long swords or chrysanthemums; others are giant-wheeled *yama* floats, uniquely decorated and pulled using impressive ropes. The floats are paraded around the city on July 17th and 24th. The floats' elaborate decorations, including tapestries imported from Europe in the sixteenth century, make the floats virtually artworks themselves. During the Gion Festival, Kyotoites exchange gifts of mackerel sushi (*saba-zushi*) and conger eel sushi (*hamo-zushi*) and enjoy a Kyoto confection associated with the Gion Festival, *chigo-mochi*, which is made of pounded glutinous rice filled with sweet and salty miso and coated with flakes of freeze-dried *mochi* that resemble ice.

祇園祭の八寸 *Gion Matsuri no Hassun*

Gion Festival *Hassun*

During Kyoto's Gion festivals, worshippers pass through a large hoop made of straw, in a ritual said to guard against ill health and disaster. Here blades of bamboo grass were wound around a bamboo ring to resemble these straw hoops, and adorned with a good-luck talisman. The *gion* festivals are also known as the "*hamo* festivals," coinciding as it does with the season when *hamo* (pike eels) lay down a rich layer of fat. *Hamo* "stick" sushi is made with grilled unseasoned *hamo*, perfectly complemented by an intensely flavored sauce. RECIPE P. 207

Naginata (halberd) *hoko* float in the Kyoto Gion Festival. A child specially chosen (*chigo*) that year is seated atop the float.

盆

O-bon, the Summer Festival for the Ancestral Spirits

In mid-August (July in some areas) the spirits of the dead are believed to visit this world. This period is known as O-bon. Welcome fires (*mukae-bi*) are lit at the entrances to homes to help a family's ancestral spirits find their way. Within the home, special offerings are placed at the Buddhist altar and "cows" and "horses" made with vegetables are displayed on a shelf. "Horses" are made of cucumbers and "cows" eggplants. One theory suggests that people wish their ancestors to arrive quickly, riding horses, but depart slowly astride cows. Another theory, meanwhile, is that spirits ride the horses while the cows carry their luggage. These customs continue to be observed even today in some families. August 16th is the day the spirits of the ancestors return to the spirit world, therefore at this time people light farewell fires (*okuri-bi*) to send off the visiting spirits.

Each year in Kyoto, the fires of O-bon are lit on a grand scale in five locations along the mountains extending from Higashiyama in the east and Kitayama in the north to Saga. These are known as the Daimonji (the big characters) or the Gosan no Okuribi (five mountain farewell fires). The principal site is the slope of Mt. Nyoigatake on the eastern side of the city, where 75 fires are lit in the shape of the character "Dai" (大, great). The fires on the other mountainsides take the shape of the characters "Myo" and "Ho" (妙 and 法, wondrous dharma of Buddhist teachings), another smaller "Dai," as well as the shapes of a boat and a *torii* (shrine gate). The fires light up the darkness of the night. The continuation of these traditions is an indication that the city's residents maintain traditional beliefs. These great farewell fires last only about 20 minutes from the time they are lit, but they beautifully and aptly embody the poignant moment when people pause to remember their ancestors.

オランダ煮 *Oranda-ni*

"Dutch-Style" Stew

Stew "Dutch-style" refers to a cooking technique in which ingredients are sautéed or fried before simmering. This makes for an intriguing texture: crisp on the outside, moist on the inside, and the use of oil ensures that even *shojin* cuisine will be filling. The technique is said to have come to Japan through trade with Holland. **RECIPE P. 208**

重陽の節句

The Chrysanthemum Festival

(Choyo no Sekku)

September 9th is a day for warding off evil spirits and praying for long life. In China there was a legend that people who put branches of oleaster (Ch. *zhuyu*; Jp. *gumi*; Ln: *Elaeagnus*) in their hair and climbed a mountain would be spared from disaster. In Japan the custom is to hang a bag containing the fruit of the oleaster tree inside the house to ward off misfortune.

Another legend brought over from China was that those who drank the dew of the chrysanthemum would live like a boy for 700 years. The ninth day of the ninth month, therefore, is celebrated by drinking sake with chrysanthemum petals in it (*kikuzake*). Placing a cotton cloth over chrysanthemum blossoms to collect the dew overnight and then using this to wipe one's body so one can attain long life became a well established custom in Japan.

One reason for these customs is that, in yin-yang cosmology, odd numbers were considered yang or "positive" numbers, and nine in particular was regarded as the strongest figure in ancient times, making "double-nine" symbolic of the greatest and longest life. Another reason is that the strong smell of the chrysanthemum is thought to drive away evil.

During this season, cooks use chrysanthemums in a variety of ways, along with the season's best vegetables and abundant mushrooms.

菊菜ひたし *Kikuna-hitashi*

Boiled Chrysanthemum Greens

An *ohitashi* boiled vegetable dish using chrysanthemum, symbol of the Choyo or chrysanthemum festival, ninth day of the ninth month in the lunar calendar. Chrysanthemum flowers are mixed in, and also used as a garnish, while *matsutake* mushroom adds a hint of autumn. **RECIPE P. 208**

冬至

The Winter Solstice (*Toji*)

The shortest day of the year is called Toji (winter solstice), and in China and Japan it was customary to consider this day the beginning of the New Year. Today, few people are familiar with such traditions, yet there still remains a sense that the date marks the changing of the seasons and special foods are eaten in hopes that they will ward off illness and misfortune.

This is the season when the *yuzu* fruit, a Japanese citrus, has ripened, and one custom is to take a bath with *yuzu*. Its aroma and nutrients are thought to be good for the body, and those who take a good hot *yuzu-yu* bath are thought to be assured of enjoying a hale and hearty winter.

In ancient China it was customary to eat adzuki bean flavored gruel on the winter solstice, the red color of the beans being a potent talisman against evil. Rice porridge with adzuki beans is a special food served on the winter solstice in Japan as well. Another food eaten on this occasion is *kabocha* squash, also called *nankin*. It was believed that foods with names ending in "-n," like *nankin*, as well as *renkon* (lotus root) and *mikan* (tangerine), were good for warding off illness if eaten on the winter solstice. No doubt this was one way of assuring that in winter, when fresh vegetables were scarce, people would obtain sufficient vegetable nutrients to stay in good health until spring.

鹿ヶ谷かぼちゃ冬至仕立

Shishigatani Kabocha Toji-jitate

Shishigatani Squash, Winter Solstice Style

Eating foods with names that contain two *n* sounds at the winter solstice is said to bring *un* (good fortune). Using ingredients with an *n* at the end such as *ninjin* (carrot), *daikon*, *renkon* (lotus root) and *ginnan* (gingko nut) is referred to as *unmori:* literally "a plate of good fortune," and has auspicious associations. The quail meat dumplings used in this dish are generally known as *uzuragan*, but in *unmori* dishes are called *jungan* (*jun* being an alternative reading of *uzura,* meaning quail), that is, with two *n* sounds. In particular, eating a dish with ten *n* sounds is said to bring worldly success.

Squash is also known as *nankin*, and is an *unmori* food. Though actually a summer crop, being high in nutrients such as vitamin A and carotene, and a long keeper, it is not only auspicious, but a smart choice of food for getting through winter. RECIPE P. 209

大晦日 New Year's Eve (*Omisoka*)

In late December, people begin preparations for greeting the New Year. Stalls are opened that sell decorations made of rice straw and other ornaments to be placed in the home to symbolically protect it from misfortune, and other items for use over the New Year must be purchased beforehand as well.

One preparation event is the *mochi-tsuki*, for *mochi* is a food central to the New Year's festivities. The tradition for obtaining in a supply of *mochi* was to steam a quantity of glutinous *mochi* rice, pound it using mortar and pestle, and shape it into edible-sized cakes for use in the holiday meals or for making the large *kagami-mochi* offering to the gods (see p. 164). As it is easier to make *mochi* in large quantities, *mochi-tsuki* are often held as gatherings of relatives or neighbors and are a good occasion for reaffirming local and family ties. Today, however, *mochi* are most often purchased in stores and rarely made at home.

Another important preparation is housecleaning. The house must be cleaned from top to bottom, and on New Year's Eve, when everyone has been busy with cleaning, the customary meal is soba noodles, which are easy to make and to consume. The soba eaten on New Year's Eve is called *toshikoshi-soba*, or "year-crossing soba" and is eaten with the wish for a life that is long, like soba noodles.

As midnight approaches, people go to their local temple to ring the temple bell, the sound of which is thought to rid them of all the misfortunes and regrets they may have accumulated during the past year and prepare them for welcoming the New Year.

年越しそば *Toshikoshi-soba*

Year-Crossing Soba Noodles

Soba noodles are consumed on New Year's Eve, in the hope that happiness will be as long and thin (i.e. modest, humble) as the noodles. Generally the noodles are served in simple form as *kake-soba* or *zaru-soba*, these being easily prepared at a time when the household is busy with cleaning and preparations for the New Year celebrations. **RECIPE P. 209**

Temple bells are rung 108 times, starting on New Year's Eve, to banish the 108 worldly desires believed to burden human existence.

Diversity in Japanese Cuisine

KUMAKURA Isao

Historian

With the Asian mainland, especially Korea, so close to the long stretch of the Japanese archipelago, other food cultures have had a strong impact on the Japanese diet throughout history. Taro root culture came to Japan from the south via the Philippines and Taiwan while wet-rice cultivation was introduced from China and Korea. Chinese food culture arrived in several waves over a period of 1,300 years starting around the sixth century. A notable example is the *shojin* cuisine introduced to temples along with Zen Buddhism in the thirteenth century. Noodles and tofu made with soybeans became an established part of the diet from around that time.

Western European influences grew strong starting in the nineteenth century. Beef and pork, not part of the diet until then, came to be served in various dishes. Vegetables adopted from the West, such as cabbage and potatoes, soon began to be grown domestically. These new ingredients were used in ways compatible with Japanese tastes, producing *wayo-setchu* dishes that were a cross of Eastern and Western cuisine—*sukiyaki* hot pot, *tonkatsu* deep-fried cutlets, and croquettes suitable for a traditional Japanese meal complete with rice and miso soup. One aspect of the diversity of Japanese cuisine, therefore, developed from the incorporation of such influences from overseas into the native diet.

Another dimension of that diversity lies in the complex geography of the archipelago, blessed by a wide variety of ingredients used in some 1,000 types of local cuisine. Sushi is a good example. The origins of sushi go back to the fermented fish known as *nare-zushi*, fermentation being a method widely used for the long-term preservation of freshwater fish in East and Southeast Asia. Shiga prefecture's *funa-zushi*, made with carp (*funa*), is a typical example. It is made with rice and salt to induce lactic acid fermentation. Rather than allowing the fish to completely ferment, the sushi is deemed ready to eat when the lactic acid has imparted a tart, slightly sour flavor (since after all, "sushi" means "sour rice") to the cooked rice. In the nineteenth century a method was devised for making sushi by mixing vinegar with the rice,

Tempura

Unagi

rather than through fermentation, resulting in the sushi we know today. This is a good example of the way dishes introduced from outside have developed in distinctive ways in Japan. Tempura, too, came into being out of the marriage of the continental method of deep-frying in oil with the seasonal ingredients available in Japan.

Noodles are another important part of Japan's food culture. Flour was introduced from mainland Asia, and once stone mills had been imported, the culture of *udon* (thick wheat noodles) and *somen* (thin wheat noodles) took off. In mountainous areas not suited to wet-rice paddy farming and where fertilizer was scarce and the soil poor, people planted buckwheat (*soba*). *Udon* and *soba* are eaten both cold and hot. *Zaru-soba* are chilled buckwheat noodles served on a bamboo-slat rack and dipped in a cool dashi-based sauce. *Udon* and *soba*, eaten with a sauce with a flavorful dashi base, is among the favorite dishes of Japanese.

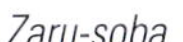

Zaru-soba

Udon

Ichi-ju San-sai

The Daily Menu of Soup and Three Side Dishes

KUMAKURA Isao

Historian

In fine restaurants, Japanese-style meals are often served on trays, one set at each place to hold chopsticks, sake cup, and the courses of the meal as they are served. These trays are the vestiges of the individual tray tables that were traditionally used for serving meals. The tray tables—called *zen*—used in households until the beginning of the twentieth century were of a size that was adequate to hold the rice bowl, bowl of soup, and one or two, at most three side dishes, plus a small saucer of pickles. The size of the tray table meant that the soup and three side dishes, along with rice, were the maximum served in ordinary home cooking. When guests were entertained and more dishes were to be served, the host would add another tray table per person. To serve especially lavish meals meant adding not just one, but two, four, or even six extra tables to the meal, although that practice is no longer seen today. When the trays were increased, there would be two or more kinds of soup and five or more side dishes. Daily family fare continues to be set apart from such fancy meals by the term *ichi-ju san-sai*—one soup, three side dishes (and the important but uncounted bowl of rice).

Both the Japanese meal served in restaurants and the food served in ordinary households embody the traditional way of eating referred to as *washoku*. The basic Japanese meal is thus household fare, the menu of which typically consists of four items: cooked rice, soup (usually but not always miso soup), side dishes, and pickles made by salting or fermentation. Traditionally, one to three side dishes were served, but today with the wealth of ingredients available, often four or even five accompany a meal. Sometimes the side dishes may include dishes derived from Western, Chinese, or other ethnic fare introduced to Japan over the last 100 years.

The content of daily household fare differs from one part of the country to another. In Kyoto, for example, home cooking is called "obanzai" and region-specific traditions linger in some parts of the country, such as having standard menus for meals on the first and fifteenth of the month. Distinctive styles of local cuisine (*kyodo ryori*) are rooted in the larger traditions of specific areas.

The one-soup, three side-dishes (*ichi-ju san-sai*) meal with rice provides a good balance of the different categories of food.

Health Benefits of Japanese Food

FUSHIKI Tohru

Scientist

The Distinctive Traits of Japanese Cuisine

Japan is one of the nations with the highest average life span in the world for both men and women, and the health benefits of Japanese food and the traditional Japanese diet have received greater and greater international attention in recent years. The traditional Japanese diet is built around a staple food of steamed rice. The word for "meal" is, in fact, the word *gohan*, which literally means "cooked rice." Rice has been revered as a sacred plant since early times, and has been favored by Japanese ever since. Miso soup and pickled vegetables—both rich in umami and saltiness—and a variety of side dishes, the majority consisting of fish or vegetables, complement the flavor of rice.

The manner in which a meal is customarily eaten is actually a key component of the traditional Japanese diet. Rather than eating each dish separately, people generally alternate between the dishes served—rice, a taste of a side dish, some soup, more rice, a bit of pickles, soup, and so on. This style of eating induces satiety after even a modest-sized meal, helping to reduce the total number of calories consumed daily. It also helps to keep oil and fat intake lower than in Western countries. For the average person who eats Japanese cuisine, oil and fat intake makes up less than 30 percent of the total calories consumed.

The many types of fish eaten as side dishes contain oils rich in unsaturated fatty acids. Beef, pork, mutton and other meats high in saturated fat, now believed to be the cause of lifestyle-related ailments, have traditionally been a less important part of the diet than in many other countries. Small and medium-sized fish rich in fatty acids like DHA and EPA are thought to have particular health benefits; fish like horse mackerel (*aji*), sardines (*iwashi*), and chub mackerel (*saba*) have been mainstays of the Japanese fishing industry for centuries. Raw vegetables are boiled in a traditional dashi stock; this reduces bulk and makes it easier to eat large amounts, boosting people's intake of fiber and micronutrients. Bean-based foods are also consumed in large amounts in the form of miso and tofu; these are believed to be effective at reducing blood sugar levels and blood pressure. Although Japanese food is high in salt, the incidence of high blood pressure and heart disease in Japan is relatively low—a phenomenon that has been called the "paradox" of the Japanese diet.

Umami: The Fifth Taste

Umami is a fundamental element of Japanese cuisine. It also plays an important role in other cuisines enjoyed around the world, no doubt because it pleases the human palate in a way that rivals the satisfaction we get from fats and sugars.

Fermented fish sauces like *nuoc mam* and *nam pla*, commonly used in Asian cuisines, have a very strong umami flavor. Records survive from ancient Rome of a comparable fermented condiment called "garum" (or "liquamen") that was made from small fish. It is believed that garum may have resembled modern anchovy sauce. Japanese cuisine evolved at a time when sweet or oily flavors were not easy to come by. Because of this, much of the flavor in Japanese food comes from umami, generally obtained from fermented foods and dashi made from kombu and *katsuobushi* bonito flakes.

Kombu, *katsuobushi*, and fermented foods—the source of Japanese umami—also have strong smells. This sensory experience, which can be an acquired taste for people accustomed to different foodways, is an important part of what makes Japanese food distinctive.

Changes in Japanese Food

Naturally, Japanese food and Japanese dietary habits have changed over the centuries. Eating patterns that excluded beef and pork were established early on in the seventh century, when the early state issued a law forbidding the consumption of meat for religious reasons. For approximately 1,200 years, until the beginning of the modern era, state law prohibited people from eating animal meat, and that factor shaped Japan's culinary traditions in a significant way. In this context, people met their energy requirements predominantly by eating grains—either rice or a mix of other grains for the poor. The diet that became the norm in Japan for hundreds of years was centered around these grains and supplemented by fish for protein and vegetables for micronutrients. In a diet with little or no fat or oil, umami and salt were vital for making food appetizing. Japan's relative isolation from the rest of the world when its borders were closed to other countries under the policy of *sakoku*, a period that lasted roughly 200 years from the early seventeenth century to the mid-nineteenth century, also helped Japanese cuisine develop in distinctive ways.

Culinary styles that made important contributions to Japanese cuisine as we know it today developed during the period when meat consumption was prohibited. *Shojin* cuisine, which evolved in Zen temples where the consumption of all animal products was forbidden for the priesthood, the refined cuisine of traditional *ryotei* restaurants, and the kaiseki *ryori* served as part of the tea ceremony all have historical roots in this period.

In the Meiji era, which began in 1868, Western foods began to enter the country. The emperor lifted the ban on meat in 1871. The range of ingredients available in Japan increased dramatically as meat, vegetables, and other products were brought in from around the world. A century later, during the period of rapid economic growth of the 1970s, a nutritionally rich and balanced diet similar to the one we know today became the norm for most of the population.

When people think of Japanese food as healthy, they are probably thinking of the average Japanese diet of the 1980s, when most people achieved an optimal balance of protein, fat, and carbohydrates. Japanese ate more rice than they do today, as well as greater quantities of fish and vegetables. By then the traditional Japanese diet had already been augmented by the introduction of imported dairy products and meat. In the decades since, however, the Westernization of the Japanese diet has perhaps gone too far. Today tastes and dietary preferences differ dramatically by age group. The prevalence of lifestyle-related diseases is increasing. This problem is also becoming more and more common in other Asian countries as the process of industrialization continues.

The Future of Japanese Food

In its most basic form, a traditional Japanese meal consists of rice as a staple food, an umami-rich miso soup, a variety of pickles, and a selection of side dishes made from fish and vegetables to complement the rice. This is the common formula for Japanese dining, which people have increasingly begun to appreciate in recent years. Although it is only natural for the nature and composition of the side dishes to evolve over time, the fundamental rice-and-side dishes pattern of Japanese cuisine is likely to persist.

Interest in Japanese food and the traditional Japanese diet has risen to new heights since "Washoku, traditional dietary cultures of the Japanese" was included on the UNESCO list of Intangible Cultural Heritage. I hope that this development will bring about renewed appreciation for Japanese food not just among people from abroad but also among Japanese themselves, and will serve as a reminder of the health benefits to be had from traditional Japanese cuisine.

Traditional Weights and Measures

NAKATA Masahiro Specialist in Japanese cuisine

Japan's traditional system of measurements (*shakkan ho*), based on units such as the *shaku* (about 30 cm), *ata* (about 15 cm), and *sun* (about 3 cm), was officially abolished in 1958 and replaced by the metric system, but in traditional arts, including cuisine, textile-making, as well as other crafts, the old units continue to be used widely.

The English system of measurement based on inches, feet, yards, and pounds is based on parts of the body, the standard inch being the length between the tip of the thumb and the first joint and the standard foot the length of the foot from the tip of the toes to the heel. Some Japanese measurements, too, are based on parts of the body. For example, the still-widely used *shaku* is double the length of the *ata*, which is based on the distance between the tip of the thumb and the tip of the index finger when the hand is spread wide. The tray or tray table (*zen*) upon which Japanese food is traditionally served is generally one square *shaku* in size. Japanese chopsticks are usually about one and a half *ata* in length. The chopsticks that are easiest for a particular individual to use are considered to be roughly 15 percent of the person's height.

Another frequently used unit of measure is the above-mentioned *sun*. The soup bowls used to serve Japanese food are generally less than four *sun* (about 12 cm) in diameter. This size is based on the diameter of the circle formed by putting together the middle fingers and thumbs of both hands. In order to make a vessel easy to hold with two hands, its size is generally made to fit within the necessary diameter. Other units based on the *sun* are also used in the kitchen as standard units for cutting, as with *gobu-giri*, or cutting ingredients into pieces half-a-*sun* (approx. 15 mm) thick.

UNITS OF WEIGHT

Shakkan units for weight	Metric system equivalents
1 *momme*	3.75 g
1 *ryo*	37.5 g
1 *kin*	600 g
1 *kan*	3.75 kg

UNITS OF LENGTH

Shakkan units for length	Metric system equivalents
1 *sun*	3.03 cm
1 *shaku*	30.3 cm
1 *ken*	180.8 cm
1 *cho*	109.09 m
1 *ri*	3927.2 m

UNITS OF VOLUME

Shakkan units for volume	Metric system equivalents
1 *shaku*	18 ml
1 *go*	180 ml
1 *sho*	1.8 L
1 *to*	18 L
1 *koku*	180 L

One course in kaiseki cuisine, the *hassun*, takes its name from a vessel eight (*hachi*) *sun* square (about 24 × 24 cm) in size. Originally the term referred to a square cedar tray that measured eight *sun* square, but eventually the term was used for the assortment of tidbits served with sake in a vessel of that size. Today the *hassun* is a dish consisting of an attractive array of seasonal appetizers served on a plate or tray.

The *go*, a traditional unit of volume, continues to be used to measure rice even today. The *go* is said to be the amount of rice a person would consume at a single meal and the estimated daily consumption of rice by one adult was said to be three *go*. The *koku*, about 150 kilograms, meanwhile, is based on the volume of rice traditionally consumed by one adult over the course of one year. Today, the average annual rice consumption for a Japanese person is about 60 kilograms (only about 1 *go* per day), which shows how rice consumption has decreased considerably as diets have diversified.

The *tawara* is the straw bale holding roughly 72 liters (approx. 60 kg) that was traditionally used to carry rice grain. One *tawara* (called *ippyo*) was considered to be the amount that a farmer could reasonably carry. Since two *tawara* represented the amount that could be carried by one horse, this unit became a convenient unit of measurement for the shipping, storage, and transport of rice. Recently, as rice farmers have grown older, bags of about 30 kilograms (a half *tawara*) are now the standard.

The list above provides the common equivalents for traditional units of measure that were once the basis of daily life in Japan.

These old *masu* boxes for measuring liquids are made of wood coated with persimmon tannins (*kakishibu*). They were branded on the side to show that they had been approved by the shogunal government. This mark was affixed only to items that fulfilled official standards.

Making Dashi

The flavor of Japanese cuisine, it would be true to say, is determined by the quality of the dashi used. Here are basic recipes for four of the most popular kinds of dashi. In addition, we also include *kobujime*, a food preparation technique that utilizes the umami of kombu.

ICHIBAN DASHI

Ichiban (primary) dashi is almost pure umami broth. The combination of kombu and *katsuobushi* boosts the umami content considerably. Made from the finest ingredients, it is devoid of the astringency that often results when dashi is prepared from other ingredients and draws out the flavor of other foods without calling too much attention to itself. The clarity and subtle aroma of ichiban dashi make it ideal for soup.

1.8 L (generous 7 cups) soft water	30 g (1 oz.) Rishiri kombu (see p. 99)	50 g (1⅔ oz.) shaved *honkarebushi* (dried bonito flakes), *chiai* (blood line) removed

1 Combine water and kombu in a pan over very low heat.

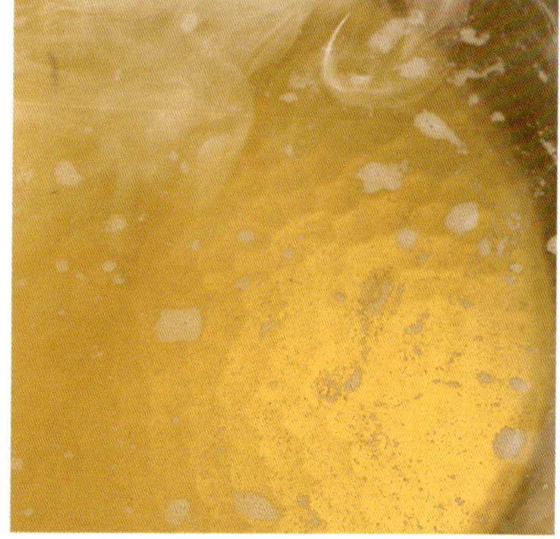

2 Slowly heat pan until the water reaches 140°F (60°C), and keep the water at that temperature for 1 hour to extract the maximum umami from the kombu.

3 Remove kombu and increase the temperature of the water to 185°F (85°C). Turn off the heat and add the bonito flakes.

4 When bonito flakes have thoroughly soaked up water, leave for about 10 more seconds, then strain through a fine sieve covered with cheese cloth. Never squeeze the bonito flakes, but let the liquid drain naturally.

NIBAN DASHI

Niban (secondary) dashi is made by simmering kombu and dried bonito flakes already used to prepare ichiban dashi, drawing out the remaining umami. It is ideal when cooking with seasonings, as when making simmered dishes and miso soup.

About 1.6 L (6⅔ cups) soft water

Kombu and *honkarebushi* previously used to prepare ichiban dashi

1. Place kombu and dried bonito flakes previously used to prepare ichiban dashi in a pan and add water.
2. Bring to boil over a high flame, then reduce to a medium heat and simmer for about 10 minutes.
3. Strain through a fine sieve covered with cheese cloth.

KOMBU DASHI

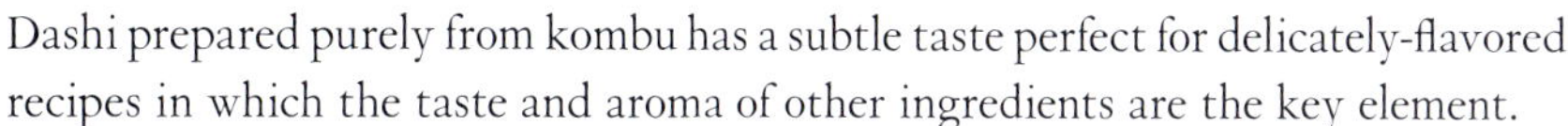

Dashi prepared purely from kombu has a subtle taste perfect for delicately-flavored recipes in which the taste and aroma of other ingredients are the key element.

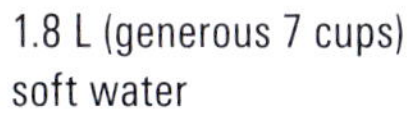

1.8 L (generous 7 cups) soft water

30 g (1 oz.) Rishiri kombu

1 Combine the water and the kombu in a pan over very low heat.

2 Slowly heat the water to 140°F (60°C) and maintain at that temperature for 1 hour to extract the maximum umami from the kombu. Remove the kombu.

SHIITAKE MUSHROOM DASHI

Dashi made from dried shiitake mushrooms is a kind of *shojin* dashi (see p. 102), offering intense aroma and umami. When not in *shojin* cuisine (which is vegetarian), it is often used in combination with dashi prepared from ingredients like kombu and *katsuobushi*.

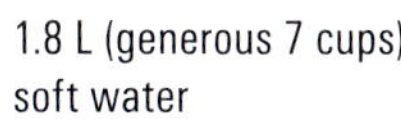

1.8 L (generous 7 cups) soft water

50 g (1⅔ oz.) dried shiitake mushrooms

1 Wash any dirt or other impurities off the shiitake mushrooms without soaking them. Place them in a bowl with the water and leave to soak overnight.

2 Strain through a fine sieve covered with cheese cloth.

KOBUJIME

Kobujime is a technique in which fish such as sea bream is sprinkled with salt and placed between sheets of kombu, so that the umami of the kombu is transferred to the fish. Tightening the flesh of the fish with sake and salt amplifies this effect. Salting also draws out excess moisture, giving sashimi—which can spoil quickly—a longer shelf life.

300 g (10 oz.) sea bream (for sashimi)

20 cm (8 in.) × 8 cm (3 in.) × 2 kombu sheets

0.8% of sea bream by weight salt (2.4 g)

100 ml (scant ½ cup) sake

1 Sprinkle both sides of sea bream with salt and set aside for about 1 hour.

2 Wet kombu with sake to make it pliable.

3 Lay a sheet of kombu in a metal tray. Arrange sea bream, sprinkle salt on top, add other sheet of kombu, and set aside for 1–4 hours.

BASIC RECIPES

Sushi Rice

PP. 186-187, 192, 202-203, 206-207

YIELDS ABOUT 2 CUPS (450 G)
Scant 1 cup (210 g) rice
1 cup plus 2 Tbsp. (270 ml) water
2.5 cm (1 in.) square kombu
2 Tbsp. sushi vinegar (recipe below)

Wash rice in two or three changes of cold water and let drain in a sieve 30 minutes before cooking. Combine kombu, water and rice in a rice cooker and steam.

Let the just-cooked rice rest for 10 minutes and transfer to a container. Pour the sushi vinegar over the rice and mix with a rice paddle using a gentle slicing and tossing motion.

Sushizu (sushi vinegar)

PP. 186-187, 192, 202-203, 206-207

YIELDS ABOUT 120 ML (½ CUP)
120 ml (½ cup) rice vinegar
20 g (⅔ oz.) sea salt
75 g (2½ oz.) sugar

Combine the ingredients in a pan and bring to a boil. Mix well and when salt and sugar dissolve, remove from the heat.
* For ¾ cup (160 f) of uncooked rice use about 2 Tbsp. of sushizu.

Tosazu

PP. 189, 193-194

YIELDS ABOUT 300 ML (1¼ CUPS)
220 ml (scant 1 cup) ichiban dashi
5 Tbsp. vinegar
1 Tbsp. *usukuchi* soy sauce
½ tsp. sugar
10 g (⅓ oz.) dried bonito flakes

Heat dashi, vinegar, usukuchi soy sauce and sugar in a pan. Just before it boils, add dried bonito flakes and turn off heat. Let cool, strain.

Amazu

PP. 186-187, 197, 200, 203-207

YIELDS ABOUT 1 L (ABOUT 4 CUPS)
200 ml (scant 1 cup) rice vinegar
2 ½ cups (600 ml) water
9 Tbsp. sugar
7 g kombu

Combine vinegar, water and sugar, add kombu and let sit for a day. Heat the mixture in a pan and when it starts to boil, turn off the heat. Let cool, then remove kombu.

Cooked miso paste

PP. 185, 204, 208

YIELDS ABOUT 2¼ CUPS (500 G)
500 g (scant 17 oz.) white miso paste
540 ml (2¼ cups) sake

Add sake to white miso paste and mix well to dissolve miso. Put in a pan over heat and stir with a wooden spoon, taking care not to burn, then simmer until the mixture returns to the original thickness of the white miso paste.

RECIPES

Ainame Nishu Endo Soup P. 11

Fat Greenling Two Ways in Pea Soup

SERVES 1

40 g (1⅓ oz.) fat greenling
3 g *udo*
1.5 g *hoshiko*
1 L (1 qt.) kombu dashi
50 g (1⅔ oz.) peas
8 g *kudzu* starch
⅓ tsp. soy sauce
Kinome to taste
Salt, pepper to taste
Potato starch as required

Make slits 5 mm (¼ in.) deep in the fat greenling, then cut in half lengthwise. Sprinkle with salt and leave for about 30 minutes. Dredge one of the two pieces of fat greenling in kudzu.

Chop udo into 3 cm (1¼ in.) pieces and peel. Cut peeled udo into 1mm (1/10 in.) strips, soak in water to remove bitterness, and drain. Grill one side of the hoshiko, cut into 2 cm (1 in.) pieces then 2 mm (⅛ in.) strips.

Place 800 ml (3⅓ cups) of kombu dashi in a pan and bring to a boil. Add scant 1 Tbsp. salt to season. Transfer half to a different pan.

Bring another pan of water to a boil, add fat greenling coated in kudzu starch and cook for about 30 seconds, then transfer into the pan containing only 400 ml (1⅔ cups) of stock and rinse off the kudzu starch. Coat the other piece of fat greenling in starch, fry in hot oil until golden, and drain off oil.

Fill a pan with water and bring to a boil, salt to taste. Boil peas for about 3 minutes, drain, use electric fan or similar to lightly blow away moisture, and rub through a sieve.

Place sieved peas in 200 ml (scant 1 cup) of boiling kombu dashi. Add salt and pepper to taste. Rub seasoned peas through a sieve again and thicken with kudzu starch mixed with water.

Place both parboiled and fried fat greenling in bowl, top with udo, hoshiko, and kinome leaves. Carefully pour in pea soup.

Tsukuri Tai-kanoko, Ika, Toro P. 13

Sashimi *Kanoko* Sea Bream, Squid, and Fatty Tuna

SERVES 2

50 g (1⅔ oz.) sea bream
50 g (1⅔ oz.) squid
50 g (1⅔ oz.) fatty tuna belly
Garnish (recipe below) to taste
Wasabi to taste
300 ml (1⅓ cups) kombu dashi

GARNISHES

Julienned squash

10 g (⅓ oz.) buttercup squash

Pare thinly, leaving skin on, cut into strips, rinse in water and form into a mound.

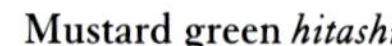

Mustard green *hitashi*

1/10 bunch mustard greens
150 ml (⅔ cup) niban dashi
About ½ tsp. salt

Wash mustard greens and cut into 1 cm (½ in.) lengths, place boiling water in pan and blanch greens. Cool in ice water, drain and soak for about 4 hours in the mixture of niban dashi and salt. Form into a bite-sized mound.

Glehnia sprigs

2 sprigs of *hamabofu* (beach silbertop or *Glehnia littoralis*)

Wash sprigs, make four evenly-spaced cuts in stems, soak in water for about 10 minutes, then roll up stems.

Edible gold leaf in *nori*

1 g *nori*
0.5 g agar powder
2 tsp. niban dashi
Edible gold leaf as required

Put niban dashi and agar powder in pan, heat until agar dissolves. Add nori, and when blended, pour into a small container to set. Cut into 1 cm (½ in.) cubes and affix gold foil to finish.

Pour boiling water only on skin side of filleted sea bream. Pour all of the kombu dashi only on skin side and chill. Make cuts 2 mm (⅛ in.) apart across and down skin to give a dappled effect, and cut into pieces about 5 cm (2 in.) thick.

Rinse squid, remove skin. Make a series of vertical cuts about 2 mm apart in outer surface, then diagonal cuts about 3 mm (⅛ in.) apart on the inside to cross-hatch. Cut into 2 cm (1 in.) wide bite-sized pieces along cuts in outer surface. Cut tuna belly into pieces 2 cm (1 in.) square, 5 mm (¼ in.) thick.

Arrange sea bream, squid and tuna on plates, garnish, and serve with wasabi on side.

Yaki Takenoko PP. 16–17

Baked Bamboo Shoots

1 bamboo shoot
Scant 1 cup rice bran
2 L (2 qts.) water

1 chili pepper
Kinome to taste
Kinome miso paste (recipe below) to taste

Kinome miso paste YIELDS ABOUT 390 G (12⅔ OZ.)

300 g (10 oz.) cooked miso paste
50 g (1⅔ oz.) *kinome*
40 g (1⅓ oz.) spinach, boiled and finely chopped
Powdered *sansho* pepper to taste

Place all ingredients in food processor and mix until smooth. Freeze and pulverize using a Pacojet.

Take bamboo shoot, skin on, slice off tip diagonally, then score once along the length of the shoot.

Place bamboo shoot, water, rice bran and chili pepper in a pan. Cover with a drop lid or parchment paper and boil until a bamboo skewer easily penetrates the bottom. Cool in pan, then rinse off rice bran. Bake boiled shoot in oven for 15 minutes at 350°F (180°C).

Cut baked shoot in half, use a kitchen torch or similar to char. Make cuts with a knife for easier eating, and sprinkle with crushed kinome. Accompany with kinome miso paste.

Reisei Mame-togan Suppon Kenchin P. 19

Chilled Turtle *Kenchin* in Mini Winter Melon

SERVES 4

1 mini winter melon
4 tiger prawns, 30 g (1 oz.) each
 450 ml (1⅔ cups) sake
 2 Tbsp. plus 2 tsp. *usukuchi* soy sauce
 1⅔ Tbsp. mirin
12 pieces of octopus 1 cm (½ in.) wide
Serves 6–8
 200 g (7 oz.) octopus (tentacles)
 450 ml (1⅔ cups) sake
 2 Tbsp. plus 2 tsp. *usukuchi* soy sauce
 2 Tbsp. plus 2 tsp. mirin
 1 Tbsp. rice vinegar
8 *satoimo* cormlets (*koimo*), 15 g (½ oz.) pieces each
 Scant ½ cup rice bran
 420 ml (1⅔ cups) ichiban dashi
 1 Tbsp. *usukuchi* soy sauce
 1⅔ Tbsp. mirin
 1 tsp. salt
 5 g sugar

Mini winter melon filling
 Flesh of 8 mini winter melons, approx. 15 g (½ oz.) each
 300 ml (1⅓ cups) ichiban dashi
 1 Tbsp. *usukuchi* soy sauce
 1 Tbsp. mirin
 About ¼ tsp. salt
300 ml (1⅓ cups) turtle soup (recipe below)
8 *shiso* flower sprigs

Turtle soup YIELDS SCANT 4 L (16 CUPS)

1 kg (35 oz.) snapping turtle meat (bone in)
1.8 L (scant 7 cups) water
540 ml (2¼ cups) sake
50 g (1⅔ oz.) ginger
10 g (⅓ oz.) kombu
300 ml (1⅓ cups) ichiban dashi
1 Tbsp. plus 1 tsp. *usukuchi* soy sauce
5 g gelatin powder
1 tsp. grated ginger juice

Remove inner membrane and pulp from winter melon. Chop flesh into 1.5 cm (½ in.) cubes and set aside. Score outside of melon all over in a criss-cross pattern, rub salt (extra) into skin, and cook for about 15 minutes. Transfer to ice water, drain when cool. Bring simmering liquid ingredients to a boil. Add melon, simmer over low heat for 2–3 minutes, then plunge pan, including cooking stock, into ice water to cool quickly.

Take the turtle meat, cut, skinned and blanched, and place in a pan with ingredients for turtle soup. Boil 20–30 minutes at high heat, strain. Combine turtle soup and ichiban dashi, heat. Season with soy sauce, add gelatin powder and simmer to dissolve. Refrigerate 1–2 hours to cool and set, then push the resulting turtle *gelée* through a sieve. Mix in ginger juice.

Remove heads from tiger prawns, devein, and skewer lengthwise (with the prawn curled up). Combine sake, soy sauce and mirin, boil off alcohol, add skewered prawns, cook for 1½ minutes, remove from heat. Cool prawns and cooking liquid, separately, strain liquid, then return prawns and marinate for 2–3 hours. Cut each prawn into 3 equal pieces.

Combine sake, usukuchi soy sauce and mirin for octopus and boil off alcohol. Add octopus, simmer for about 1½ minutes, and remove from heat. Strain cooking liquid, return octopus, marinate for 2–3 hours. Chop into 1 cm (½ in.) pieces.

Top and tail koimo to a uniform size, pare. Wrap rice bran in a bleached cotton cloth. Fill a pan with water, soak cloth, and knead so that the rice bran comes out. Add koimo, bring to a boil. Cook for about 20 minutes until pierced easily using a bamboo skewer. Fill pan again with water, add koimo. Bring to a boil, then plunge into cold water, and take out. Place koimo, dashi, salt, soy sauce, mirin and sugar in a pan, simmer for about 10 minutes over low heat. Cut in half.

Arrange prawns, octopus, koimo and mini winter melon flesh in hollowed out melon, pour over the turtle *gelée*. Pluck shiso flowers and sprinkle them on top.

Natsu no Hassun P. 20

Summer *Hassun*

Eel "Yawata-maki" Style SERVES 10

2.5 × 20–22 cm (1 × about 8½ in.) long eel
25 cm (10 in.) burdock root (thin and long slightly longer than the eel for easier rolling. trim any leftover ends after rolling)
Simmering liquid
 3 L (3 qts.) ichiban dashi
 250 ml (generous 1 cup) soy sauce
 300 g (10 oz.) sugar
Two pinches powdered *sansho* pepper
Basting sauce
 200 g (7 oz.) unseasoned grilled eel bones
 900 ml (3⅔ cups) de-alcoholized sake
 1 L (4 cups) mirin
 200 ml (¾ cup) *usukuchi* soy sauce
 70 ml (⅓ cup) soy sauce
 1 Tbsp. starch syrup
 40 g (1⅓ oz.) coarse granulated sugar

Place all ingredients in a pan, bring to a boil over high heat. Once boiling, reduce heat to medium and simmer until ⅒ of original volume.

Bring simmering liquid to a boil, add burdock root (uncut) and simmer for about 10 minutes until tender and flavor is absorbed.

Position burdock root in center of eel, pierce core of burdock root with a metal skewer, roll up and grill front and back for 3 minutes each over a high flame. Remove skewer, steam for 20 minutes at 195°F (100°C). When cool, insert a skewer in center of the eel once again, pour basting sauce on top, and grill over medium heat (paying particular attention to placing sides not browned at top and bottom to ensure all four sides are browned). When tiny bubbles start to appear in the sauce, turn eel over and baste again, then twice more on each side (a total of four times), grilling 3 minutes each time.

Cut 2 cm (1 in.) piece for each serving, and sprinkle sansho on top.

New Lotus Root Wrapped in Lake Biwa Trout SERVES 3

30 g (1 oz.) Biwa trout, sliced in 3 thin pieces
1 baby cucumber, lightly pickled
 1 baby cucumber
 1 L (4 cups) 1.5% saltwater solution
 4 × 4 cm (2 × 2 in.) pieces of kombu
 1 Tbsp. *usukuchi* soy sauce
2 mm (⅛ in.) × 3 slices lotus root

100 ml (scant ½ cup) sweet vinegar
3 honeywort (*mitsuba*) stalks
Vinegared egg yolk
  1 egg yolk
  1 Tbsp. water
  1 Tbsp. water sugar
  A dash of *usukuchi* soy sauce
  Small quantity of salt
  1 tsp. *sudachi* juice

Pickle the cucumber: trim baby cucumber slightly at ends, wash in water. Place on cutting board, rub with salt (extra) and roll around. Leave for 20 minutes. Rinse, then immerse in the saltwater for 2 hours. Add kombu and usukuchi soy sauce, leave aside for 2 hours.

Make kobujime using the Biwa trout: sprinkle slices of trout with a little salt, place on a 10 × 10 cm (4 × 4 in.) piece of kombu (extra) moistened with 2 Tbsp. of sake (extra), then wiped with a cloth or paper towel on both sides, fold kombu over and leave for 2 hours. Wrap trout around pieces of pickled cucumber cut into 3 cm × 1 cm (1¼ × ½ in.) chunks.

Make vinegared egg yolk, mix all ingredients until blended. Peel new lotus root and cut into 2 mm (⅛ in.) slices. Cook for about 10 seconds in boiling water, then steep in sweet vinegar for an hour. Wrap in Biwa trout, place lotus root marinated in sweet vinegar on top, tie with honeywort, and pour vinegared egg yolk over top.

Koimo in Mitarashi Glaze — SERVES 30

30 *satoimo* cormlets (*koimo*)
400 ml (1⅔ cups) ichiban dashi
2 Tbsp. plus 2 tsp. soy sauce
3 Tbsp. plus 1tsp. mirin
15 g (½ oz.) sugar
30 *kinome*
Kudzu starch as required
Mitarashi glaze
  400 ml (1⅔ cups) ichiban dashi
  2 Tbsp. plus 2 tsp. soy sauce
  3 Tbsp. plus 1 tsp. mirin

Dissolved kudzu starch(add 30 g [1 oz.]kudzu starch to 60 ml [¼ cup] water and leave for 2 hours to dissolve).

Rub satoimo with a cloth, peel, place in pan with water and some uncooked rice (extra) (80 g [2⅔ oz.] rice to 2 L [2 qts.] water), and boil until tender (satoimo will be tender and hard to break).

Bring dashi to a boil, flavor with soy sauce, salt, sugar and mirin, simmer for about 15 minutes over medium heat, and allow to cool.

Make the mitarashi glaze. Place dashi, mirin and soy sauce in a pan, heat, and thicken with kudzu starch.

Dredge satoimo in kudzu (extra) and fry for 2 minutes at 350°F (180°C), dip in mitarashi glaze, coating thoroughly, and top with kinome.

Sushi Wrapped in Simmered Pike Eel — SERVES 2

18 g (⅔ oz.) pike eel, sliced thinly into 8 pieces, then cut each piece in half again
10 g (⅓ oz.) sushi rice
2 red *shiso* stalks, chopped roughly
Scant 1 Tbsp. toasted sesame
10 g (⅓ oz.) ginger
2 Tbsp. plus 2 tsp. sweet vinegar
Wasabi to taste
Salt to taste
Small amount *umeboshi* flesh

Boil water, place pike eel on surface of water for about 10 seconds so that only the skin is submersed, then quickly dip whole piece in and remove to plunge into water. Remove promptly and drain on cloth, allow to cool slightly, transfer to steel tray or similar, season flesh lightly with salt, and leave for 30 minutes.

Cook the sushi rice. Take red shiso, briefly cooked in boiling water and drained, and chop finely. Mix with toasted sesame seeds. Peel new ginger, boil for 1 minute, and marinate in sweet vinegar for half a day.

Mix shiso and sesame into sushi rice. Form a rice ball for one, top with a little wasabi, and wrap eel around. Place umeboshi in the center.

Edamame with Sweet Tofu Dressing in Chinese Lantern Flowers — SERVES 1

1 Chinese lantern flower (use scissors to remove fruit, open up flower)
5–6 beans black bean edamame
30 g (1 oz.) sponge gourd
Sweet tofu dressing (yields about 1⅓ kg [about 44 oz.]
  1 kg (35 oz.) drained tofu
  150 g (5 oz.) sesame paste
  40 g (1⅓ oz.) salt
  150 g (5 oz.) sugar
Marinade
  450 ml (scant 2 cups) ichiban dashi
  2 Tbsp. plus 1 tsp. *usukuchi* soy sauce
  2 Tbsp. plus 1 tsp. mirin

Place black bean edamame (in pods) in a mortar, and add a little salt and water. Grind to remove any fine bristles. Parboil in boiling water for about 7 minutes, drain and leave to cool, and remove pods and membranes.

Chop gourd into rounds, cook in boiling water for about 5 minutes, cool and marinate in the stock for 2 hours.

Make sweet tofu dressing. Place all ingredients in food processor and blend until smooth. Mix beans and slices of gourd with 1 tsp. of the sweet tofu dressing.

Kohaku-yose amber jelly — SERVES 20

10 tiger prawns
4 okra pods
80 g (2⅔ oz.) sea urchin
270 ml (1 cup plus 2 Tbsp.) jelly liquid (recipe below)

Jelly liquid

400 ml (1⅔ cups) ichiban dashi
2 tsp. *usukuchi* soy sauce
About ½ tsp. salt
Small quantity of sugar
18 g (⅔ oz.) agar powder

Remove heads from prawns, devein, and cook for 2½ minutes in boiling water. Cut each prawn into 4 equal pieces. Chop ends off okra, then cut in half crosswise. Rub with salt (extra) to remove fine bristles. Blanch in boiling water for 1½ minutes, plunge into chilled water, transfer to sieve and drain. Use a bamboo skewer to remove seeds, holding cut surface under running water. Cut each okra half into 5 equal slices.

Place all ingredients of jelly liquid in a pan over high heat. When mixture comes to a boil, skim, then cool to 100°F (40°C).

Pour the cooled jelly containing prawn, okra and sea urchin respectively into separate molds (approx. 3 × 3 × 2.5 cm [1¼ × 1¼ × 1 in.]), refrigerate until set.

Simmered Green *Ume* Plums in Jelly — SERVES 35

35 green *ume* about medium size

Syrup for plums

1.8 L (generous 7 cups) water
600 g (20 oz.) sugar

Place water and sugar in pan and simmer over low heat for 15 minutes. Cool to 100°F (40°C)

Syrup for jelly

400 ml (1⅔ cups) water
200 g (7 oz.) sugar
2 Tbsp. plus 2 tsp. lemon juice
100 ml (⅓ cup plus 4 tsp.) plum wine
90 g (3 oz.) agar powder

Place green (unripe) Japanese plums in 7% saltwater solution and leave for 5 days. When plums have turned yellow, soak an additional day in fresh water, pierce skins with a needle, place plums in a copper pan full of water (add a copper plate as well and the copper will cause a chemical reaction that returns the plums to their original green color after boiling), bring to a boil, then cook over low heat for about 5 minutes (this will ensure the plums stay whole). Remove from heat and leave for an hour to allow the green color to completely return. Soak for another 12 hours in water.

Transfer plums to a stainless steel pot, bring to a boil, and simmer for 5 minutes or so over low heat to eliminate any copper odor or taste. Soak for half a day in water. Make syrup for plums. Place water and sugar in pan and simmer over low heat for 15 minutes. Cool to 100°F (40°C), add plums, cover with a paper lid, leave for 1 hour for flavors to penetrate, then simmer for 5 minutes over medium heat.

Make the jelly: place jelly syrup ingredients in a pan, bring to a boil over high heat, skim, and allow to cool slightly. Pour jelly into tins 5 cm (2 in.) square, 3 cm (1¼ in.) high and refrigerate until set. Top plums in syrup with slices of jelly.

Kamasu Sugiita-yaki P. 23

Barracuda in Smoldering Cedar Shavings

SERVES 4

2 barracuda (*karamasu*)
4 shiitake mushrooms
Marinade
  2 Tbsp. plus 2 tsp. de-alcoholized sake
  1 Tbsp. plus 2 tsp. water
  1 tsp. soy sauce
  ½ tsp. *usukuchi* soy sauce
  ½ tsp. mirin
8 cedar shavings (soak in water overnight)
Bamboo bark (tear to make twine) as required
2 *sudachi*

Miso *Yuan-ji* (yields about 1½ kg [50 oz.])
1 kg (35 oz.) white miso
Miso marinade base
  180 ml (⅔ cup plus 4 tsp.) water
  180 ml (⅔ cup plus 4 tsp.) sake
  90 ml (⅓ cup plus 2 tsp.) mirin
  2 Tbsp. soy sauce
  5 Tbsp. *usukuchi* soy sauce
  ½ *yuzu* zest

Make miso Yuan-ji. Place all miso marinade base ingredients in a pan, bring to a boil, and when alcohol has evaporated off, remove from heat and allow to cool. Cut yuzu zest into suitably-sized pieces. Mix miso marinade base and yuzu zest into white miso.

Fillet barracuda and remove fine bones. Wipe off any moisture and marinate in miso Yuan-ji for 12 hours. Trim bases off shiitake mushrooms and steep in marinade for 1 hour.

Rounding the ends of the barracuda slightly, place on a length of cedar shaving pre-soaked in water, making sure no fish extends beyond the edges. Arrange shiitake on top. Place another shaving over fish and shiitake and bind with the bamboo twine.

Bake for 15–20 minutes in the oven at 350°F (180°C). When cooked, remove from oven, light cedar with a kitchen torch, and serve with half a sudachi.

Hangetsu Fuchidaka P. 25

Half-moon *Fuchidaka*

Sea Bream and Prawn-Sushi Chrysanthemum Style — SERVES 4

4 thin strips sea bream, 10 g (⅓ oz.) each
1⅔ Tbsp. vinegar for bream
2 tiger prawns
1⅔ Tbsp. sweet vinegar for prawns
8 *kinome*
1 egg yolk
160 g (5⅓ oz.) sushi rice

Cook sushi rice. Wash sea bream in water and fillet, remove abdominal bones and divide into back and belly. Skin, pare flesh into thin slices. Sprinkle with salt (1.5% of bream by weight), set aside for at least 15 minutes, and rinse in vinegar (1⅔ Tbsp.). Boil prawns in plenty of saltwater solution (2%), peel, rinse in sweet vinegar (1⅔ Tbsp.) and chop in half.

Add egg to boiling water, boil for 10 minutes until hard-boiled. Drop into ice water to cool, then sieve the egg yolk only.

Wet a piece of bleached cotton or similar and wring. Place 20 g (⅔ oz.) of sushi rice on the cloth, top with one kinome leaf and some slices of bream and shape into a ball. Place egg yolk in center. Repeat with prawns (making 4 pieces each of bream and prawn-sushi).

Hajikami Pickled Ginger Shoot — SERVES 20

20 *hajikami* ginger shoots
Sweet vinegar

Thinly peel white portion of ginger shoots. Blanch shoots in boiling water for about 10 seconds, transfer to sieve and salt (extra) lightly. When shoots have cooled, marinate in sweet vinegar for 5 hours.

Grilled Barracuda with Miso *Yuan*-yaki Baste — SERVES 4

4 barracuda (filleted), 30 g (1 oz.) each
80 ml (⅓ cup) de-alcoholized sake
Miso *Yuan-ji* base
  4 Tbsp. plus 1 tsp. mirin
  1 Tbsp. plus 2 tsp. *usukuchi* soy sauce
  1 Tbsp. plus 2 tsp. soy sauce
  100 g (3⅓ oz.) coarse-grained miso
  ½ *yuzu*

Make the Yuan-ji : combine de-alcoholized sake, mirin, usukuchi soy sauce and regular soy sauce, and add miso and finely-chopped yuzu.

Marinate barracuda in Yuan-ji for 2–5 days in refrigerator. Remove barracuda and wipe off miso etc. Grill over low-to-medium flame for 8 minutes on each side.

Maitake Mushrooms Dressed in Wasabi — SERVES 4

80 g (2⅔ oz.) *maitake* mushrooms
80 ml (⅓ cup) ichiban dashi
½ tsp. *usukuchi* soy sauce
½ tsp. soy sauce
½ tsp. wasabi

Trim bases from maitake mushrooms. Heat oven to 390°F (200°C), bake maitake for 5 minutes. When cooked, tear into pieces such that they can be easily picked up with chopsticks.

Add regular soy sauce and usukuchi soy sauce to ichiban dashi. Add baked maitake and mix in wasabi.

Fallen Leaves — SERVES 4

2 mm (⅛ in.) sweet potato slices
1 *kuchinashi* (dried gardenia pod)
1 L (4 cups) water

Cut sweet potato slices into maple and gingko leaf shapes.

Crush gardenia pod and add to water. When water turns yellow, add maple and gingko leaf cutouts, remove when dyed yellow, and leave to dry overnight. Fry for 1 minute in oil at 325°F (160°C)

Nori-wrapped Elbow Crab Fried Flour in Rice — SERVES 8

200 g (7 oz.) elbow crab meat
1 sheet *nori*
5 honeywort (*mitsuba*) stalks
20 g (⅔ oz.) cake flour
½ egg white, beaten lightly
30 g (1 oz.) glutinous rice flour

Lay nori on a sushi mat, crab meat on top. Place honeywort in center and roll up. Use finger to spread egg white (extra) on nori to seal.

Brush with cake flour, Coat with egg white and then rice flour. Fry for about a minute in oil at 340°F (170°C), cut in 1.5 cm (½ in.) lengths.

Roast Candied Chestnuts — SERVES 10

10 chestnuts
100 ml (scant ½ cup) water
80 g (2⅔ oz.) sugar
1 *kuchinashi* (dried gardenia pod)
1 L (4 cups) water

Use a knife to peel outer and inner skins from chestnuts, add to water containing crushed gardenia pod, bring to a boil, then reduce heat to medium and cook for 15 minutes until color turns to yellow. Steep in cold water for about 30 minutes and drain in sieve.

Bring water and sugar to a boil, add chestnuts and cook for about 5 minutes. Allow to cool in syrup, and leave for at least 12 hours. Remove chestnuts from syrup and char using a kitchen torch.

Fried Gingko Nuts and *Mukago* Needle Skewer on Pine — SERVES 4

8 gingko nuts
8 *mukago* (wild yam propagules)
4 pine needles

Fry gingko nuts and mukago for 2 minutes in oil at about 300°F (150°C). Skewer on pine needles.

Ebi taro — SERVES 8

2 *ebi* taro tubers
20 g (⅔ oz.) sugar
About ¼ tsp. salt
1 Tbsp. plus 1 tsp. *usukuchi* soy sauce
1 Tbsp. mirin
600 ml (2½ cups) simmering liquid
  2 L (2 qts.) niban dashi
  30 g (1 oz.) *katsuobushi*
  100 ml (scant ½ cup) sake
  2 Tbsp. plus 2 tsp. mirin

Peel ebi taro thickly, keeping the shape of the tubers and ensuring all fibers are removed. Fill a pan with water used to wash rice (i.e. cloudy liquid containing starch), add ebi taro and place on heat, covering with parchment paper or similar that can sit directly on liquid. Bring to a boil, reduce heat to low, and cook for about 12 minutes. When cooked through, rinse in cold water and cool thoroughly.

Drain ebi taro and cut in half lengthwise. Place all ingredients of simmering liquid in a pan, boil for 15 minutes, then strain. Add simmering liquid, bring to a boil, then reduce heat to low, add sugar, salt, usukuchi soy sauce and mirin, simmer for about 10 minutes to enable flavors to be absorbed, then cool in liquid. When cool, chop ebi taro into pieces 4 × 2.5 cm (2 × 1 in.) long.

Sweetfish Simmered in *Sansho* Pepper — SERVES 3

3 sweetfish with roe
200 ml (scant 1 cup) sake
10 g (⅓ oz.) sugar
1 Tbsp. plus 2 tsp. soy sauce
1 Tbsp. plus 2 tsp. mirin
20 g (⅔ oz.) *sansho* pepper *tsukudani* (commercial product)
500 ml (generous 2 cups) *bancha* coarse tea

Grill sweetfish 8 minutes on one side, 4 on other side over a medium flame, without seasoning. Transfer to a pan, add coarse tea. Place parchment paper on top of liquid, bring to a boil, reduce heat to medium and simmer until skulls are soft (about 5 hours, topping up liquid with water as needed). Add sake, sugar, soy sauce, mirin and sansho and simmer until liquid is glossy.

Steamed Conger Eel — SERVES 5-6

3 conger eels (about 210 g [7 oz.])
Steaming liquid
  300 ml (1¼ cups) sake
  200 ml (scant 1 cup)
  5 Tbsp. plus 2 tsp. soy sauce

Split conger eels open, remove abdominal and other bones and dorsal fin. Pour hot water over side with skin and plunge into cold water to de-slime.

Place sake and mirin in a pan, bring to a boil, add soy sauce, return to a boil, then remove from heat.

Place prepared conger eels in a tray, add steaming liquid and place in steamer for 30 minutes. Allow to cool, remove from liquid and chop into 2 cm (1 in.) pieces.

Yuba — SERVES 4

5 sheets *yuba*
200 ml (scant 1 cup) simmering liquid (see *ebi* taro above for quantities and instructions)
1 tsp. sugar
Small amount salt
1 tsp. *usukuchi* soy sauce
1 tsp. mirin
Bamboo string

Bundle yuba with bamboo string.

Place yuba and simmering liquid in a pan, bring to a boil, add sugar, salt, usukuchi soy sauce and mirin and cook for 5 minutes. When cool, cut into 4 cm (2 in.) pieces.

Snowpeas — SERVES 5

10 snowpeas
150 ml (⅔ cup) simmering liquid (see *ebi* taro above for quantities and instructions)
About ½ Tbsp. sugar
Small amount salt
1 tsp. *usukuchi* soy sauce

Trim stalk ends from snowpeas, blanch and rinse in cold water.

Place simmering liquid, sugar, salt and soy sauce in a pan, bring to a boil, add drained snowpeas, and when pan returns to a boil (about 20 seconds), remove from heat and stand in cold water to cool.

Amadai Awa-mushi P. 27

Tilefish Steamed with Millet

SERVES 10

10 tilefish pieces, 35 g (1 oz.) each
4 shiitake mushrooms
2 chestnuts, outer shells and inner skins removed
10 *aomi* daikon radishes
⅓ *Kintoki* carrot
½ bunch chrysanthemum leaves
100 g (3⅓ oz.) *awa* millet

35 g (1 oz.) *Domyoji* rice flour
1 *yuzu* zest, cut into pine needle-sized strips
Shiitake cooking stock
  180 ml (⅔ cup plus 4 tsp.) ichiban dashi
  2 tsp. *usukuchi* soy sauce
Marinade for daikon and *Kintoki* carrot
  720 ml (3 cups) ichiban dashi
  4 tsp. *usukuchi* soy sauce
  1 scant tsp. salt
Millet dumpling stock
  150 ml (½ cup plus 2 Tbsp.) ichiban dashi
  1 tsp. *usukuchi* soy sauce
  Small amount salt
Chrysanthemum leaves *an* sauce
  1 L (4 cups) ichiban dashi
  5 tsp. *usukuchi* soy sauce
  1 scant Tbsp. mirin
  1 tsp. salt

Dissolved *kudzu* starch as required (dissolve 500 g [17 oz.] *kudzu* starch in 900 ml [(3⅔ cups)] water)

Remove bases from shiitake and cut each mushroom into 6 equal pieces. Add to cooking stock and cook 2–3 minutes over medium heat. Cut chestnuts into 7 mm (¼ in.) cubes, sprinkle on salt (0.5% by weight) and steam for 5–6 minutes at 100°F (40°C).

Peel daikon radishes and cut into small daikon shapes. Blanch, then plunge into cold water. Chop carrot into 3 mm × 10 cm (⅛ × 4 in.) sticks and sprinkle with a little salt (extra). When softened, tie together in pairs using a third stick. Soak in water for 5 minutes to remove salt, blanch and plunge into cold water. Drain daikon and carrot and steep in marinade for 1–2 hours.

Divide chrysanthemum into leaves and stalks. Bring a pan of water to a boil, add leaves, and when it starts to a boil again, remove leaves and squeeze out moisture. Boil stalks for 1 minute in boiling water then remove and squeeze out moisture. Purée stalks and leaves in food processor, then use a Pacojet to freeze and pulverize.

Sprinkle tilefish all over with salt (2% by weight) and set aside for 4–5 hours. Open so that millet dumplings can be wrapped inside.

Bring millet dumpling stock to a boil. Add boiled stock to millet and Domyoji flour in a bowl and mix well. Cover with plastic wrap and steam for 2–3 minutes at 190°F (90°C). When cool, divide into 10 equal pieces, stuff with shiitake and chestnut, and roll into balls. Wrap these millet dumplings in tilefish. Place in a dish and steam for 4–5 minutes at 190°F (90°C).

Make the chrysanthemum green *an* sauce: place all ingredients except kudzu into a pan and bring to a boil. Add dissolved kudzu starch, then frozen and pulverized chrysanthemum greens.

Top steamed tilefish with daikon radish and carrot (reheat first), and pour chrysanthemum sauce over top. Garnish with yuzu zest cut into fine needles.

Kamo Shinjo Usugori-jitate P. 29

Duck Dumplings in Icy Pond

SERVES 4

⅓ grated turnip
1 whole turnip, peeled into a cylinder 10 cm (4 in.) in diameter
3 cm (1¼ in.) Kujo green onion
4 *yomogi* mochi
2 *kuwai*
8 *Kintoki* carrot slices, cut into plum blossom shape
½ tsp. ginger juice
Small amount edible gold leaf
5 g *kuchinashi* (dried gardenia pod)
8 *yuzu* peels, cut into plum blossom shape
Duck dumplings
 100 g (3⅓ oz.) duck breast
 10 g (⅓ oz.) *tsukuneimo* yam
 40 g (1⅓ oz.) white fish *surimi*
 Small amount powdered *sansho* pepper
 1 tsp. soy sauce
Simmering liquid
 540 ml (2¼ cups) ichiban dashi
 Scant 1 Tbsp. *usukuchi* soy sauce
 ½ tsp. salt
Broth
 600 ml (2½ cups) ichiban dashi
 Scant 1 Tbsp. *usukuchi* soy sauce
 ½ tsp. salt
 1½ Tbsp. dissolved *kudzu* starch (dissolve 500 g [17 oz.] *kudzu* starch in 900 ml [(3⅔ cups)] water)

Peel whole turnip into a cylinder 10 cm (4 in.) in diameter, and cut into slices 2 mm (⅛ in.) thick. Grate the ⅓ turnip, add a little salt to the turnip juice, heat until translucent, cool, and skim off scum. Add sliced turnip to this turnip juice and simmer for 10 minutes at 140°F (60°C) .

Grill the yomogi mochi. Grill the Kujo green onion and chop into 2 cm (1 in.) lengths. Split arrowhead bulbs in half lengthwise, and peel into the shape of a votive tablet. Dye using the kuchinashi in boiling water, brand with Chinese calendar symbol and cook for 4–5 minutes in simmering liquid.

Cut carrot into plum blossom shapes and cook for 4–5 minutes in simmering liquid. Place dumpling ingredients in a mortar and blend thoroughly.

Place half the broth in a pan, bring to a boil, drop in spoonfuls of the duck dumpling mix and cook through. Bring remaining broth to a boil in a separate pan, add grilled Kujo green onion, cook for 1–2 minutes then remove. Add 150 ml (⅔ cup) of dashi from pan used to make dumplings, and ginger juice to taste, then thicken with kudzu paste.

Arrange a dumpling, piece of grilled onion, a yomogi mochi, and arrowhead in bowl. Pour in broth.

Top with a slice of turnip resembling ice, making sure there are no air pockets, and sprinkle with plum blossom carrot slices, yuzu and gold leaf.

Ayu Shio-yaki P. 51

Salt-Grilled Sweetfish

SERVES 6

6 sweetfish
Rock salt to taste

Place fresh sweetfish on skewers and sprinkle with salt to taste. Grill over charcoal until fragrant, and arrange in serving dish.

Sansai Tosazu-ae P. 55

Wild Vegetables in Tosazu Vinegar

SERVES 4

150 g (5 oz.) bamboo shoot
⅓ cup rice bran
700 ml (scant 3 cups) water
½ red chili pepper
8 *kogomi*
8 *taranome*
2 shoots *fuki*
½ stem *yamaudo*
12 *katakuri*
12 stems *tsukushi* (horsetail)
Kinome to taste
Marinade for *kogomi* and *taranome*
 300 ml (1⅓ cups) ichiban dashi
 2 tsp. *usukuchi* soy sauce
 Small amount salt
Tosazu *gelée*
 200 ml (scant 1 cup) Tosazu
 2.5 g gelatin powder

Make Tosazu *gelée*. Place Tosazu and gelatin powder in a pan and heat until gelatin dissolves. Allow to cool, pour into a 21 × 21 cm (8½ × 8½ in.) mold, cool overnight to set, then push through a sieve.

Wash kogomi, taranome and katakuri to remove any dirt. Blanch kogomi and katakuri, then plunge briefly into cold water, and drain. Cut crosses into the stalks of the taranome, and chop kogomi and katakuri into 3 cm (1¼ in.) lengths. Remove fibers from fuki, cut into 4.5 cm (2 in.) lengths. Boil a pan of water, blanch fuki, plunge briefly into cold water, drain. Peel yamaudo, chop roughly into longish pieces. Dip in 4% saltwater solution, drain.

Boil bamboo shoot as follows. Place bamboo shoot (skin on), water, rice bran and chili pepper in a pan. Cover with drop lid or parchment paper directly on surface and boil until a bamboo skewer easily pierces the base of the shoot. Cool in pan, remove bamboo shoot. Remove any remaining skin, cut shoot into 1 × 3 cm (½ × 1¼ in.) chunks.

Boil marinade for kogomi and taranome, then allow to cool. Marinate kogomi and taranome for an hour. Fry tsukushi without coating or seasoning for 3–4 minutes at 325°F (160°C), drain off oil and salt lightly (extra).

Mix crushed kinome into Tosazu vinegar gelée. Add bamboo shoot, taranome, katakuri, kogomi, fuki, yamaudo and tsukushi, and combine gently.

Seri to Aigamo Gomadare-gake P. 55

Roast Duck and Dropwort with Sesame Dressing

SERVES 5

125 g (4 oz.) dropwort
150 g (5 oz.) fillet of duck
Approx. 270 g (9 oz.) special sesame dressing (recipe below)
Stock for duck
 600 ml (2¼ cups) sake
 100 ml (scant½ cup) mirin
 100 ml (scant½ cup) soy sauce
Marinade for dropwort
 450 ml (1⅔ cups) ichiban dashi
 2 Tbsp. plus 2 tsp. *usukuchi* soy sauce
 2 Tbsp. plus 2 tsp. mirin

Special sesame dressing APPROX. 50 PORTIONS

500 g (scant 17 oz.) firm tofu, drain off liquid
90 g (3 oz.) sesame
1 Tbsp. plus 1 tsp. salt
150 g (5 oz.) sugar
20 g (⅔ oz.) *karashi* mustard

Place all ingredients in food processor and mix until smooth.

Cut roots from dropwort, wash section near roots thoroughly. Mix ichiban dashi, soy sauce and mirin. Parboil dropwort and marinate in the stock for an hour. Cut into 5 cm (2 in.) lengths.

Fry duck thoroughly skinside down, drain off oil, immerse quickly in water, then drain. Make stock for duck. Flambé sake and mirin to burn off alcohol, add soy sauce. Add to 150 ml (⅔ cup) of the stock and braise 30 minutes at 150°F (65°C) in a steam convection oven.

Pierce braised duck skin and flesh with two metal skewers to bleed. Allow to cool. Use ice to chill the braising juices, and when the fat on the juices turns white and hard, skim off. Immerse duck in the stock (cooled) and braising juices, and leave for a day. Slice into 5 mm (¼ in.) pieces.

Arrange duck and dropwort on dish and finish with sesame dressing.

Hassun P. 75

Hassun

Whitebait Grilled in Bottarga Powder — SERVES 4

20 whitebait
About ¼ tsp. salt
2 tsp. egg white
1 tsp. bottarga powder (commercial product)

Rinse whitebait quickly and drain. Sprinkle with salt and set aside for 30 minutes. Using thin bamboo skewers, skewer in groups of five, piercing each through both head and gut. Sun-dry for half a day.

Grill 5 minutes and 3 minutes respectively on each side, over a low to medium flame, to dry surface of whitebait. Brush egg white on one side, dredge with bottarga powder, then grill for another minute over a low to medium flame. Cut heads off whitebait, remove skewers and arrange on dish.

Angelica Buds in Black Sesame Sauce — SERVES 5

10 Japanese angelica buds
50 ml (3 Tbsp. plus 1 tsp.) ichiban dashi
Scant 1 tsp. *usukuchi* soy sauce
Scant 1 tsp. soy sauce
½ tsp. mirin
2 tsp. toasted sesame seeds

Trim a little of the woody base from angelica buds and peel. Score base of each with a cross, plunge into water, then drain.

Place dashi in a pan and heat, adding soy sauces and mirin. When boiling, add buds. Boil over a medium flame for about a minute until the base of each bud can be pierced with a bamboo skewer. Transfer to a bowl along with cooking liquid, and stand in ice water to cool. Leave for half a day.

Place sesame seeds in a mortar and grind coarsely. Add 1 Tbsp. of cooking liquid and buds, then combine. Serve two buds per person.

Shokado Bento P. 82

Shokado Bento Box

Hassun — SERVES 4

Salmon roe in soy sauce marinade

100 g (3⅓ oz.) salmon roe
90 g (3 oz.) salt
100 ml (scant ½ cup) niban dashi
1 tsp. soy sauce

Dissolve 90 g (3 oz.) salt in 3 L (3 qts.) water. Transfer 1 L (4 cups) of saltwater solution to a pan and heat to 175°F (80°C). Add roe to 300 ml (1⅓ cups) of the remaining (cooled) saltwater solution, and remove any sinews or other extraneous material. Drain. Blanch by plunging into the heated saltwater and then quickly removing. Drain immediately. Add roe to 300 ml (1⅓ cups) of remaining saltwater solution, remove sac, working roe with hand in a similar fashion to washing rice, and changing saltwater as many times as required until roe is clean. Drain in a sieve.

Bring niban dashi and soy sauce to a boil in a pan, then allow to cool. Add roe and marinate for 3 hours in refrigerator to allow flavors to be absorbed.

Steamed chicken with *tonburi* seeds — SERVES 4

40 g (1⅓ oz.) *tonburi* (*Bassia scoparia*) seeds
10 g (⅓ oz.) chicken
10 g (⅓ oz.) *nagaimo* mountain yam, grated, or ground using mortar and pestle
Tosa shoyu seasoned base
- 2 Tbsp. niban dashi
- 1 Tbsp. plus 1 tsp. soy sauce
- Scant 2 tsp. mirin
- 2 tsp. sake
- 2 g kombu
- 1 g *katsuobushi*

Place Tosa shoyu base ingredients in a pan, bring just a boil, then strain through paper towel and cool.

Rinse tonburi seeds, drain on a finely-woven cloth or similar. Salt chicken lightly (salt extra) and steam for about 5 minutes over medium heat. Cut into 5 mm (¼ in.) cubes and cool.

Combine tonburi, chicken and nagaimo, and add a little Tosa shoyu (extra) to taste.

Atsuyaki tamago layered omelet — SERVES 20

10 egg yolks
120 ml (½ cup) mirin
About ½ tsp. salt
6 g *nagaimo* mountain yam (grated, or ground using mortar and pestle)
80 g (2⅔ oz.) white fish *surimi* (commercial product)

Place surimi in mortar and grind, adding mirin, egg yolks, salt and nagaimo, mixing well, then strain through a fine sieve. Place strained batter in a heatproof dish. Bake for 2½ hours at 190°F (90°C), then cool.

Chestnuts in syrup — SERVES 3

3 chestnuts
300 ml (1⅓ cups) water
1 *kuchinashi* (dried gardenia pod), crushed
50 g (1⅔ oz.) rock sugar

Peel chestnuts, place in a pan, add plenty of water, bring to a boil and boil for about 10 minutes, until easily pierced by a bamboo skewer. Transfer to water and soak for about 10 minutes to eliminate any lingering astringency. Simmer boiled chestnuts, water, crushed kuchinashi and rock sugar over a low flame for about 20 minutes, then allow to cool.

Ox tongue in sweet soy sauce — SERVES 6

100 g (3⅓ oz.) ox tongue (one whole piece)
1.5 L (generous 6 cups) sake
Base
- 200 ml (scant 1 cup) cooking liquid (after cooking tongue 2 hours in pressure cooker)
- 1 Tbsp.mirin
- 20 g (⅔ oz.) sugar
- 1 Tbsp. plus 2 tsp. soy sauce
- 5 g ginger

¼ onion
1 Tbsp. oil

Place ox tongue and sake in pressure cooker, cook for about 2 hours (under pressure). Cut onion into 1 cm (½ in.) slices. Heat oil in frying pan and sauté.

Place ox tongue base ingredients and sautéed onion in a pan, simmer for about 15 minutes over medium heat, strain through a sieve, and transfer to another pan. Cut the pressure-cooked ox tongue into bite-sized pieces, add to pan and simmer over medium heat for about 5 minutes. Allow to cool.

Simmered sweet potato — SERVES 5

½ sweet potato
Base
- 180 ml (⅔ cup plus 4 tsp.) water
- 100 g (3⅓ oz.) rock sugar
- 4 g lemon
- ½ *kuchinashi* (dried gardenia pod)

Chop sweet potato into bite-sized pieces and trim corners off each. Place in pan with plenty of water and boil until easily pierced with a bamboo skewer. Transfer to cold water for about 10 minutes to remove any bitter taste. Place sweet potato base ingredients and parboiled sweet potato in a pan and simmer for 10 minutes at medium heat. Remove sweet potato and cool.

Tender-cooked abalone — SERVES 4

200 g (7 oz.) abalone
1 L (4 cups) water
About ½ tsp. salt
8 g kombu

Rinse abalone thoroughly, place with water in pressure cooker, cook for about 20 minutes at high pressure. Remove abalone, wipe clean, and transfer to another pan.

Strain abalone cooking juices, place in abalone pan with salt and kombu, simmer for about an hour over a low flame. Let abalone cool in cooking liquid (remove kombu after simmering for about 10 minutes). Chop abalone into bite-sized pieces.

Tiger prawn in sweet soy sauce SERVES 1

1 tiger prawn
Base
- 90 ml (scant ½ cup) de-alcoholized sake
- 1 Tbsp. sugar
- About ½ tsp. salt

Remove head of tiger prawn, devein, plunge into boiling water for about 40 seconds, then peel. Place tiger prawn base ingredients in pan, bring to a boil, allow to cool, add the prawn and marinate in refrigerator for about 12 hours.

Satoimo **taro steamed in its skin** SERVES 4

4 *satoimo* cormlets (*koimo*)
2 g *Daitokuji natto*

Wash satoimo taro, slice off a small piece from the base of each, then steam satoimo for about 15 minutes. Scoop out a small hole in each, and stuff with Daitokuji natto.

Gingko nuts on pine needle skewer SERVES 1

3 gingko nuts
Small amount salt

Remove shell and membrane from gingko nuts, fry for 1 minute in oil at 340°F (170°C) to heat through. Drain off oil, and add a dash of salt to finish.

Salt-grilled tilefish SERVES 1

20 g (⅔ oz.) white tilefish (fillet)
Small amount salt

Cut tilefish into bite-sized pieces, place on skewer and sprinkle with salt. Set aside for about 10 minutes, then grill over charcoal.

Simmered Stuffed Tofu Balls and Vegetables SERVES 2

"Hiryuzu" tofu balls
- 25 g (scant 1 oz.) white fish *surimi* (commercial product)
- 10 g (⅓ oz.) burdock root (*gobo*)
- 15 g (½ oz.) carrot
- 10 g (⅓ oz.) shiitake mushrooms
- 10 g (⅓ oz.) *kikurage* wood ear mushrooms, soaked in water to rehydrate
- 25 g (scant 1 oz.) *nagaimo* mountain yam (grated, or ground using mortar and pestle)
- 170 g (5⅔ oz.) tofu
- 1 Tbsp. plus 1 tsp. oil
- 1 egg yolk
- 3 gingko nuts
- 3 lily bulbs

Base
- 300 ml (1⅓ cups) niban dashi
- 2 Tbsp. plus 2 tsp. mirin
- 2 Tbsp. plus 2 tsp. soy sauce
- Small amount *katsuobushi* (wrap in gauze)
- Small amount *kudzu* starch (dissolved in water)
- 1 Tbsp. oil

Cut shiitake into thick 2 cm (1 in.) strips, peel carrot and cut to the same size. Prepare burdock root *sasagaki* style, (i.e. in shaved strips). Heat oil in frying pan, fry vegetables and shiitake until tender, allow to cool. Cut kikurage into 2 cm (1 in.) strips.

Bring a generous pan of water to a boil, add tofu, boil for about 2 minutes, remove and drain. Mix until smooth using a hand mixer or whisk, transfer to sieve, cover with a cloth and allow to cool.

Place egg yolks and 1 Tbsp. oil in food processor, blend well, add surimi, tofu and yamaimo, mix and transfer resulting dough to a bowl. Mix in sautéed vegetables and kikurage.

Fry gingko nuts in oil (extra) for 1 minute at 340°F (170°C), drain, cool and cut in half. Chop lily bulbs into bite-sized pieces, sprinkle with a little salt (extra) and steam for about 3 minutes. Add gingko nuts and lily bulb to dough, roll into bite-sized balls, fry in oil at 350°F (180°C) until golden, and drain.

Place hiryuzu base ingredients in a pan, bring to a boil, add fried tofu balls, and simmer for 5 minutes.

1 shiitake mushroom
Base
- 200 ml (scant 1 cup) niban dashi
- Generous 1 Tbsp. mirin
- Scant 1 Tbsp. *usukuchi* soy sauce
- 1 Tbsp. plus 2 tsp. soy sauce
- 2 g kombu

Remove stalk from shiitake, wipe clean. Fry in oil for 1 minute at 340°F (170°C), then cut into bite-sized chunks. Place shiitake base ingredients in a pan, add fried shiitake, simmer for 10 minutes and cool. Simmer for a further 10 minutes, cool (simmering twice ensures the flavors penetrate completely).

1 *satoimo* taro
Base
- 300 ml (1⅓ cups) niban dashi
- 4 Tbsp. mirin
- 1 tsp. salt
- 2 g kombu

Wash satoimo, peel, soak in water for about 10 minutes. Place in pressure cooker with satoimo base ingredients, cook under high pressure for 3 minutes.

40 g (1⅓ oz.) *Kintoki* carrot
Base
- 200 ml (scant 1 cup) niban dashi
- 20 g (⅔ oz.) sugar
- 1 Tbsp. plus 2 tsp. *usukuchi* soy sauce
- Dash soy sauce
- 2 g kombu

Peel Kintoki carrot, chop into bite-sized pieces, place in a pan with plenty of water, boil for 2 minutes. Place carrot base ingredients in a pan, bring to a boil, add parboiled Kintoki carrot, simmer for about 5 minutes, cool. Refrigerate for 12 hours to allow flavors to be absorbed.

¼ bunch spinach
Base
- 100 ml (scant ½ cup) niban dashi
- About ½ tsp. salt

Wash spinach, cut into bite-sized pieces. Bring 3% saltwater soliution (1 Tbsp. salt in 500 ml [generous 2 cups] water) to a boil, add spinach and blanch for a minute and a half. Plunge into water, pat dry. Place spinach base ingredients in a pan, bring to a boil, add spinach. Arrange on plate while still warm.

⅒ of 1 *yuzu*

Remove inner white pith from yuzu peel, cut into thin 2.5 cm (1 in.) strips. Place tofu balls, shiitake, satoimo, Kintoki carrot and spinach in dish, top with yuzu peel.

Sashimi Selection SERVES 1

35 g (1 oz.) sea bream
40 g (1⅓ oz.) Ise lobster
30 g (1 oz.) squid
⅒ bunch *mizuna* (Japanese mustard greens)
Base
- 100 ml (scant ½ cup) niban dashi
- About ½ tsp. salt

170 g (5⅔ oz.) *kabocha* squash
Small amount olive oil
Wasabi to taste

Skin sea bream, cut into bite-sized pieces for sashimi. Chop lobster into bite-sized pieces, place on skewer and brush with olive oil. Grill over burner until scorched, cool. Cut crosshatching in squid, and chop into 3 cm pieces.

Cut mizuna into 3 cm (1¼ in.) lengths, boil 3% saltwater solution (1 Tbsp.salt in 500 ml [generous 2 cups] water), add mizuna, blanch for about 40 seconds, plunge into cold water, drain. Place mizuna base ingredients in a pan, bring to just under a boil, cool, add mizuna and refrigerate for 3 hours. Julienne squash in 2 cm (1 in.) strips, soak in water for 10 minutes and drain.

Arrange sea bream, lobster, squid, mizuna and squash on dish, serve with wasabi on side.

Sea Bream "Stick" Sushi and Tuna Belly Sushi SERVES 3

150 g (5 oz.) sea bream (belly)
200 g (7 oz.) tuna belly (cut for sashimi)
2 *nori*, 15 × 22 cm (6 × 8½ in.) each
2 cups sushi rice
Scant 1 Tbsp. wasabi
50 g (1⅔ oz.) kombu
1 tsp. salt

Sprinkle about ½ tsp. salt over sea bream, sandwich in kombu and set aside for 2 hours. Remove bream from kombu, place on sushi mat, add wasabi, then rice, and roll. Cut into 2 cm (1 in.) pieces.

Cut tuna belly into 1 cm (½ in.) lengths. Place nori, rice, wasabi and a length of tuna on sushi mat in that order, roll, and cut into 2 cm (1 in.) pieces.

Kakure Ume P. 87

Hidden Plum

SERVES 10

10 large *umeboshi*
800 ml (3⅓ cups) ichiban dashi
Generous 1 Tbsp. *usukuchi* soy sauce
About 1 tsp. salt
10 g (⅓ oz.) *katsuobushi*
Shirako cream
500 g (scant 17 oz.) sea bream milt
100 ml (scant ½ cup) sake
1 tsp. sesame paste
2 tsp. vinegar
About ½ tsp. salt
Scant 1 tsp. *usukuchi* soy sauce
10 peach blossoms

Prick plums all over with a needle and soak in water overnight to remove saltiness. Place in plenty of fresh water and cook for 20–30 minutes over low heat. Transfer plums to cold water and soak until water is cool.

Add soy sauce and salt to dashi to season (adjust depending on saltiness of plums), add cooked plums. Place katsuobushi wrapped in gauze or similar on top instead of a drop lid (*oigatsuo*), simmer over a very low flame for about 15 minutes to allow flavors to absorb into plums. Cool plums in cooking liquid.

Sprinkle shirako with 1% salt by weight, and set aside for an hour. Sprinkle with sake, steam for 10–15 minutes at 190°F (90°C). Place sieved shirako, sesame paste, salt and soy sauce in a food processor and mix into a thick cream.

Pour cream over individual drained plums and top with a peach blossom.

Kamasu Miso Yuan-yaki P. 91

Grilled Barracuda with Miso Yuan-yaki Baste

(SEE P. 187)

Amadai Sumashi-jitate P. 98

Tilefish in Clear Broth

SERVES 4

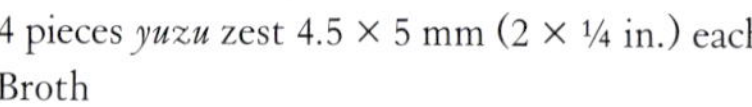

4 tilefish fillets, 60 g (2 oz.) each with any darker flesh near backbone removed
4 field mustard stalks
4 small sheets dried sea cucumber ovaries (*bachiko*)
4 pieces *yuzu* zest 4.5 × 5 mm (2 × ¼ in.) each
Broth
100 ml (scant ½ cup) ichiban dashi
Scant 1 Tbsp. *usukuchi* soy sauce
½ tsp. salt
Marinade
90 ml (scant ½ cup) ichiban dashi
½ tsp. *usukuchi* soy sauce
0.5 g salt

Blanch the field mustard and plunge into cold water. Squeeze out moisture, steep in marinade for 1–2 hours. Sprinkle tilefish with salt (extra: 1% by weight), grill close to a high flame for 4–5 minutes on skin side first then on other side for the same amount of time.

Place tilefish in bowl skin side up, accompanied by bachiko and field mustard, and top with yuzu zest. Pour broth in bowl carefully around tilefish.

Okoze Maru-jitate P. 100

Devil Stinger in "Turtle Style" Broth

SERVES 4

1 devil stinger
4 blocks *yomogi* tofu (recipe below)
8 *kogomi* (ostrich fern)
10 g (⅓ oz.) *sansho* pepper flower
12 ginger petals (thin slices of ginger cut into flower petal shape)

***Yomogi* tofu** SERVES 12

40 g (1⅓ oz.) *yomogi* (dried)
750 ml (3 cups plus 2 Tbsp.) kombu dashi
100 g (3⅓ oz.) sesame paste
120 g (4 oz.) *kudzu* starch

Place kombu dashi, sesame paste, and kudzu in a pan. Heat over a medium flame, working while mixing with a whisk. When the mixture begins to thicken, reduce to low heat and stir for about 20 minutes with a wooden spoon, until thick and sticky.

To finish add yomogi moistened with a little water, blend in quickly, pour into mold and allow to cool naturally until set. Cut into 3 × 4 cm (1¼ × 2 in.) pieces.

***Maru-jitate* broth**

5 cm (2 in.) square piece kombu
450 ml (scant 2 cups) water
300 ml (1¼ cups) sake
1 Tbsp. *usukuchi* soy sauce
Small amount salt

***Kogomi and sansho* pepper flower cooking liquid**

300 ml (1¼ cups) ichiban dashi
⅓ tsp. *usukuchi* soy sauce
About ½ tsp. salt

Cut devil stinger into three pieces, fillet, then remove fine bones at 2 mm–3 mm (⅛ in.) intervals. Sprinkle with salt (extra) 1% by weight of fish then dredge with kudzu (extra). Blanch for about 10 seconds in boiling water, then plunge into ice water (coating in kudzu makes for a better mouthfeel, and seals in the flavor of the fish). Plunge the offal (head, bones etc.) into boiling water then into cold water (blanching), then remove any blood or foreign matter.

Place water and kombu for maru-jitate broth in a pan with blanched devil stinger offal and heat. Add sake just before it comes to a boil, and simmer for about 10 minutes over low heat. Add usukuchi soy sauce and salt to season as desired. Strain through bleached cotton or similar.

Blanch kogomi and sansho pepper flower. Heat cooking liquid, add blanched kogomi and sansho, leave on heat for about 30 seconds. Steam fish flesh for 5 minutes in a steamer at 190°F (90°C). Arrange devil stinger, kogomi, sansho and ginger petals in bowl, pour 150 ml (⅔ cup) of broth around fish.

Unagi Ushio-jitate P. 101

Eel in Salt Broth

SERVES 2

1 eel
100 g (3⅓ oz.) winter melon
20 g (⅔ oz.) wasabi
3 *shiso* flowers

500 ml (generous 2 cups) kombu dashi
Broth
500 ml (generous 2 cups) niban dashi
About 1 tsp. salt
½ tsp. soy sauce

Split eel into halves, and chop one half into 3 cm (1¼ in.) chunks. Salt chunks generously and leave for 15 minutes. Rinse off salt, quickly pour on boiling water to "frost," and cool in ice water. Use a pot scourer to wash any white slime off the eel's surface, and dry with a cloth.

Place eel chunks and kombu dashi in a pan and heat. Reduce heat to low just before stock comes to a boil, and simmer for about 10 minutes, skimming as required.

Place remaining half of eel on a skewer, and sear on side. Steam for 20 minutes in steamer, remove fine bones while still hot, and let cool.

Chop wasabi into 2.5 cm (1 in.) pieces then fine strips, soak in water for about 10 minutes, drain.

Thinly peel winter melon, cross-hatch skin side with a knife, and cut into bite-sized pieces. Boil water, add salt to taste (½ tsp.per 500 ml [generous 2 cups] water), parboil melon for about 15 minutes, then marinate in the broth for 3 hours.

Place grilled eel back on a skewer, steam for about two minutes. Salt lightly, grill skin side over a high flame until fragrant, and cut into bite-sized pieces.

Place winter melon in pot of broth to warm briefly, then arrange in bowl. Top with steamed eel, place wasabi alongside, then garnish with the shiso flowers. Season 280 ml (1 cup plus 2 Tbsp.) of the eel and kombu dashi soup with salt and soy sauce to taste, and pour into bowl.

Hiryuzu-wan P. 103

Hiryuzu Tofu Dumplings

SERVES 4

1 block tofu, about 330 g (11 oz.)
60 g (2 oz.) finely grated *yamatoimo* mountain yam
20 g (⅔ oz.) julienned carrot
20 g (⅔ oz.) *kikurage* wood ear mushrooms
8 lily bulbs
4 gingko nuts
8 *warabi* (bracken)
8 *fukinoto* (butterbur buds)
Generous 1 Tbsp. *kudzu* starch

2 tsp. *usukuchi* soy sauce
About ½ tsp. salt
15 g (½ oz.) finely chopped ginger
Skin of *fukinoto* to taste
About ½ tsp. black sesame

Shojin dashi

1 L (4 cups) water
10 g (⅓ oz.) Rishiri kombu
2 dried shiitake mushrooms
40 g (1⅓ oz.) soybeans
5 g *kampyo* (dried gourd shavings)
15 g (½ oz.) dried daikon radish

Steep dried shiitake in 300 ml (1¼ cups) of water overnight to rehydrate. Toast soybeans over a low flame for about 25 minutes. Rub kampyo thoroughly with salt (extra) then wash off.

Place water and kombu in a pan, leave for 2 hours to extract umami from the kombu. Add all other ingredients, simmer for 20 minutes over low heat, strain.

Simmering liquid

1 L (4 cups) kombu dashi
1 Tbsp. plus 2 tsp. sugar
About 1 tsp. salt
1 Tbsp. plus 2 tsp. *usukuchi* soy sauce

Steam tofu at 210°F (100°C) for 10 minutes, place a weight on top to drain well. When about half the original weight, add grated yamatoimo and kudzu starch to tofu and grind until smooth. Season with soy sauce and salt, and mix in carrot and kikurage.

Add lily bulbs and gingko nuts, shape gently, roll in black sesame seeds and fry 2 minutes in oil at 350°F (180°C). When fried, pour boiling water over top to remove oil. Add to the simmering liquid and simmer over low heat for 2 minutes.

Place warabi in 2 L (2 qts) hot water with 1 tsp. of baking soda dissolved in it, leave overnight, remove any dirt and fine hairs, and cut off hard roots.

Arrange hiryuzu and warabi in dish. Season 100 ml (scant ½ cup) of warmed shojin dashi with usukuchi soy sauce and salt, thicken with kudzu starch (extra) and pour into dish. Serve with lightly grilled fukinoto skin and ginger.

Hamaguri Shinjo P. 105

Hamaguri Clam Dumpling

SERVES 6

12 *Hamaguri* clams
80 g (2⅔ oz.) *udo*, cut into sticks
80 g (2⅔ oz.) carrot, cut into sticks
200 g (7 oz.) white fish *surimi*
80 ml (⅓ cup) kombu dashi

80 ml (⅓ cup) ichiban dashi
Zinbaso as required
Kinome to taste

Steam clams for 3 minutes at 210°F (100°C), remove meat from shells (with surrounding viscera and mantle still attached), clean as required and chop roughly. Mix chopped clam meat into surimi thinned with kombu dashi and steam for 10 minutes at 190°F (90°C). Set steamed clam juice aside for later use.

Rehydrate zinbaso by first steeping in water for 30 minutes, then plunging into boiling water for about 10 seconds. Boil water in another pan, add carrot sticks, udo and rehydrated zinbaso, boil for about 2 minutes. Plunge into ice water and drain. Heat zinbaso, carrot and udo in remaining kombu dashi (just until warm).

Place a steamed clam dumpling in dish. Top with kinome leaves. Combine 80 ml (⅓ cup) of ichiban dashi and 2 Tbsp. plus 2 tsp. steaming juices and carefully pour around dumpling.

Hassun Kuro-oke Akikusa-kazari P. 107

Hassun in a Black Barrel with Autumn Wildflowers

Salt-Grilled Kobujime Style Beef — SERVES 10

100 g (3⅓ oz.) beef sirloin
1 tsp. salt
Scant 1 tsp. wasabi
10 cm (4 in.) square piece kombu

Prepare the kobujime: chop meat into 2.5 cm (1 in.) cubes, sandwich in kombu, sprinkle with salt, and set aside for two hours.

Remove meat from kombu, place on a skewer, cook until medium over high charcoal flame. When cooked, top with wasabi.

Vinegared Abalone — SERVES 10

2 abalone
3 L (3 qts.) water
Generous 1 tsp. salt
10 g (⅓ oz.) kombu
1 bunch *komatsuna* (Japanese mustard spinach)
Tosazu seasoned vinegar base
100 ml (scant ½ cup) niban dashi
1 Tbsp. plus 1 tsp. mirin
3 Tbsp. vinegar
1 Tbsp. plus 2 tsp. soy sauce
2 g kombu

1 g *katsuobushi*
5 g gelatin

Rinse abalone thoroughly, place with water in pressure cooker and cook at high pressure for about 20 minutes. Remove abalone, wipe clean and transfer to another pan. Add strained cooking juices from abalone, generous 1 tsp. salt, and 30 g (1 oz.) kombu to pan containing abalone, simmer over low heat for about an hour, allow to cool (remove kombu after about 10 minutes of cooking). When cool, remove abalone and chop into 1 cm (½ in.) pieces.

Chop komatsuna into 2 cm (1 in.) pieces, place 3% saltwater solution (30 g [1 oz.] salt in 1 L [4 cups] water) in a pan, bring to a boil, add komatsuna, and blanch for 2 minutes. Plunge into cold water, drain.

Place Tosazu seasoned vinegar base ingredients in pan, bring just to a boil, strain through paper towel, and cool. Add gelatin, return to heat until gelatin dissolves. Refrigerate until set.

Arrange abalone and komatsuna in dish, top with the Tosazu vinegar jelly.

Salmon Roe in Soy Sauce Marinade (SEE P. 190)

Matsutake Mushroom *Hitashi* SERVES 10

100 g (3⅓ oz.) *matsutake* mushrooms
1 bunch chrysanthemum leaves
Base
200 ml (scant 1 cup) niban dashi
About 1 tsp. salt
Small amount *katsuobushi*

Wash matsutake, sprinkle with a little salt (extra), grill 2 minutes over hot charcoal, cut into 1 cm (½ in.) slices. Chop chrysanthemum leaves into 1 cm (½ in.) lengths. Boil 3% saltwater solution (30 g [1 oz.] salt in 1 L [4 cups] water), add chrysanthemum leaves, blanch for 1 minute. Steep in cold water for 3 minutes, remove, and cool.

Place base ingredients in a pan, bring just to a boil, cool, add chrysanthemum leaves and marinate in refrigerator for 3 hours.

Arrange chrysanthemum leaves and matsutake on dish, top with bonito shavings.

Prawns and Sea Urchin SERVES 10

5 prawns
40 g (1⅓ oz.) sea urchin
Scant 1 tsp. wasabi

Remove heads from prawns and devein, place on bamboo skewers to prevent curling during cooking. Boil 3% saltwater solution(30 g [1 oz.] salt in 1 L [4 cups] water), add prawns and boil for 20 seconds. Peel, chop each into two 2.5 cm (1 in.) chunks, cool. Top each piece of prawn with 4 g of sea urchin, followed by wasabi.

Potato in Egg Yolk Miso Marinade SERVES 10

40 g (1⅓ oz.) potato
2 egg yolks
Miso marinade base
100 g (3⅓ oz.) coarse-grained white miso
Generous 1 Tbsp. mirin

Make the egg yolk miso marinade: place base ingredients in a bowl and mix. Prepare a sheet of gauze and layer egg yolks, gauze and miso marinade base on a tray in that order, then refrigerate for 3 days. Chop potato into thin 2 cm (1 in.) strips, fry in oil at 325°F (160°C) until crisp.

Remove egg yolks from miso marinade base, cut into 1 cm (½ in.) cubes (yolks will have hardened in the marinade). Wrap fried potato around yolk pieces, forming balls.

Squid in Salted Bonito Entrails SERVES 10

200 g (7 oz.) squid, cut for sashimi
150 g (5 oz.) bonito entrail base (commercial product)

Cut crosshatching into squid, then chop into 2.5 cm (1 in.) cubes. Marinate in entrail base for about 10 minutes. Place squid on skewers and char over burner.

Goshiki-ae P. 114

Five-Color Salad

SERVES 4
100 g (3⅓ oz.) daikon radish
100 g (3⅓ oz.) *Kintoki* carrot
80 g (2⅔ oz.) cucumber
80 g (2⅔ oz.) crab stick
5 g Suizenji *nori* (dried)
¼ tsp. toasted sesame seeds
80 g (2⅔ oz.) Tosazu vinegar *gelée* (see p. 189)
1 tsp. grated ginger juice
½ tsp. *yuzu* juice

Soak Suizenji nori in water for about 12 hours. Cut cucumbers in half lengthwise, deseed. Cut daikon radish, Kintoki carrot, cucumber, crab and nori into 3.5 cm × 5 mm (1¼ × ¼ in.) lengths. Soak daikon and carrot in 3% saltwater solution, and cucumber in 2% saltwater solution for 15 minutes each. Wrap in gauze or similar, squeeze out moisture.

Place daikon, carrot, cucumber, nori and crab in a bowl. Dress with Tosazu vinegar *gelée*, ginger juice, and yuzu juice. Arrange in dish and sprinkle toasted sesame seeds on top.

Nishime P. 117

Simmered Vegetable Stew

SERVES 4
30 g (1 oz.) dried shiitake (add 300 ml [1⅓ cups] of water to rehydrate)
200 g (7 oz.) *satoimo* taro
½ cup rice bran
100 g (3⅓ oz.) *konnyaku*
150 g (5 oz.) lotus root
100 g (3⅓ oz.) *Kintoki* carrot
50 g (1⅔ oz.) burdock root
6 snowpeas
10 g (⅓ oz.) ginger
Snowpea marinade
90 ml (scant ½ cup) ichiban dashi
½ tsp. *usukuchi* soy sauce
0.5 g salt
Simmering liquid
Generous 2 cups ichiban dashi
1⅔ Tbsp. sugar
2 Tbsp. mirin
½ Tbsp. *usukuchi* soy sauce
1 Tbsp. soy sauce

Bring a pan of water to a boil, add snowpeas. When water returns to a boil, remove from heat and plunge snowpeas into cold water, then quickly remove and drain. Bring marinade to a boil then allow to cool. Add snowpeas and marinate for 2 hours.

Soak dried shiitake in the 300 ml (1¼ cups) of water for about half a day to rehydrate. Remove stalks. Top and tail satoimo slightly, peel.

Wrap rice bran in a bleached cotton cloth. Fill a pan with water, steep cloth in water and knead so that bran comes out. Add satoimo and bring to a boil. Cook for about 20 minutes until easily pierced by a bamboo skewer. Fill another pan with water, add boiled satoimo. Bring to a boil then transfer satoimo to cold water. Remove.

Cut konnyaku into 5 mm (¼ in.) slices. Cut a slit in the center of each slice, take one edge and push (twist) it through this slit. Boil a pan of water, add konnyaku. When water boils once again, remove from heat and drain.

Peel lotus root, trimming into a flower shape. Cut into 7 mm (⅓ in.) slices, soak in water to remove astringency. Peel carrot and chop roughly. Cut burdock root into 4.5 cm (2 in.) lengths.

Place satoimo, carrot, shiitake, lotus root, burdock root, konnyaku and dashi in a large pan, place a drop lid or parchment paper on top and heat over a high flame. When boiling, reduce heat to medium. When carrot and lotus root are tender, add sugar, usukuchi and regular soy sauce, and mirin, and simmer until most of the simmering liquid has evaporated.

Arrange in dish, add peeled and finely chopped ginger to finish.

Togan Manju P. 118

Winter Melon Dumplings

SERVES 14

1 winter melon
60 g (2 oz.) lily bulb
70 g (2⅓ oz.) *kikurage* wood ear mushrooms (rehydrated)
14 hairy crab legs
½ *yuzu*
Scant 30 g (1 oz.) ginger, finely julienned
Marinade
 700 ml (scant 3 cups) ichiban dashi
 1 tsp. *usukuchi* soy sauce
 About 1 tsp. salt
 2 tsp. sugar
 5 slice ginger, 5 mm (¼ in.) each
Cooking stock for *kikurage*
 220 ml (scant 1 cup) ichiban dashi
 Generous 1 Tbsp. *usukuchi* soy sauce
 Generous 1 Tbsp. mirin

Ginger *an* sauce

420 ml (1⅔ cups) ichiban dashi
1 tsp. *usukuchi* soy sauce
About ½ tsp. salt
1 tsp. sugar
Dissolved *kudzu* starch as required (dissolve 20 g [⅔ oz.] *kudzu starch* in 4 Tbsp. water)
1 Tbsp. ginger juice

Place dashi, soy sauce, salt and sugar in a pan, bring to a boil and dissolve sugar and salt. Thicken using the kudzu dissolved in water.

Split melon in half lengthwise, cut into 10 cm (4 in.) square cubes, remove seeds and peel thinly. Crosshatch for a decorative effect, coat with about 15 g (½ oz.) salt, and leave for 30 minutes. Fill a copper pan with water, bring to a boil, add melon, cover surface with thick paper towel and boil 10 minutes at medium heat. Plunge melon into chilled water, drain.

Take kikurage, rehydrated in advance, blanch for 1 minute over medium heat in boiling water, and simmer for 2 minutes in the warmed stock. Steam lily bulb for 10 minutes at 190°F (95°C).

Scoop out centers of melon pieces, stuff with kikurage and lily bulb. Wrap in gauze and form into a round shape, then steep for half a day in marinade.

Wash crabs thoroughly, sprinkle 1 tsp. salt on apron and leave for 10 minutes. Cook crabs for 20 minutes over medium heat, shell side down, and when cooled remove flesh from shell.

Take out melon, remove gauze, pour warmed ginger an sauce on melon, grate zest of yuzu and sprinkle with melon. Serve with crab and finely chopped ginger.

Tai Kabura P. 118

Stewed Sea Bream and Turnip

SERVES 4

1½ sea bream heads
6 turnips
½ bunch chrysanthemum leaves
⅓ *yuzu* zest
1 L (4 cups) sake
About ½ tsp. salt
Simmering liquid for sea bream
 5 Tbsp. plus 1 tsp. soy sauce
 20 g (⅔ oz.) sugar
400 ml (1⅔ cups) turnip stock (see p. 196)
Marinade
 180 ml (⅔ cup plus 4 tsp.) ichiban dashi
 Scant 1 tsp. *usukuchi* soy sauce
 About ¼ tsp. salt

Blanch chrysanthemum leaves and plunge into cold water. Squeeze out moisture, steep in marinade for 2 hours.

Rinse sea bream heads, removing any scales, blood, etc. Pour boiling water over to blanch them. Place in a pan with sake, cover with a drop lid or parchment paper on surface. Bring to a boil, add sugar and soy sauce in that order, simmer.

Cook turnips in another pan as follows. Peel turnips and cut in half. Place turnip stock and turnips in a pan, simmer until turnips are tender. When cooking liquid for sea bream is reduced to about ⅓ the original volume, transfer 120 ml (½ cup) of this liquid to the turnip pan. Simmer turnips a little longer, then transfer 200 ml (scant 1 cup) of liquid from the turnip pan to the sea bream pan. Add 2 g of salt to turnip pan, remove from heat, and allow to cool. Continue to simmer sea bream heads with drop lid on until only a little liquid remains.

Arrange sea bream heads, turnips and chrysanthemum leaves in a dish, and top with fine strips of yuzu zest.

Ise ebi Gusoku-ni P. 119

Ise lobster Cooked in the Shell

SERVES 3

1½ Ise lobsters, 500 g (scant 17 oz.)
300 ml (1¼ cups) sake
100 ml (scant ½ cup) lobster soup
110 g (3⅔ oz.) white miso
2 tsp. grated ginger juice
9 snowpeas
90 ml (scant ½ cup) ichiban dashi
½ tsp. *usukuchi* soy sauce
Small amount salt
1 slice ginger, thinly cut
Dash soy sauce
Lobster soup
 150 g (5 oz.) lobster shell, roasted golden in oven
 10 g (⅓ oz.) kombu
 900 ml (3¾ cups) water
 300 ml (1¼ cups) sake

Split lobster in half, devein. Using strips of dried bamboo bark or similar, bind up legs, feelers and tail. Place all ingredients of lobster soup in pan over low heat and simmer until reduced to about ⅓ original volume.

Arrange lobster in pan, add sake and lobster soup, cover with a drop lid or parchment paper on surface, place on heat. Cook, moving the pan to bring the liquid up over the lobster from time to time, until the meat becomes slightly opaque. Remove from pan, and remove meat from shells.

Add ichiban dashi and lobster soup to cooking liquid (making up to 800 ml [3⅓ cups] combined), stir in the white miso. Return lobster shells to broth and cook for a few minutes to bring out further flavor. Remove shells, return meat to pan and heat for about 30 seconds. Remove and cut into pieces of a suitable size for eating.

Return meat to shells, arrange on dish with snowpeas. Pour a generous serving of broth seasoned with soy sauce and ginger juice around lobster and garnish with ginger.

Takenoko to Wakame Takiawase P. 120

Simmered Bamboo Shoot and Wakame

SERVES 1

50 g (1⅔ oz.) bamboo shoot
15 g (½ oz.) *wakame*
3 broad beans
1 g *kinome*
⅓ tsp. thinly-shaved *katsuobushi*
300 ml (1¼ cups) kombu stock
2 Tbsp. sake
3 pieces kombu, 5 cm (2 in.) each
About ½ tsp. salt
Soy sauce to taste
Oil as required
Base
 400 ml (1⅔ cups) niban dashi
 Scant 2 tsp. soy sauce
 1 generous tsp. *uskcuchi* soy sauce
 2 tsp. sake

Parboil bamboo shoot in appropriate amount of nuka (rice bran) for 1 hour, drain. When cool, peel and soak in water for about 10 minutes. Remove tip of the shoot, chop rest into pieces 5 cm (2 in.) thick and about 2 cm (1 in.) long.

Place pieces of shoot in a pan, add kombu dashi, sake, two pieces of the kombu, and bring to a boil. Once boiling, skim, reduce heat to medium, and cook for about 10 minutes. Add 2 g salt, remove kombu, then cook for another 10 minutes or so. Wrap half of the bonito flakes in muslin cloth and add. Leave for about 2 minutes.

Pour all of the wakame base and remaining piece of kombu into a pan, bring to a boil and skim. Reduce heat to a low flame, and when the color of the kombu changes, add the wakame and cook for about 10 minutes.

Sprinkle salt on broad beans to taste and steam for 2 minutes. Heat oil in frying pan and sear over high heat.

Arrange bamboo shoot, wakame and broad beans in a dish, pour generous quantity of base used to cook bamboo shoot and garnish with thinly-shaved katsuobushi and kinome.

Fuyuyasai Takiawase P. 121

Simmered Winter Vegetables

SERVES 4

- 5 small turnips
- 300 ml (1¼ cups) ichiban dashi
- ½ Tbsp.salt
- Generous 1 Tbsp. *usukuchi* soy sauce
- Generous 1 Tbsp. mirin
- 300 ml (1¼ cups) turnip stock
  - 250 g (1⅔ oz.) peel from turnips
  - 1.2 L (5 cups) water
  - 5 g kombu

Cut turnips in half lengthwise and peel. Mix all ingredients of turnip stock and cook over a low flame until reduced to ⅔ original volume. Add to combined dashi and turnip stock, braise for about 20 minutes at 210°F (100°C).

Transfer to a pan, add salt, usukuchi soy sauce and mirin, and cook for about 10 minutes over a low flame.

- 2 *ebi* taro
- 1 L (4 cups) ichiban dashi
- About 1 tsp. salt
- 2 Tbsp. *usukuchi* soy sauce
- 35 g (1 oz.) sugar
- 10 g (⅓ oz.) *katsuobushi*

Peel ebi taro into a hexagonal shape. Braise in starchy water used to wash rice (extra) for 20–30 minutes at 210°F (100°C). Transfer to cold water. Boil hot water, return ebi taro, cook.

Combine dashi, salt, soy sauce and sugar, bring to a boil once. Place ebi taro and boiled dashi in a dish, wrap katsuobushi in gauze and place on top. Cover with plastic wrap and cook for 30 minutes at 185°F (85°C).

- 5 pieces *Kintoki* carrot, 15 g (½ oz.) each
- 2 Tbsp. *usukuchi* soy sauce
- Scant 1 Tbsp. mirin
- 300 ml (1⅓ cups) *Kintoki* carrot stock
  - 250 g (1¼ oz.) *Kintoki* carrot peel, tops etc.
  - 1.2 L (5 cups) water
  - 5 g kombu

Combine all ingredients and cook over low heat until reduced to ⅔ original volume. Take peeled and roughly chopped carrot pieces and simmer in Kintoki carrot stock until tender. Add usukuchi soy sauce and mirin, simmer for a few more minutes.

- ½ bunch chrysanthemum leaves
- 180 ml (⅔ cup plus 4 tsp.) ichiban dashi
- Scant 1 tsp. *usukuchi* soy sauce
- About ¼ tsp. salt

Blanch chrysanthemum leaves, plunge into cold water. Squeeze out moisture and marinate in a mixture of the dashi, usukuchi soy sauce, and mirin for 1–2 hours.

- 3 pieces Horikawa burdock root, 20 g (⅔ oz.) each
- 200 ml (scant 1 cup) ichiban dashi
- Generous 1 Tbsp. *usukuchi* soy sauce
- Scant 2 tsp. mirin

Chop burdock root, boil in starchy water used to wash rice (extra). When tender, rinse in cold water, then boil hot water, return burdock and continue to cook again. Combine with the dashi, soy sauce, and mirin and simmer over low heat for 5–6 minutes.

- 6 pieces Kujo green onion, 4 cm (2 in.) each
- 180 ml (⅔ cup plus 4 tsp.) ichiban dashi
- Scant 2 tsp. *usukuchi* soy sauce
- About ¼ tsp. salt
- Scant 1 tsp. mirin

Grill green onion without seasoning, then marinate in a mixture of dashi, soy sauce, salt and mirin for 3–4 hours.

Arrange separately cooked vegetables in dish, and add 150 ml (⅔ cup) of turnip stock. Garnish with thin strips of yuzu peel.

Nimonowan Sumashi-jitate P. 122

Simmered Bowl of Clear Broth

SERVES 4

- 300 g (10 oz.) abalone
- 60 ml (¼ cup) abalone liquid
- 60 ml (¼ cup) sake
- 2 Tbsp. *usukuchi* soy sauce
- Scant 1 Tbsp. mirin
- 600 ml (2¼ cups) ichiban dashi
- Generous 1 Tbsp. soy sauce
- About ½ tsp. salt
- 4 *urui* (young hosta heads), chopped into 3 cm (1¼ in.) pieces, blanched and rinse in water.
- 5 g thinly cut ginger

300 ml (1¼ cups) cooking base

- 1.4 L (scant 6 cups) niban dashi
- 300 g (10 oz.) dried tuna flakes (*magurobushi*)
- 1 cup plus 4 Tbsp.mirin
- 800 ml (3⅓ cups) sake

Place all ingredients in a pan, simmer for 15 minutes, and strain.

Yomogi Tofu

- 150 g (5 oz.) sesame paste
- 200 g (7 oz.) frozen *yomogi*
- 5 g dried *yomogi*
- 70 g (2⅓ oz.) *kudzu* starch
- 40 g (1⅓ oz.) bracken starch
- 800 ml (3⅓ cups) niban dashi

Dissolve sesame paste in niban dashi. Strain dissolved sesame paste, kudzu and bracken starch, and place in a pan.

Stir thoroughly from bottom of pan, place over a medium flame. When mixture starts to bubble, reduce heat to low, and cook about 20 minutes, working with a spatula or similar. Pour into tin and refrigerate until set.

Remove shells and livers from abalone, and de-slime. Place in a pan with plenty of water, parboil for 6 hours. When tender, transfer to fresh water, saving cooking liquid.

Place abalone, cooking base and sake in a pan, bring to a boil, add mirin and usukuchi soy sauce, allow to cool, and leave overnight. Cut urui stalks into 5 cm (2 in.) pieces, blanch, and rinse in water.

Cut yomogi tofu into suitably-sized cubes, steam over a medium flame for 6 minutes to warm through. Cut abalone into pieces 1 cm (½ in.) wide, add to 60 ml (¼ cup) of cooking juice that has been set aside, and warm through.

Make the broth. Heat 600 ml (2¼ cups) of niban dashi, add 60 ml (¼ cup) of sake, generous 1 Tbsp. usukuchi soy sauce, scant 1 tsp. soy sauce, and about ½ tsp. salt to flavor.

Arrange yomogi tofu, abalone, urui, ginger in bowl in that order, pour in broth.

Naruto Hamo Kudzu-tataki P. 123

Naruto Conger Eel in *Kudzu* Coating

SERVES 4

- 100 g (3⅓ oz.) conger eel, cut into 35 pieces, then each piece cut again into two pieces of equal size.

2 okra pods
2 bamboo fungi, rehydrated by soaking in water
8 burdock root, cut into lengths 3 × 1 cm (1¼ × ½ in.) in diameter
1 large abalone mushroom, chopped into 8 equal pieces
20 g (⅔ oz.) *kudzu* starch
Peel 4 *yuzu* slices, flesh remove

Broth

500 ml (generous 2 cups) ichiban dashi
⅓ tsp. *usukuchi* soy sauce
About ½ tsp. salt

Boil dashi, add soy sauce and salt to flavor.

Kombu dashi for burdock root

400 ml (1⅔ cups) water
4 g kombu

Place water in a pan, add kombu and soak overnight. Heat over a medium flame, and when dashi reaches 175°F (80°C) (take care as a higher heat than this will cause flavor to deteriorate), remove kombu.

Clear broth

700 ml (scant 3 cups) ichiban dashi
⅔ tsp. *usukuchi* soy sauce
½ tsp. salt

Boil dashi, add soy sauce and salt to flavor.

Salt thinly-sliced conger eel lightly. Dredge each slice in kudzu starch, roll up and secure with a toothpick. Boil water, add conger, boil at slightly below medium heat for 3 minutes. Rub okra with salt to remove fine bristles, blanch for 2 minutes over high heat in boiling water, remove ribs and seeds from the inside and pound thoroughly.

Rehydrate bamboo fungi: boil 1 L (4 cups) of water, add 1 tsp. vinegar, add fungi and remove from heat. Cover pan with paper towel and leave for about 10 minutes until fungi are rehydrated. Place in water to remove any impurities or musty odor.

Boil half (250 ml [generous 1 cup]) of the broth, add fungi and simmer for 2 minutes over medium heat.

Add 5 g rice bran (extra) and burdock root to 1 L (4 cups) of water. Bring to a boil and simmer for 4 minutes over high heat. Using a needle or similar, scoop out cores from burdock root pieces, place cored burdock root in boiled kombu dashi and simmer for 5 minutes over a medium flame. When tender, season with 1 tsp. usukuchi soy sauce and about ¼ tsp. salt.

Boil remaining broth (250ml), add abalone mushroom and simmer for 2 minutes at medium heat.

Steam conger eel (190°F [90°C] for 7 minutes), bamboo fungi (190°F for 5 minutes), burdock root (190°F for 5 minutes), abalone mushroom (190°F for 5 minutes) and okra (190°F for 1 minute) all separately, and arrange in bowl. Top with yuzu zest, and add 120 ml (½ cup) of warmed clear soup to bowl.

Amadai Miso Yuan-yaki P. 125

Tilefish Miso *Yuan-yaki*

SERVES 4

4 pieces tilefish
Miso *Yuan-ji*
2 Tbsp. plus 2 tsp. de-alcoholized sake
4 Tbsp. plus 1tsp. mirin
2 Tbsp. *usukuchi* soy sauce
2 Tbsp. soy sauce
100 g (3⅓ oz.) coarse-grained white miso
½ *yuzu*

Make the miso Yuan-ji : combine de-alcoholized sake, mirin, usukuchi and regular soy sauce, and coarse-grained white miso. Add the peel from the yuzu, cut into suitably-sized pieces, tilefish and marinate 2–5 days in refrigerator. Remove tilefish and use hands to wipe off any miso etc. on surface.

Grill front of tilefish for 6 minutes over a medium flame, then other side for 3 minutes.

Moroko Tsuke-yaki P. 126

Biwa Gudgeon Grilled with Soy-based Sauce

SERVES 3

27 roe-carrying Biwa gudgeon
2 broad beans
Basting sauce
300 ml (1⅓ cups) mirin
Scant 1 cup soy sauce
2 Tbsp. *tamari* soy sauce
70 ml (generous ¼ cup) sake

Make basting sauce. Place all ingredients in a pan and simmer down to about ⅒ volume.

Carefully scale fish using a cook's knife. Rinse in water and skewer under jaw and in front of tail fin. Stand with head facing down and turn several times to cook straight. When both sides are cooked, pour on basting sauce twice each side. Lastly, stand head up and grill thoroughly until heated right through.

When cooked, arrange in dish. Serve with broad beans lightly salted and steamed 6–8 minutes (time will depend on size of beans) at 210°F (100°C).

Kamo nasu Edamame Miso Dengaku P. 126

Kamo eggplant in Edamame *Dengaku* Miso Glaze

SERVES 4

1 large Kamo eggplant
4 purple asparagus
2 *myoga* ginger shoot
200 ml (scant 1 cup) sweet vinegar
Oil as required

Edamame miso

(enough for about 20 servings)

500 g (scant 17 oz.) edamame
170 g (5⅔ oz.) white miso
20 g (⅔ oz.) salt

Rub edamame with salt (extra) to remove fine bristles. Bring 2 L (2 qts.) water with salt to a boil, add edamame, boil for about 7 minutes, and drain in sieve. When cool, remove pods and membranes, place in food processor, and process into a paste. Mix edamame paste and miso.

Cut top off eggplant, then cut in half lengthwise, and again crosswise (making 4 pieces of equal size). Peel so as to form a striped pattern (of alternating peeled and unpeeled sections) and place each piece on a metal skewer (lengthwise)

Place eggplant in a frying pan with about 1 cm (½ in.) of oil in bottom, cover, and steam-bake for about 5 minutes over a low flame. Flip each side twice to cook right through.

Baste with 20 g (⅔ oz.) of edamame miso per serving and sear surface over flame. Chop bottom ⅓ off asparagus spears, then cut rest of each spear into two chunks of equal size. Brush with oil, sprinkle with a little salt (extra), grill.

Chop myoga in half, quickly pour boiling water over it, then transfer to sieve and salt lightly. When cool, marinate in 200 ml (scant 1 cup) of sweet vinegar for 2 hours or more.

Arrange eggplant on dish, add asparagus and ginger.

Ochiba-yaki P. 127

Grilled Autumn Leaf Medley

SERVES 10

500 g (scant 17 oz.) tilefish
10 prawns
10 chestnuts
20 gingko nuts
7.5 g *kuchinashi* (dried gardenia pod), crush lightly the day before and soak in 400 ml (1⅔ cups) water.
40 g (1⅓ oz.) rock sugar

Chop tilefish into approximately 40 g (1⅓ oz.) chunks, place on skewers, sprinkle with salt, set aside for about 10 minutes, then grill over a high flame for about 4 minutes until skin is fragrant and crisp. Peel heads of prawns, trim tip of head, place each prawn on a separate skewer. Fry just head in oil for about 1 minute at 340°F (170°C), raise temperature to 350°F (180°C), and fry entire prawn until fragrant. Drain off oil, sprinkle with salt (about ½ tsp. per 350 g [11⅔ oz.] of prawns).

Peel chestnuts, place in pan with plenty of water, bring to a boil, then reduce to medium heat, and cook for about 10 minutes. When soft enough to pierce easily with a bamboo skewer, transfer to water for about 10 minutes to remove any lingering astringency. Place chestnuts, water, gardenia pod and rock sugar in a pan, simmer over low heat for about 20 minutes, allow to cool.

Remove shell and skin from gingko nuts, fry for 1 minute in oil at 340°F, drain, sprinkle with salt (about ¼ tsp. for 20 gingko), pierce with pine needles, trim needles to same, suitable length.

Lay autumn leaves (chestnut, kudzu, gingko etc.) in dish, and arrange tilefish, prawns, chestnuts and gingko nuts on top.

Nanohana-mushi Uni-an P. 129

Steamed Field Mustard Blossom in Sea Urchin Sauce

SERVES 13

- 50 g (1⅔ oz.) field mustard
- 450 g (15 oz.) soy pulp (*okara*)
- 65 g (2 oz.) white fish *surimi*
- 80 g (2⅔ oz.) fresh *yuba*
- 15 g (½ oz.) *kikurage* wood ear mushrooms, rehydrated
- 65 g (2 oz.) carrot
- 30 g (1 oz.) lily bulb
- 60 ml (¼ cup) cream
- Scant 1 tsp. *usukuchi* soy sauce
- Dash salt for lily bulb
- 190 g (scant 7 oz.) grated wasabi
- 26 field mustard stems and 26 flowers for garnish
- 120 g (4 oz.) raw sea urchin for sea urchin sauce
- 13 pieces raw sea urchin, 5 g each
- Sea urchin paste
  - 350 g (11⅔ oz.) salted sea urchin
  - ½ egg yolk
- Sea urchin sauce base
  - 1.2 L (5 cups) ichiban dashi
  - 2 Tbsp. *usukuchi* soy sauce
  - Generous 1 tsp.salt
  - Dissolved Tbsp. 3 *kudzu* starch (dissolve 500 g [scant 17 oz.] *kudzu* in 900 ml [3¾ cups]water)
  - 100 ml (scant ½ cup) ichiban dashi
- Soy pulp mixture
  - 500 g (scant 17 oz.) soy pulp
  - 500 ml (generous 2 cups) ichiban dashi
  - 200 ml (scant 1 cup) sake
  - Generous 1 Tbsp. *usukuchi* soy sauce
  - 2 Tbsp. mirin
  - About 1 tsp. salt
- Simmering liquid for field mustard
  - 540 ml (2¼ cups) ichiban dashi
  - 1 Tbsp. *usukuchi* soy sauce
  - ½ tsp. salt
- Simmering liquid for carrot
  - 60 ml (¼ cup) ichiban dashi
  - 1 tsp. *usukuchi* soy sauce
  - About ¼ tsp. salt
- Simmering liquid for *kikurage* wood ear mushrooms
  - 100 ml (scant ½ cup) ichiban dashi
  - ½ tsp. *usukuchi* soy sauce
  - 0.5 g salt

Cook the soy pulp as follows. Bring ichiban dashi to a boil, add soy pulp and simmer until pulp reverts to its original harder consistency. Add usukuchi soy sauce, mirin, and salt to season. Process surimi, soy pulp, yuba, and usukuchi soy sauce in food processor until smooth.

Bring simmering liquid to a boil, cool. Boil field mustard in boiling water, transfer to ice water, drain. Marinate in the stock for 1–2 hours, then chop into small pieces. Soak kikurage in water to rehydrate. Boil water, add kikurage, and when water returns to a boil, cook for 2–3 minutes. Remove and drain. Bring simmering liquid to a boil, add kikurage, boil for 2–3 minutes, leave to cool in liquid so flavors absorb. Chop carrot into 5 mm (¼ in.) cubes. Boil water, add carrot, when water returns to a boil, cook for 2–3 minutes. Remove and drain. Boil simmering liquid for carrot, add carrot, boil for 2–3 minutes, leave to cool in liquid so flavors soak in. Peel one segment of lily bulb off at a time, steam for 5–6 minutes at 210°F (100°C) and sprinkle with salt.

Place dough from food processor in a bowl, mix in boiled kikurage, carrot, and steamed lily bulb, and form into balls of 50–60 g (2 oz.) per person. Spread finely-chopped field mustard blossom on a piece of bleached cotton or similar, place ball of dough in top, squeeze into a tea-cloth shape. Steam 3–4 minutes at 210°F (100°C).

Make the sea urchin sauce as follows. Mix ingredients for sea urchin paste. Bring sea urchin sauce base to a boil, add kudzu starch. Add sea urchin paste and chopped raw sea urchin (120 g [4 oz.]) and combine.

Arrange steamed "tea cloths" in dish, pour sea urchin sauce over top. Garnish with 5 g of raw sea urchin per person, and pour in grated wasabi in dashi. Decorate with field mustard.

Wakakusa-mushi P. 130

Spanish Mackerel Steamed with Spring Herbs

SERVES 5

- 75 g (2⅓ oz.) Spanish mackerel (*sawara*)
- 2–3 (approx. 125 g [4 oz.]) field mustard, boil in salted water and drain
- 10 stalks *tsukushi* (horsetail)
- 100 g (3⅓ oz.) fresh *yuba*
- 2 egg whites
- Salt to taste

Gin-an

- 350 ml (1½ cups) ichiban dashi
- About ½ tsp. salt
- ½ tsp. *usukuchi* soy sauce
- ½ tsp. grated ginger juice
- Dissolved *kudzu starch* (dissolve 15 g [½ oz.] in 2½ Tbsp. water)

Heat dashi and add salt, soy sauce, and ginger. Thicken with kudzu slurry.

Sprinkle Spanish mackerel with salt and set aside for 6 hours. Steam for 12 minutes at 190°F (90°C), skin while hot and allow to cool. Chop into bite-sized pieces.

Mix fresh yuba, field mustard and lightly-beaten egg whites to make egg-white paste. Place Spanish mackerel in dish, pour over egg-white paste, steam for 5 minutes at 190°F. Pour over gin-an and serve with horsetail.

Tamba-mushi P. 131

Tamba-mushi

SERVES 4

- 18 large Tamba chestnuts, boiled and sieved
- 2 Tamba chestnuts, boiled
- 40 Tamba adzuki beans
- 80 g (2⅔ oz.) Tamba *matsutake* mushroom
- 80 g (2⅔ oz.) grilled barracuda
- 2 slices of lily bulbs
- 12 *kuchinashi* (dried gardenia pod)
- ½ egg white
- 1 tsp. grated ginger juice
- Cooking liquid for chestnuts
  - 300 ml ichiban dashi
  - 3 Tbsp. *usukuchi* soy sauce
- 2 Tbsp. sugar

Gin-an

- 240 ml (1 cup) ichiban dashi

About ½ tsp.salt
½ tsp. *usukuchi* soy sauce
Dissolved *kudzu starch* (dissolve 10 g [⅓ oz.] in 2 Tbsp. water)

Heat dashi and add salt, soy sauce. Thicken with kudzu paste.

Peel shells and skins from chestnuts, place in a pan, add 1.8 L (generous 7 cups) water and 12 crushed gardenia pods, bring to a boil, then reduce heat to medium, and cook for 15 minutes to color chestnuts. Drain, then push 18 of the chestnuts through sieve. Set aside 2 chestnuts and place in water.

Add 300 ml (1¼ cups) of boiled hot water to adzuki, steam for 45 minutes at 210°F (100°C), and allow to cool. Steam lily bulbs for 10 minutes at 190°F (95°C). Cut matsutake mushrooms vertically into four equal pieces, and halve stalks if long.

Rinse barracuda in water, divide into three pieces, sprinkle with salt, about 1.5% barracuda's weight (about ¼ tsp.) and set aside for 6 hours. Place on metal skewer and grill over high flame, but not too close, 3 minutes on skin side, 2 on flesh, then cool and cut into 420 g (14 oz.) pieces.

Place cooking liquid for chestnuts in pan, use to cook two reserved chestnuts over medium heat for about 5 minutes, cool. Beat egg white and mix into sieved chestnut meat to make dough.

Add usukuchi soy sauce and salt to ichiban dashi for gin-an and heat. Add matsutake and heat through for approximately 1 and a half minutes.

Place chestnut dough on steamed lily bulb and grilled barracuda, and sprinkle with adzuki. Arrange matsutake gin-an in front. Chop each of the whole cooked chestnuts into four, and place two pieces on top of chestnut dough. Steam for 8 minutes at 210°F (100°C), thicken matsutake gin-an with kudzu paste, and add ginger juice.

Aki no Fukiyose mori P. 133

Autumn *Fukiyose* Medley

SERVES 4

½ Naruto *Kintoki* sweet potato
2 *kuchinashi* (dried gardenia pod)
4 large *kuwai*
½ lotus root
2 leaves spinach
160 g (5⅓ oz.) tilefish
80 g (2⅔ oz.) *matsutake* mushrooms
80 g (2⅔ oz.) log-grown *maitake* mushrooms
12 g (⅓ oz.) *arareko* fine cracker crumbs (recipe right)
10 g (⅓ oz.) *panko* breadcrumbs

½ lemon, cut in comb shape
80 g (2⅔ oz.) grated daikon radish
⅓ tsp. cayenne pepper
1 *sudachi*
Iridashi dipping sauce
200 ml (scant 1 cup) ichiban dashi
1 Tbsp. *usukuchi* soy sauce
½ tsp. salt
25 g (1 oz.) *katsuobushi*

Fine cracker crumbs

65 g (about 2 oz.) plain rice crackers, unsalted

Place rice crackers in oven and bake for 2 minutes at 570°F (300°C), turn over, and bake a further 2 minutes. When cool, place in a plastic bag or similar and crush finely with a rolling pin. Shift using a fine sieve.

Gingko Naruto sweet potato

Chop sweet potato into 5 mm (¼ in.) rounds, cut into 8 leaf shapes. Crush gardenia pods and place in 300 ml (1⅓ cups) of water, bring to a boil, cook sweet potato pieces for 1 minute to color. Wipe with a cloth, then fry (without coating of any sort) in oil for 4 minutes at 300°F (150°C).

Pinecone arrowhead bulbs

Peel each bulb into an octagonal shape (*happomuki*), cut base to a point, and make alternate cuts on bulb to form a pinecone pattern. Fry for 6 minutes in oil at 300°F (150°C), then at 375°F (190°C) until golden.

Crispy lotus root

Peel lotus root, cut into 5 mm (¼ in.) slices, and rinse to remove any bitterness. Pat dry, place on a bamboo mat, and allow to dry naturally for about 2 hours (turn over after 1 hour and continue to dry. Avoid exposing to any natural or artificial breeze). Brush on a very thin layer of kudzu starch (extra) and fry 4–5 minutes in oil at 300°F (150°C).

***Matsutake* tilefish roll**

Lightly salt (extra) tilefish and set aside for 30 minutes. Using a kitchen knife, remove the base of the matsutake, quarter along length and arrange two pieces each "top and tail" style. Place matsutake on a spinach leaf, wrap, then place on top a quarter of the tilefish, wrap in plastic wrap and steam for 3 minutes at 210°F (100°C). Tidy into a tube shape, coat in flour, egg white, and panko breadcrumbs (extra), fry in oil for 1 and a half minutes at 340°F (170°C), then cut in half. Make another roll in the same fashion, and cut this in half too.

***Maitake* tilefish roll**

Lightly (extra) salt tilefish and set aside for 30 minutes. Clean any dirt off maitake, cut in half and arrange "top and tail" style. Wrap in tilefish. Steam for 3 minutes at 195°F (100°C), then coat in flour (extra), egg white (extra) and cracker crumbs, fry for 1 and a half minutes in oil at 340°F (170°C), then cut in half. Make another in the same fashion, and cut this in half too.

Mix grated daikon and cayenne pepper to make *momiji-oroshi* condiment. Cut sudachi decoratively in half (see photo p. 133). Make iridashi dipping sauce: heat ichiban dashi in pan, add soy sauce and salt to flavor. Wrap katsuobushi in paper towel and place in pan(*oigatsuo*). Bring to a boil before use.

Arrange a half matsutake tilefish roll and half maitake tilefish roll on dish. Add gingko leaf shapes, arrowhead bulb, and lotus root to make fukiyose medley, and garnish with persimmon leaf or pine needles (decoration only as required). Position *momiji-oroshi* and sudachi in front. Pour iridashi into separate dish and place on side (mix to taste with *momiji-oroshi* and use for dipping).

Meitagarei Kara-age P. 134

Deep-Fried Finespotted Flounder

SERVES 4

2 finespotted flounder
4 asparagus
½ onion
2 green *shiso* leaves
1 Tbsp. sesame oil
Sweet and sour sauce
150 ml (⅔ cup) ichiban dashi
Scant 2 tsp. *usukuchi* soy sauce
Scant 2 tsp. soy sauce
1 Tbsp. citrus juice
20 g (⅔ oz.) grated daikon
5 g finely chopped *naganegi* onion
15 g (½ oz.) *kudzu* dashi paste (mixed with 1 Tbsp. ichiban dashi)

Gut finespotted flounder, rinse in water. Sprinkle with salt and set aside for 30 minutes or more. Dry in sun for about 2 days. Chop off head and tail, slit down middle and open out. Fillet, leaving edges intact. Trim woody roots from asparagus, and peel just the section near the root.

Peel onion, then halve onion and chop finely. Rinse under running water, gently squeeze out water, and mix in shiso chopped into thin strips. Add sesame oil to make marinade.

Combine sweet and sour sauce ingredients (excluding the kudzu dashi paste). Bring to a boil, add kudzu dashi paste to thicken.

Dredge flounder in potato starch (extra), fry for 2 minutes in oil at 350°F (180°C). Roll bones in flour and fry until crisp (5 minutes at 350°F). Coat asparagus with tempura batter (extra) and fry for 2 minutes at 340°F (170°C).

Spread onion mix in dish, and arrange flounder—cut in two after frying—and asparagus on top. Serve with the crisp turbot bones, and sweet and sour sauce on the side.

Ainame Arareko-age Sakura-an P. 135

Fried Greenling in Cracker Crumbs with Cherry Blossom Sauce

SERVES 4

8 pieces fat greenling, slice into thin strips 5 mm (¼ in.) wide, then 4 cm (2 in.) long

60 g (2 oz.) *arareko* fine crackers crumbs (recipe p. 199)

5 Japanese angelica buds (*taranome*)

Salt to taste

Cherry blossom *an*

360 ml (1½ cups) ichiban dashi

80 g (2⅔ oz.) lily bulb paste (steam bulbs for 8 minutes at 190°F [95°C] and mash)

10 salted cherry blossoms

Red food coloring powder (commercial product) as required

Pinch of salt

Dissolved *kudzu starch* (dissolve 10 g [⅓ oz.)] in 2 Tbsp. water)

Batter for *taranome*

45 g (1⅔ oz.) cake/pastry flour

100 ml (scant ½ cup) water

½ large egg white

Sprinkle fat greenling with salt. Dredge fat greenling in cracker crumbs and fry in oil for 2 minutes at 350°F (180°C).

Make cherry blossom an. Add lily bulb paste, finely-chopped salted cherry blossoms, and red food coloring powder to dashi, and thicken with kudzu. Coat angelica buds lightly in batter, fry for 1 minute 30 seconds at 350°F (180°C), salt lightly.

Pour cherry blossom an (approx. 80 ml [⅓ cup]) into dish, place fat greenling on top, and arrange angelica buds in front.

Waka-ayu Nanban-zuke Kinome-oroshi P. 135

Young Sweetfish "Nanban-zuke" Style Served with Grated *Sansho* Pepper Leaves

SERVES 1

15 g (½ oz.) young sweetfish

2 lengths *naganegi* onion, 5 cm (2 in.) each

Nanban-zuke base (10 servings)

300 ml (1⅓ cups) de-alcoholized sake

200 ml (scant 1 cup) de-alcoholized mirin

100 ml (scant ½ cup) *usukuchi* soy sauce

200 ml (scant 1 cup) water

3 Tbsp. plus 1 tsp. *Chidori*-brand vinegar

1 chilli pepper

Kinome-oroshi

2 *kinome*

12 g (about ⅓ oz.) grated (lightly strained) daikon radish

Pierce sweetfish "odori-kushi" style (i.e. to look as if swimming) with a metal skewer, grill, and when charred remove skewer. Fry for about 2 minutes in oil at 340°F (170°C).

Heat Nanban-zuke base until hot, add grilled spring onion and marinate freshly fried fish. Arrange on dish and serve with kinome-oroshi.

Shogatsu no Hassun P. 139

New Year *Hassun*

Ryuhi-maki Sushi

1 sheet *ryuhi* kombu, 18 × 24 cm (7 × 9½ in.)

240 g (1⅓ oz.) sea bream, filleted, and with any darker flesh near backbone removed

Vinegar for *ryuhi-maki*

480 ml (2 cups) rice vinegar

120 ml (½ cup) *usukuchi* soy sauce

80 g (2⅔ oz.) sugar

30 g (1 oz.) ginger

½ tsp. salt

100 ml (scant ½ cup) sweet vinegar

Rinse bream and fillet. Skin and cut into 7 mm (⅓ in.) strips. Salt 2% by weight and set aside for an hour or more. Assemble vinegar for ryuhi-maki, marinate fish for 15 minutes, drain off all juices.

Bring a pan of water to a boil, add julienned ginger, bring back to a boil then remove. Drain in a sieve and sprinkle with salt. When cool, marinate in sweet vinegar for 2 hours.

Place ryuhi-kombu on sushi mat and spread fish in an oblong shape at front (bottom half, of kombu). In front of the bream (bottom half, above bream) place vinegared ginger, making this the core and roll up. Trim off ends and cut into 12 × 1.2 cm (5 × about ½ in.) pieces.

Kintoki Carrot and Tilefish, Salmon and Turnip Swirls

SERVES 5

50 g (1⅔ oz.) tilefish, filleted, and with any darker flesh near backbone removed

A piece *Kintoki* carrot, 9 × 15 cm (3½ × 2 in.) pared *katusramuki* "roll paper" style

50 g (1⅔ oz.) ginger

15 g (½ oz.) smoked salmon

A piece turnip, 9 × 15 cm (3½ × 2 in.) pared *katsuramuki* "roll paper" style

3 g *yuzu* zest

100 ml (scant ½ cup) each rice vinegar for tilefish and smoked salmon

100 ml (scant ½ cup) each sweet vinegar for *Kintoki* carrot and turnip

50 ml (scant ¼ cup) sweet vinegar for ginger

Wash and fillet tilefish. Skin, salt 2% by weight, and set aside for an hour or more. Pare Kintoki carrot and turnip into *katsuramuki*, marinate separately in 3% saltwater solution for an hour or more. Drain, marinate in sweet vinegar for 2 hours.

Peel ginger and julienne. Boil a pan of water, add julienned ginger, and when water returns to a boil, remove pan from heat, drain and salt ginger (about 0.5% by weight). When cool, marinate in sweet vinegar for 2 hours. Steep tilefish and smoked salmon separately in vinegar for about 5 minutes, cut into 5 mm (¼ in.) thick pieces.

Arrange cut tilefish on carrot strip, add ginger for center, and roll into a stick 2.5 cm (1 in.) in diameter. Trim off ends and cut into 5 equal pieces.

Cut yuzu zest into thin strips. Arrange cut salmon on turnip strip, make yuzu the center, and roll in the same manner as the carrot and tilefish. Trim off ends and cut into 5 equal pieces.

Plum Blossom Carrot

SERVES 4

4 cm (2 in.) chunk *Kintoki* carrot

250 ml (generous 1 cup) ichiban dashi

1 Tbsp. *usukuchi* soy sauce

½ Tbsp. mirin

From carrot, cut 4 plum blossom shapes each 2 mm (⅛ in.) thick. Bring dashi to a boil, add carrot and simmer for about 5 minutes over a medium flame. When tender, add soy sauce and mirin, simmer for a further 2–3 minutes. Allow to cool in cooking liquid so flavors are absorbed.

Kombu with Herring Roe

SERVES 4

4 pieces kombu, 15 g (½ oz.) each with herring roe attached

"First" marinade and "main" marinade

360 ml (1½ cups) ichiban dashi

2 Tbsp. plus 2 tsp. *usukuchi* soy sauce

2 Tbsp. plus 2 tsp. mirin

5 g *katsuobushi*

Cut kombu with herring roe into slabs 2 × 3 × 1 cm (1 × 1¼ × ½ in.). Soak in 600 ml (2½ cups) of water for half a day to remove salt.

Make the marinades as follows. Bring dashi, soy sauce and mirin to a boil, add katsuobushi and remove from heat. When cool, strain and divide marinade in two. Use half the marinade ("first" marinade) to soak drained kombu for 2–3 hours.

Remove kombu and soak in remaining

("main") marinade for 2–3 hours (moisture in the kombu will be released in the first lot of marinade, hence the two rounds of marinating will prevent the flavor being diluted).

Mini *Kuwai* SERVES 4

8 *kuwai*
5 *kuchinashi* (dried gardenia pod)
600 ml (2½ cups) water
Simmering liquid
  170 ml (⅔ cup plus 2 tsp.) ichiban dashi
  Scant 1 tsp. *usukuchi* soy sauce
  1 scant tsp. mirin
  About ¼ tsp. salt

Pare each kuwai into a hexagonal shape. Crush gardenia pods and add to water. Bring to a boil, reduce heat to medium, add kuwai and cook for 3–4 minutes to color the bulbs. Remove kuwai and drain. Fry for a minute, as is, at 350°F (180°C), drain off oil.

Bring simmering liquid to a boil, add fried kuwai, simmer for 5–6 minutes at medium heat.

Chishato Pickled in Sake Lees SERVES 10

1 *Chishato* (type of lettuce stem)
750 g (25 oz.) sake lees
250 ml (generous 1 cup) de-alcoholized sake
Generous 4 Tbsp. soy sauce
2 Tbsp. plus 2 tsp. mirin
1 Tbsp. salt

Cut chishato into 4 cm (2 in.) lengths, and peel thickly. Bring a pan of water to a boil, add chishato, boil for about a minute, drain, and cool in a sieve or on a rack.

Mix de-alcoholized sake, soy sauce, mirin, and salt thoroughly into sake lees. Spread half this mixture in a tray or similar, add a layer of gauze over the top, then arrange chishato on top of this, then another layer of gauze, and the rest of the sake lees mix. Set aside for about 12 hours.

Simmered Abalone SERVES 4

4 abalone in shell, 350 g (11⅔ oz.) each
Simmering liquid
  1.6 L (6⅔ cups) sake
  800 ml (3⅓ cups) water
  1 tsp. sugar
  Scant 2 tsp. *usukuchi* soy sauce

Remove abalone from shells, scrub off any sliminess or extraneous matter, and remove the beaks.

Bring simmering liquid to a boil, add abalone. When abalone is tender, simmer for a further hour or so until only a little liquid remains. Take out abalone and cut into pieces 5 mm (¼ in.) thick.

Place abalone and chishato on willow skewers.

Dried Sardines SERVES 12

300 g (10 oz.) dried sardines
10 pieces *Kintoki* carrot, 10 cm × 2 mm (4 × ⅛ in.)
Simmering liquid (yields about 1L [4 cups])
  840 ml (3½ cups) sake
  6 Tbsp. soy sauce
  2 Tbsp. *usukuchi* soy sauce
  2 Tbsp. *tamari* soy sauce
  60 g (2 oz.) sugar
  210 g (7 oz.) *mizuame* syrup
  About ½ tsp. powdered *sansho* Japanese pepper

Arrange sardines on a heat-proof dish and microwave 3–4 minutes to dry.

Bring simmering liquid ingredients to a boil to evaporate off alcohol. Transfer just under 2 Tbsp. plus 2 tsp. of this liquid and ½ tsp. oil (extra) to another pan and place on heat. When it has boiled down slightly and taken on a syrupy consistency, add sardines and mix together. Spread sardines on a tray or similar to cool.

Cut Kintoki carrot into long thin strings, soak in 3% saltwater solution for at least an hour, drain. When sardines have cooled, tie into bundles of 5 or 6 using carrot. Trim off any excess.

Black Soybeans

200 g (7 oz.) black soybeans
2 L (2 qts.) water used to wash rice
First batch of syrup
  400 g (14 oz.) sugar
  1.8 L (generous 7 cups) water
Second batch of syrup
  800 g (29⅔ oz.) sugar
  1.8 L (generous 7 cups) water

Soak beans overnight in rice water with a little lye and a couple of rusty nails (extra). Put pan on heat and simmer over 1–2 days at low heat, occasionally topping up water, until beans are soft enough to rub between fingers.

Change water and repeat this process 2–3 times. On the third, place first batch of syrup in a pan, and bring to a similar temperature to the simmering beans. Gently transfer beans from simmering pan to pan of syrup. When boiling, simmer 4–5 minutes, remove from heat, and leave overnight.

Place second batch of syrup in a pan, heat, and when cooled to about same temperature as the beans left overnight, gently transfer beans to pan containing second lot of syrup. Bring to a boil, reduce heat to low, simmer for about 15 minutes, allow to cool in liquid.

Egg Yolk in Miso SERVES 4

4 eggs
Miso marinade base
  210 g (7 oz.) white coarse-grained miso
  2 Tbsp. de-alcoholized sake
  ½ tsp. mirin
12 black sesame seeds

Cook eggs for 1 hour–1 hour 10 minutes at 160°F (70°C) in hot water or steam-convection oven. Break eggs into a bowl of water, wash away whites, take out just the yolks.

Mix miso marinade base ingredients thoroughly. Spread ⅓ of miso marinade base in a tray or similar, cover with a layer of gauze, then arrange yolks on top. Cover with another layer of gauze, and the remaining ⅔ of the miso mix (placing the greater proportion of miso on top helps the flavors to absorb better). Set aside for about 12 hours.

Warabi Cuttlefish SERVES 4

80 g (2⅔ oz.) *mongoika* (cuttlefish)
3 egg yolks
About ¼ tsp. salt
10 g (⅓ oz.) *aonori* seaweed

Skin cuttlefish and remove fin, viscera etc., then peel membrane from both sides. Cut into 10 × 5 × 5 cm (4 × 2 × 2 in.) pieces. Skewer into rolls to resemble warabi.

Grill cuttlefish quickly over a high flame, one minute for each side. Spread with lightly-beaten egg yolks and grill over low heat, holding not too close, until egg yolk has dried. Brush on more yolk and repeat grilling (repeat a total of three times). The third time, rub aonori over just the curved part of the cuttlefish, on top of the egg yolk, before grilling. When cooked, cut into 5 mm (¼ in.) thick pieces.

Pomfret in Miso SERVES 4

4 pieces pomfret fillet, 40 g (1⅓ oz.) each
Miso marinade base
  250 g (8⅓ oz.) white coarse-grained miso
  170 ml (⅔ cup plus 2 tsp.) de-alcoholized sake
  2 tsp. mirin

Cut slits in skin of pomfret. Combine miso marinade base ingredients, marinate fish in bed for a day.

Remove fish, skewer, grill skin side first for 6–7 minutes over a low flame, not too close, then turn over and cook a further 6–7 minutes.

To Serve

Lay 2 sprays of nandina and 1 of *yuzuriha* (*Daphniphyllum macropodum*) on plate, arrange *hassun* components on top. Garnish with 2 pine needles, and another 2 needles in silver and gold.

Setsubun no Hassun P. 143

Hassun for Setsubun

Daikon Box TO MAKE 1 DAIKON BOX

Daikon radish, cut into a box shape measuring 5.5 × 5.5 cm (2¼ × 2¼ in.) and 4.5 cm (2 in.) high, with the center carved out

3 field mustard stalks
25 g (scant 1 oz.) soybeans
15 g (½ oz.) *Kintoki* carrot
Marinade for 40 field mustard stalks
 600 ml (2½ cups) niban dashi
 1 scant tsp. salt
 1 Tbsp. *usukuchi* soy sauce
Hiiragi (false holly)

Halve field mustard stalks, parboil and marinate for 2 hours, then chop into 2 cm (1 in.) pieces. Soak 100 g (3⅓ oz.) of soybeans in water overnight and discard liquid. Add 500 ml (generous 2 cups) of fresh water, heat to boiling point, remove from heat, cover with lid while hot, and leave to cool for 3 hours. Then take 200 ml (scant 1 cup) of niban dashi, add 100 ml (scant ½ cup) of the liquid from the soybeans, season with about ½ tsp. salt and 1 tsp. usukuchi soy sauce, and simmer over a low flame for about 15 minutes.

Dice 150 g (5 oz.) of carrot, blanch, add 600 ml (2¼ cups) of ichiban dashi, a scant 1 tsp. salt, 1 Tbsp. usukuchi soy sauce and simmer about 5 minutes over low heat.

Arrange soybeans, Kintoki carrot and field mustard in daikon box, and garnish with false holly.

Sea Cucumber Dressed with Viscera

SERVES 10

1 sea cucumber (*namako*)
50 g (1⅔ oz.) *konowata* (salted sea cucumber viscera)
50 g (1⅔ oz.) *konoko* (dried sea cucumber ovaries)
50 g (1⅔ oz.) *nagaimo* mountain yam
20 g (⅔ oz.) coarse tea leaves

Soak sea cucumber overnight in water to rehydrate, and when swollen to double the size, chop off the mouthpart. Slit lengthwise, and when the insides are visible, use a spoon or similar to remove the viscera containing sand. To 1 L (4 cups) water add coarse tea leaves, and soak sea cucumber for about an hour until tripled in size, adding water as needed.

Place sea cucumber in a pan, add 500 ml (generous 2 cups) of niban dashi and 4 Tbsp. plus 1 tsp. soy sauce, simmer for about 15 minutes over low heat. Dress with konowata and konoko and top with roughly-chopped nagaimo.

Kuwai in Votive Picture Style

SERVES 10

5 *kuwai*
5 *kuchinashi* (dried gardenia pod)

Cut bulbs to make 10 votive picture shapes. To 1 L (4 cups) water add 5 gardenias pod (for coloring), bring to a boil, add bulbs cut into shapes and boil for 5 minutes, allow to cool and acquire color, then rinse in water.

Place 600 ml (2½ cups) niban dashi, 1 scant tsp. salt, and 2 Tbsp. usukuchi soy sauce in a pan, add cut kuwai and simmer for 10 minutes at medium heat.

Simmered Sardines "Red Plum Style"

FOR 15 FISH

15 fresh sardines
Simmering liquid
 1.2 L (5 cups) water
 200 ml (scant 1 cup) sake
 400 ml (1⅔ cups) mirin
 200 ml (scant 1 cup) soy sauce
 2 Tbsp. sugar
11 small (with stones) pickled plums
100 g (3⅓ oz.) sliced ginger

Scale sardines, cut off heads, slit bellies, and gut, then wash out thoroughly. Place fish in pressure cooker, add simmering liquid, and cook under pressure for 15 minutes.

Sea Bream "Otafuku" Sushi

MAKES 1

10 g (⅓ oz.) thinly sliced sea bream (for sashimi use)
Pinch of salt
2 pieces kombu, 5 × 5 cm (2 × 2 in.)
20 g (⅔ oz.) cooked sushi rice
⅒ of a 30 g (1 oz.) pickedled plum flesh, mashed
piece *oboro* kombu (pickled shaved kombu), 3 × 1 cm (1¼ × ½ in.)

Make kobujime. Place sea bream kobujime on sushi rice, bind with a length of cotton twine to hold in place. Place oboro kombu over about top ⅓ of the sushi to form hair, and use plum flesh to make the mouth.

Miso-flavored Salmon Roe in Kumquat Pot

SERVES 6

3 large, fully ripe kumquats
70 g (2⅓ oz.) salted salmon roe
Miso marinade base for 20 portions
 200 g (7 oz.) raw salmon roe (*ikura*)
 600 g (20 oz.) white whole-grain miso
 2 Tbsp. plus 2 tsp. mirin

Cut kumquats in half crosswise, scoop out flesh and pips.

Place salted salmon roe in lukewarm 110°F (45°C) water and break up by hand, dividing into membrane and eggs (ikura). Discard membrane. Add ikura to chilled 2% concentration saltwater solution (about ½ tsp. salt per 200 ml [scant 1 cup]) and leave for about an hour. Remove from saltwater solution, place in fresh water to chill, then place between gauze and marinate in miso marinade base for 24 hours.

Serve in scooped-out kumquats.

Fried Prawns "Golden Staff" Style

SERVES 5

5 tiger prawns
Salt to taste
10 g (⅓ oz.) red and white *mijinko* (coarse glutinous rice flour), available commercially in red and white (mix 1 Tbsp. white and ½ tsp. red)

Remove heads from prawns, devein. Peel, leaving tails attached. Salt lightly, pierce each with bamboo skewer to straighten. Dredge completely in the rice flour, fry for 1 minute 30 seconds in oil at 340°F (170°C).

Hime Chirashi P. 145

Scattered Spring Sushi Fit for a Princess

SERVES 4–6
350 g (11⅔ oz.) sushi rice

Shiitake, *Koyadofu*, *kampyo*
 20 g (⅔ oz.) dried shiitake mushroom
 20 g (⅔ oz.) *Koyadofu* (dried)
 20 g (⅔ oz.) kampyo (dried shaved gourd)

Soak shitake in 500 ml (generous 2 cups) of water for half a day to rehydrate. Soak Koyadofu in water to rehydrate, use a bleached cotton cloth or similar to squeeze out moisture. Rinse kampyo thoroughly in water, sprinkle with salt to taste and rub in. Soak in water to remove salt, then add a little salt (extra) to boiling water, blanch and transfer to cold water. Use a cloth or similar to squeeze out moisture.

Process rehydrated shiitake, Koyadofu and kampyo in food processor until finely chopped. Bring to a boil 300 ml (1¼ cups) of ichiban dashi, 150 ml (⅔ cup) of water used to rehydrate shiitake, 75 ml (⅓ cup) soy sauce and 35 g (1 oz.) sugar, add finely chopped ingredients and cook until stock has completely evaporated. Mix 50 g (1⅔ oz.) of the cooked ingredients into the sushi rice.

Simmered conger eel

2 eels, 400 g (14 oz.) each
Simmering liquid
 450 ml (1⅔ cups) sake
 450 ml (1⅔ cups) water
 150 ml (⅔ cup) soy sauce
 150 ml (⅔ cup) mirin
 10 g (⅓ oz.) sugar

Split eels, fillet and remove fins. Blanch to remove sliminess. Bring simmering liquid to a boil, add eels, return to a boil and simmer for 4–5 minutes. Remove from heat, leave in stock, and when no longer piping hot, remove eels and allow to cool.

Finely chop portion (30 g [1 oz.]) to be mixed into sushi rice. Chop portion (20 g [⅔ oz.]) for topping into 2.5 cm (1 in.) cubes.

Kinshi tamago Thin ribbons of omlet

3 eggs
0.1 g salt
1 tsp. oil

Heat oil in a non-stick frying pan, pour in a thin layer of egg, and when one side is cooked, turn over and cook other side. Cut into thin strips about 4 cm (2 in.) × 1 mm (1/10 in.).

Diced carrot

20 g (⅔ oz.) *Kintoki* carrot
Marinade
 180 ml (⅔ cup plus 4 tsp.) ichiban dashi
 1 tsp. *usukuchi* soy sauce
 About ¼ tsp. salt

Chop carrot into 5 mm (¼ in.) cubes. Boil marinade, reduce to medium heat, add carrot, and cook for about 5 minutes. Remove from heat, leave for 2 hours in marinade to allow flavors to be absorbed.

Flower petal ginger

20 g (⅔ oz.) ginger
2 Tbsp. plus 2 tsp. sweet vinegar

Pare skin from ginger, cut into petal shapes 2 mm (⅛ in.) thick. Boil a pan of water with salt about 0.5% by weight, add ginger, when water returns to a boil remove from heat, and transfer ginger to a sieve to cool. When cooled, steep in sweet vinegar for 2 hours.

Udo in plum vinegar

8 cm (3 in.) *udo*
2 Tbsp. plus 2 tsp. sweet vinegar
⅓ *umeboshi*

Peel udo and chop into 7 mm (⅓ in.) cubes. Boil a pan of water with salt (about 0.5% by weight) and add udo. When water returns to a boil remove from heat, and transfer udo to a sieve to cool. Mash umeboshi, add to sweet vinegar, add cooled udo and marinate for 2 hours.

"Glossy" tiger prawns

4 tiger praws
Simmering liquid
 450 ml (1⅔ cups) sake
 2 Tbsp. plus 2 tsp. *usukuchi* soy sauce
 2 Tbsp. mirin

Remove heads from prawns and devein. Insert a skewer on belly side, from head end.

Bring simmering liquid to a boil, add prawns, boil for about a minute and a half, remove prawns, cool separately in stock. When both are cool, remove skewer, return prawns to stock, marinate for 2–3 hours to allow flavors to be absorbed. Peel prawns and chop in 2 cm (1 in.) pieces.

Broad beans, green peas

8 broad beans pod, remove membrane
40 g (1⅓ oz.) green peas, remove from pods
Marinade each
 180 ml (⅔ cup plus 4 tsp.) ichiban dashi
 1 tsp. *usukuchi* soy sauce
 1 tsp. mirin
 About ¼ tsp. salt

Sprinkle salt (about 0.5% by weight) on broad beans and steam for 3–4 minutes at 210°F (100°C). Bring water containing about 0.5% salt by weight to a boil, add green peas, and boil for 5–6 minutes. Drain and cool in sieve.Combine marinade ingredients, add broad beans and cooled green peas, and steep for 2 hours.

Warabi

12 *warabi*
Scant ¼ tsp. lye
Simmering liquid
 220 ml (scant 1 cup) ichiban dashi
 1 generous tsp. *usukuchi* soy sauce
 ½ tsp. mirin
 Scant ¼ tsp. salt

Trim hard base off shoots. Rub with salt (extra) to remove any fine hairs, rinse off salt, and drain. Place in a heatproof dish, sprinkle with lye. Pour enough boiling water over to soak, and leave until cool (this eliminates any lingering bitterness). Rinse in water, and if the shoots seem tough, cook in boiling water for about 30 seconds, then transfer to sieve and drain. * If using boiled warabi, there is no need to treat to eliminate bitterness. Bring simmering liquid to a boil, add shoots, then quickly remove. When stock has cooled, return shoots and marinate for 1–2 hours.

30 g (1 oz.) *Atsuyaki tamago* layered omelet (commercial product), chop into about 1 cm (½ in.) cubes.
⅓ (1 g) *nori* sheet, toast both sides of sheet over a direct flame, holding not too close to flame, and tear into 1 cm (½ in.) pieces
3 g *yuzu* zest, chop into 3 mm (⅛ in.) cubes
Scant 1 tsp. toasted sesame
18 *kinome*

To Serves

Mix simmered eel, shiitake-Koyadofu-kampyo mix, yuzu zest, and toasted sesame into sushi rice. Transfer to dish, and top with nori and kinshi tamago (in that order from bottom). Spread other ingredients over top. Finish with kinome.

Hanami-ju PP. 148–149

Flower-viewing *Bento* Stack

FIRST TIER

Cod Roe Cake 22 × 22 × 4 CM (8½ × 8½ × 2 IN.) TIN

800 g (26⅔ oz.) cod roe (*tarako*)
200 g (7 oz.) lily bulb
250 g (8⅓ oz.) white fish *surimi*
3 eggs
800 ml (3⅓ cups) sake
2 Tbsp. plus 2 tsp. *usukuchi* soy sauce
2 Tbsp. plus 2 tsp. mirin
Kinome to taste

Remove surface blood from tarako, slit sac and turn inside out. Add to boiling water and boil until tarako rises to surface. Transfer to cold water, and when cool, strain in a sieve, removing membrane and any extraneous material.

Squeeze tarako thoroughly (in a cloth or similar) to remove moisture, then place in a pan with sake, soy sauce and mirin. Bring to a boil, reduce to medium heat, and cook until most of the liquid has gone.

Remove one segment at a time from lily bulb, cut into bite-sized pieces, steam for 4–5 minutes at 210°F (100°C), sprinkle with 0.2 g salt.

Place surimi, strained tarako and eggs in food processor, process until smooth. Transfer this mixture to a bowl, add steamed lily bulb, combine, and pour into mold. Cover with plastic wrap, steam at 210°F (100°C) for 40 minutes, then remove plastic wrap, and steam for a further 10 minutes. Cut into suitably-sized pieces for eating.

Butterfly *nagaimo* mountain yam SERVES 4

100 g (3⅓ oz.) *nagaimo* mountain yam
1 egg yolk
5 g *katsuobushi*
Simmering liquid
 180 ml (⅔ cup plus 4 tsp.) ichiban dashi
 1 tsp. *usukuchi* soy sauce
 ½ tsp. mirin
 10 g (⅓ oz.) sugar
 0.5 g salt

Cut nagaimo into 1.5 cm (½ in.) slices, and carve into butterfly shapes. Blanch, plunge into cold water, drain.

Place nagaimo and simmering liquid in a pan, place katsuobushi wrapped in gauze or similar on top, in place of a drop lid (*oigatsuo*), and simmer over low heat for 7–8 minutes. Steam egg yolk for 5 minutes at 210°F (100°C) and push through a sieve. Use a double boiler or bowl in hot water to cook until scrambled. Dredge nagaimo with egg.

Conger Eel Swirls SERVES 5

5 conger eels, 250 g (8⅓ oz.) each
Simmering liquid
 400 ml (1⅔ cups) sake
 400 ml (1⅔ cups) water
 100 ml (scant ½ cup) soy sauce
 100 ml (scant ½ cup) mirin
 10 g (⅓ oz.) sugar

Split eels, fillet and remove fins. Blanch to remove sliminess. Trim each eel to 25 cm (10 in.) in length. Roll up, starting from tail end, and tie in a cross (parcel style) using twine made by tearing bamboo bark, or similar.

Bring simmering liquid to a boil, add eels, return to a boil, and simmer for about 15 minutes. Remove from heat, leave in stock to cool, and when no longer piping hot, remove eels, cool, and undo twine.

"Glossy" Tiger Prawns (SEE P. 203)

Avocado in Miso YIELDS ABOUT 330 G (11 OZ.)

1 avocado
210 g (7 oz.) coarse white miso paste

Split avocado in half, remove stone, and scoop out flesh in balls. Bring a pan of water to a boil, add vinegar (extra, 3% of water volume), blanch avocado quickly, plunge into ice water, remove and drain on paper towel or similar.

Spread ⅓ of miso paste thinly in a tray, place avocado on tray in between two pieces of gauze, then cover with remaining ⅔ of miso, and marinate for about 12 hours.

"Wind in The Pines" Chicken Loaf
MAKES 22 × 22 × 4 CM (8½ × 8½ × 2 IN.) TIN

800 g (29⅔ oz.) minced chicken
1 tsp. salt
800 g (29⅔ oz.) white fish *surimi*
200 g (7 oz.) "white" chicken liver
55 g (1⅔ oz.) *hatcho* miso paste
6 egg yolks
380 ml (1½ cups) de-alcoholized sake
180 g (6 oz.) raisins (soak in 200 ml [scant 1 cup)] of brandy for half a day)
200 g (7 oz.) pine nuts
30 g (1 oz.) poppy seeds

Cut chicken livers in half, remove blood vessels. Rinse in water, drain in sieve. Salt (0.5% by weight) and set aside for a day. Add salt to minced chicken, mix thoroughly until sticky. Sprinkle liver with sake (extra), steam for about 10 minutes at 210°F (100°C), and push through sieve.

Place surimi, chicken mince, liver, hatcho miso and de-alcoholized sake in food processor and mix well. Roast pine nuts in oven until golden. Place in a bowl with mashed raisins. Pour in mixture from food processor and mix well. Pour this batter into tin, bake for 1 hour at 300°F (150°C). Sprinkle with poppy seeds.

Egg Yolk in Miso (RECIPE P. 201)

***Yuba* and Kombu Roll**

1 piece fresh *yuba*, 10 × 14 cm (4 × 5½ in.)
1 piece kombu left over from making ichiban dashi, 10 × 10 cm (4 × 4 in.)
Simmering liquid
  360 ml (1½ cups) ichiban dashi
  2 Tbsp. *usukuchi* soy sauce
  10 g (⅓ oz.) sugar

Bring half of simmering liquid ingredients to a boil, add kombu and simmer for 10 minutes over medium heat. Set aside to cool.

Place kombu on yuba (making kombu layer slightly smaller for easier rolling), roll up from bottom and tie with bamboo bark twine or similar.

Bring remaining simmering liquid to a boil in a pan, add yuba roll. When boiling again, cook for 1–2 minutes over a low flame. Remove from heat and cool in liquid. When cool, remove roll and cut into 1.5 cm (½ in.) slices.

***Warabi* Cuttlefish** (RECIPE P. 201)

Lily Bulb Petals

½ lily bulb
20 g (⅔ oz.) salmon roe (*ikura*)
Marinade
  1 tsp. de-alcoholized sake
  3 Tbsp. water
  ½ tsp. *usukuchi* soy sauce
  1 tsp. soy sauce
  1 tsp. mirin
  2 g *katsuobushi*

Bring salmon roe marinade ingredients to a boil, add katsuobushi, remove from heat and allow to cool. When cool, strain, and marinate roe for about an hour.

Peel one segment at a time from lily bulb and cut into petal shapes. Steam for 5–6 minutes at 210°F (100°C) and sprinkle with 0.2 g salt. Place roe on each piece of lily bulb.

***Udo* Petals** MAKES 10

About 5 cm (2 in.) long piece *udo*
3 Tbsp. plus 1 tsp. water
0.1 g red food coloring powder
3 Tbsp. plus 1 tsp. sweet vinegar

Cut udo into petal shapes and soak thoroughly in water. Dissolve food coloring in water, add udo and marinate for 2 hours.

SECOND TIER

***Iidako* Octopus**

3 *iidako* octopi (*octopus ocellatus*)
Simmering liquid
  300 ml (1¼ cups) water
  2 Tbsp. *usukuchi* soy sauce
  2 Tbsp. soy sauce
  2 Tbsp. plus 2 tsp. mirin
  15 g (½ oz.) sugar

Rinse octopi in water, cut off heads and tentacles, remove ink sac, beak, eyes etc. Plunge briefly into boiling water to blanch, rinse off any ink. Thread the (severed) head sacs with skewers to keep the contents from falling out.

Bring simmering liquid ingredients to a boil, reduce heat to low, add just heads, simmer for 10–15 minutes and remove. Next add tentacles, bring to a boil, remove. Allow head and tentacles to cool.

Cool stock as well, and when cool, return heads and tentacles, and marinate for 3 hours. Chop into suitably-sized pieces for eating.

Bamboo Shoot with *Kinome* Miso Paste

80 g (2⅔ oz.) bamboo shoot, peeled and trimmed flesh
60 g (2 oz.) squid
80 g (2⅔ oz.) *udo*
Kinome miso (yields about 380 g [12⅔ oz.])
  300 g (10 oz.) cooked miso
  50 g (1⅔ oz.) *kinome*
  30 g (1 oz.) spinach
  Small amount powdered *sansho* pepper
Simmering liquid
  100 ml (scant ½ cup) ichiban dashi
  1½ tsp. *usukuchi* soy sauce
  1½ tsp. mirin
2 Tbsp. sake
½ tsp. *usukuchi* soy sauce

Make the kinome miso as follows. Prepare cooked miso and cool. Boil spinach, squeeze out moisture and process into a paste. Put kinome and spinach paste in a mortar, grind together thoroughly, add cooled cooked miso, grind some more, and sprinkle with sansho.

Chop bamboo shoot into 1 cm (½ in.) cubes, cook in simmering liquid until liquid evaporates. Chop squid into 1 cm (½ in.) cubes. Bring sake and usukuchi soy sauce to a boil, broil squid, and remove. Peel udo thickly, cut into similar sized pieces to bamboo shoot and squid.

Place udo, drained bamboo shoot and squid in a bowl, add 80 g (2⅔ oz.) of kinome miso and combine.

Salmon Roe with Marinade

1 kg (35 oz.) salmon roe (*ikura*), frozen
15 g (½ oz.) *katsuobushi*
Marinade
  450 ml (1⅔ cups) ichiban dashi
  450 ml (1⅔ cups) water
  2 Tbsp. *usukuchi* soy sauce
  2 Tbsp. plus 2 tsp. soy sauce
  2 Tbsp. plus 2 tsp. mirin

Defrost salmon roe. Bring roe marinade to a boil, add katsuobushi, and remove from heat. Cool and strain, then marinate roe for an hour.

Broad Beans in Tofu Dressing

YIELDS ABOUT 480 G (16 OZ.)

8 broad beans, remove from pod, peel off membrane

Tofu dressing

1 block (420 g [14 0z.]) *momen* (firm) tofu

2 tsp. sesame paste

1 Tbsp. *usukuchi* soy sauce

1 Tbsp. sugar

Drain as much water as possible off tofu (tofu will have a final weight of about 180 g [6 oz.]). Steam beans for 3–4 minutes at 210°F (100°C), sprinkle with salt (0.5% by weight).

Process dressing ingredients until smooth. Mix into steamed beans.

Eel Burdock Root Roll

2 eels, 300 g (10 oz.) each

5 burdock roots

240 ml (1 cup) sake

2 Tbsp. *usukuchi* soy sauce

2 Tbsp. soy sauce

2 Tbsp. mirin

0.5 g powdered *sansho* pepper

Kinome for garnish as required

Basting sauce

Eel bones and heads from 2 (extra) eels

1.8 L (generous 7 cups) sake

240 ml (1 cup) soy sauce

2 Tbsp. plus 2 tsp. *tamari* soy sauce

600 ml (2½ cups) mirin

Chop eel bones and heads into suitably-sized pieces and grill until golden brown.

Place grilled bones and head in a pan with sake, and mirin, bring to a boil over a high flame, and boil until alcohol from sake and mirin evaporates. Add soy sauce and simmer over low heat, until reduced to ⅔ volume. Add tamari soy sauce, remove from heat, and strain.

Split eels, fillet and remove fins. Blanch to remove sliminess. Divide filleted eels into two equal segments lengthwise, with head and tail attached. Make a 1 cm (½ in.) cut in the tail of each, join two together, placing the head of one through the slit in the tail of the other, pulling both sides to make one long piece. Repeat to make another.

Divide each burdock root into four. Place burdock root in a pan, sprinkle with sake, broil over a high flame, shaking the pan. Add usukuchi soy sauce and mirin, reduce heat to medium and cook until most of the liquid has gone.

Roll burdock root in eel around a metal skewer, then use twine made from bamboo bark or similar to tie in the middle and at both ends. Make another roll the same way. Pierce with metal skewers in a fan shape and grill for 6–7 minutes each side close to a high flame, without seasoning. Pour on the basting sauce and grill both sides over a low flame, holding further away and drying sauce (sauce will be dry when it no longer drips off during basting). Repeat 3 or 4 times, grilling to a glossy golden brown.

Remove bamboo twine and cut rolls into 2 cm (1 in.) pieces. Sprinkle with sansho, top with kinome.

Trout Miso *Yuan*-yaki

SERVES 5

5 trout fillet, 40 g (1⅓ oz.) each

Miso *Yuan-ji*

1 kg (35 oz.) coarse white miso

Miso marinade base

180 ml (⅔ cup plus 4 tsp.) water

180 ml (⅔ cup plus 4 tsp.) sake

5 Tbsp. mirin

2 Tbsp. soy sauce

5 Tbsp. *usukuchi* soy sauce

½ *yuzu* zest

Bring all miso marinade base ingredients to a boil, boil until alcohol evaporates off, remove from heat, and cool. Chop yuzu zest into suitably-sized pieces.Mix miso marinade base and yuzu zest into coarse white miso. When cool, add trout, and marinate for 16 hours.

Remove trout, place on skewer, and grill skin side for 6–7 minutes over a low flame, not holding too close. Turn over and repeat on other side.

Carrot Petals

MAKES 5

2 cm (1 in.) carrot

Cut carrot into plum blossom shapes. Cook for about a minute in boiling water to which a little vinegar has been added (extra: 2 Tbsp. vinegar to 1 L [4 cups] water). Drain and sprinkle with salt (0.5% by weight) (extra). When carrot has cooled, marinate for 2 hours in sweet vinegar (extra).

THIRD TIER

Sea Urchin in Clam Shell

SERVES 4

4 clam shells

210 g (7 oz.) raw sea urchin

About ½ tsp. rock salt

Clean clam shells, fill with sea urchin. Sprinkle with 0.5 g of rock salt per clam, and bake in the oven for 10 minutes at 390°F (200°C).

Salt-Grilled Tilefish

SERVES 4

4 tilefish fillets, 40 g (1⅓ oz.) each with darker flesh near backbone removed

8 *kiinome*

Salt tilefish (1% by weight) and set aside for an hour.

With skin side up, curl ends of each piece slightly inward and skewer. Grill both sides close over a high flame, for 4–5 minutes each, skin side first. Remove skewers and sprinkle with crushed kinome.

Myoga Ginger Buds in Sweet Vinegar

SERVES 4

4 *myoga* ginger shoot

100 ml (scant ½ cup) sweet vinegar

Split myoga in half lengthwise. Cook for about a minute in boiling water to which a little vinegar has been added (extra: 2 Tbsp. vinegar to 1 L [4 cups] water). Drain and sprinkle salt (0.5% by weight) on surface (red part only).

When cool, marinate for 2 hours in sweet vinegar.

Scallop Grilled in Egg Yolk

SERVES 10

10 scallop adductor muscles (*kaibashira*), 25 g (scant 1 oz.) each

6 egg yolks

About ¼ tsp. salt

About ½ tsp. black sesame seeds

Remove sinews, tougher parts etc. from scallops (leaving just round adductor muscle in center), and pierce sideways with skewers. Grill both sides for 2–3 minutes each over a high, close flame.

Brush egg yolk with salt on scallops and grill 2–3 minutes over a low flame, holding skewer further away, to dry egg yolk. Repeat 3–4 times, then sprinkle with black sesame seeds to finish.

Vinegared Lotus Root

SERVES 8

80 g (2⅔ oz.) lotus root

100 ml (scant ½ cup) sweet vinegar

Peel lotus root, trimming into a flower shape. Cut into 5 mm (¼ in.) slices. Cook for about a minute in boiling water to which a little vinegar has been added (extra: 2 Tbsp. vinegar to 1 L [4 cups] water). Drain and sprinkle salt (0.5% by weight) on surface. When cool, marinate for 2 hours in sweet vinegar.

Tilefish Grilled with *Karasumi* Powder

SERVES 5

5 tilefish fillets, 50 g (1⅔ oz.) each, darker flesh near backbone removed

1 egg white (beat, then strain through gauze or similar)

50 g (1⅔ oz.) *karasumi* (cured mullet roe) powder

Salt tilefish (0.8% by weight) and set aside for an hour. Place karasumi in oven at 210°F (100°C)–250°F (120°C) for 30 minutes to dry. Remove membrane, blood vessels etc., grate to make powder.

Pierce tilefish with flat skewers, grill for 4–5 minutes each side over a high, close flame, skin side first. Brush with egg white, sprinkle with karasumi powder, and grill close over a low flame until golden.

Udo Petals (RECIPE P. 204)

Plum Blossom Carrot MAKES 5

3 cm (1¼ in.) long piece of carrot

Cut carrot into plum blossom shapes. Cook for about a minute in boiling water to which a little vinegar has been added (extra: 2 Tbsp. vinegar to 1 L [4 cups] water). Drain and sprinkle salt (0.5% by weight) on surface.

When carrot has cooled, marinate for 2 hours in 2 Tbsp. sweet vinegar.

FOURTH TIER

Conger Eel Sushi Stick SERVES 8

2 pieces simmered conger eel, 16 cm (6¼ in.) each (recipe below)

2 portions sushi rice, 150 g (5 oz.) each

10 *sansho* peppercorns

2 Tbsp. plus 2 tsp. sweet vinegar

Simmered conger eel

2 conger eels, 400 g (14 oz.) each

450 ml (1⅔ cups) sake

450 ml (1⅔ cups) water

150 ml (⅔ cup) soy sauce

150 ml (⅔ cup) mirin

10 g (⅓ oz.) sugar

Split conger eels, fillet and remove fins. Blanch to remove sliminess.

Bring sake, water, soy sauce, and mirin to a boil, add conger eels, and when pan returns to a boil, simmer for 4–5 minutes. Remove from heat, cool in cooking juices. When no longer piping hot, remove conger eels, and cool.

Briefly boil peppercorns and drain. When cool, steep in sweet vinegar for 2 hours.

Form sushi rice (one stick's worth) into a 16 cm (6¼ in.) rod, place simmered eel on top. Cut stick into 8 equal portions. Repeat to make another stick. Top both with peppercorns in sweet vinegar.

Sea Bream *Kinome* Sushi SERVES 4

80 g (2⅔ oz.) sea bream

150 g (5 oz.) sushi rice

1 sheet *shiroita* kombu, 22 × 25 cm (8½ × 10 in.)

18 *kinome*, 10 to mix into sushi rice plus 8 for garnish

100 ml (scant ½ cup) sweet vinegar

300 ml (1¼ cups) rice vinegar

Cook sushi rice. When cool, mix in crushed kinome. Heat white sheet kombu through in boiling water to which vinegar has been added (2 Tbsp. to 1 L [4 cups] water), drain. When cool, steep in sweet vinegar for 2 hours. Form sushi rice into a 16 cm (6¼ in.) rod.

Marinate sea bream (skin on) in vinegar for about 30 minutes. Remove skin, cut bream into 8 pieces of equal thickness.

Arrange pieces of bream on damp cotton cloth, place sushi rice on top, use cloth to form a sushi stick. Top with kinome, then kombu, which has been drained thoroughly after marinating. Cut stick into 8 equal pieces.

"Gold Foil" Sushi Roll SERVES 4

Usuyaki tamago thin omelet

- 3 eggs
- 0.1 g salt

200 g (7 oz.) sushi rice

50 g (1⅔ oz.) simmered dried shiitake, *Koyadofu* and dried *kampyo* gourd (see resipe p. 144)

2 tsp. toasted sesame seeds

3 g *yuzu* zest, cut into 3 mm (⅛ in.) squares

5 stems honeywort

Mix simmered conger eel, simmered shiitake, Koyadofu and kampyo mix, yuzu and sesame seeds into sushi rice.

Prepare the omelet: beat eggs lightly, strain through gauze or similar, mix in salt. Heat 1 tsp. oil in a non-stick frying pan, pour eggs in a thin layer, and when one side is cooked, turn over and cook other. Trim into a 16× 12 cm (6¼ × about 5 in.) piece. Blanch honeywort and drain.

Form sushi rice into a 16 cm (6¼ in.) stick, roll in the cooked egg, and tie with the blanched honeywort. Cut into 5 equal pieces.

Mackerel Sushi SERVES 4

200 g (7 oz.) salted mackerel (if using fresh mackerel, salt 3% by weight)

150 g (5 oz.) sushi rice

1 sheet *shiroita* kombu, 22 × 25 cm (8½ × 10 in.)

300 ml (1¼ cups) rice vinegar

100 ml (scant ½ cup) sweet vinegar

Fillet mackerel, marinate in rice vinegar for 40 minutes – 1 hour. Wipe off moisture and remove skin. Dip shiroita kombu in boiling water to which vinegar has been added (2 Tbsp. to 1 L [4 cups] water), drain. When cool, steep in sweet vinegar for 2 hours.

Form sushi rice into a 16 cm (6¼ in.) rod, cut mackerel and kombu to fit dimensions of sushi and place on top, first mackerel, then kombu. Cut into 5 equal pieces.

Young Crimson Sea Bream in Cherry Leaves SERVES 5

2.5 young crimson sea bream (*kasugodai*), 100 g (3⅓ oz.) each

5 portions sushi rice, 15 g (½ oz.) each

5 salted cherry tree leaves

100 ml (scant ½ cup) rice vinegar

10 ginger petal (recipe p. 203)

Fillet fish, salt (1.5% by weight), and set aside for an hour. Marinate in rice vinegar for 5 minutes.

Use sushi rice (15 g [½ oz.] each portion) and vinegared sea bream to make *nigiri-zushi*, and wrap in cherry leaves. Sprinkle with ginger petals.

Ginger Shoots in Sweet Vinegar SERVES 5

5 *hajikami* ginger shoots

100 ml (scant ½ cup) sweet vinegar

Cook shoots for about a minute in boiling water to which vinegar has been added (extra: 2 Tbsp. vinegar to 1 L [4 cups] water). Drain and salt surface (just red parts) with salt 0.5 g by weight. When shoots are cool, marinate in sweet vinegar for 2 hours.

Chimaki-zushi PP. 150–151

Sushi Wrapped in Bamboo Leaves

MAKES APPROXIMATELY 24

240 g (8 oz.) sea bream

720 g (24 oz.) sushi rice

Kinome to taste

Pickling vinegar (yields about 520 ml [generous 2 cups])

- 450 ml (1⅔ cups) vinegar
- Generous 4 Tbsp. *usukuchi* soy sauce
- 60 g (2 oz.) sugar

Place all ingredients in a pan, heat until sugar dissolves, remove from heat, and cool.

Marinate bream (skin on) in pickling vinegar for about 30 minutes. Skin and pare into thin slices. Cool sushi rice, mix in crushed kinome.

Take about 30 g (1 oz.) of sushi rice, top with one piece of bream, and press into *nigiri-zushi*. Wrap sushi in bamboo leaf in a cone shape, tie with silver and gold *mizuhiki* cords. Repeat for rest of ingredients. Once again using *mizuhiki*, tie sushi packages into bundles of 6.

Tanabata Mukae P. 155

Tanabata Temptation

SERVES 2

Simmered Abalone

160 g (5⅓ oz.) abalone

30 g (1 oz.) chrysanthemum leaves

20 g (⅔ oz.) ginger

Kombu, salt, sake to taste

250 ml (generous 1 cup) Tosazu jelly
- 210 ml (scant 1 cup) niban dashi
- 3 Tbsp. plus 1 tsp. de-alcoholized mirin
- 2 Tbsp. plus 2 tsp. Chidori-brand vinegar
- 3 Tbsp. plus 1 tsp. soy sauce
- 2 tsp. *usukuchi* soy sauce
- 1 tsp. *katsuobushi*
- 10 g (⅓ oz.) kombu
- 7 g for 300 ml (1¼ cups) of water gelatin

Marinade
- 300 ml (1¼ cups) niban dashi
- Scant ½ tsp. salt

Clean abalone in water and place in pressure cooker. Fill to the brim with water. Cook in pressure cooker for about 30 minutes, transfer contents to a pot, add 5 g kombu, ½ tsp. salt and 2 Tbsp. sake, and simmer gently for about an hour until abalone is tender. Allow to cool.

Mix the ingredients of marinade. Wash chrysanthemum leaves, chop into 2 cm (1 in.) pieces. Blanch by plunging in boiling water and then into ice water to cool. Drain and marinate for 3 hours. Chop ginger into thin 2 cm (1 in.) strips, soak briefly in water, and drain. Chop abalone into 3 cm (1¼ in.) cubes about 1 cm (½ in.) thick, and arrange on plate. Arrange chrysanthemum leaves in front of abalone, top with Tosazu jelly to taste, followed by the spears of ginger.

Place niban dashi, mirin, katsuobushi and kombu in a pan, and bring to a boil. Add Chidori vinegar and soy sauces, boil once more, then strain through paper towel and cool.

When cool, add gelatin and heat until gelatin dissolves. Cool again, and sieve.

Satoimo Taro Stalk Sesame Cream

40 g (1⅓ oz.) *satoimo* taro stalk (*zuiki*)
50 g (1⅔ oz.) sesame seeds
½ tsp. sugar
1 Tbsp. plus 1 tsp. de-alcoholized sake
½ tsp. soy sauce
Pine nuts to taste
Marinade
- 200 ml (scant 1 cup) niban dashi
- Scant ½ tsp. salt

Mix the marinade ingredients. Peel taro stalk. To blanch, immerse for about 5 minutes in salted boiling water (about ½ tsp. salt for 500 ml [generous 2 cups]), then plunge into ice water. Drain, then marinate for about 3 hours.

Lightly toast sesame seeds, place in blender, and process into a smooth paste. Add sugar and de-alcoholized sake, mix lightly, and strain while warm. Add soy sauce to taste. Toast pine nuts for about 10 minutes in oven at 325°F (160°C), and chop in half.

Chop satoimo taro stalk into 5 mm (¼ in.) lengths 3 cm (1¼ in.) thick. Top with sesame cream to taste, and finish with pine nuts.

Prawn in Fish Innards

2 prawns
200 ml (scant 1 cup) *shuto* base (commercial product)
Small amount green *yuzu*
Small amount spring onion
300 ml (1¼ cups) kombu stock
About ½ tsp. salt
2 Tbsp. sake

Remove heads from prawns, pierce backs with toothpicks and straighten out.

Place kombu stock in a pan, season with salt and sake (about ½ tsp. salt per 500 ml [generous 2 cups] water). Take half of stock from pan and cool. Add prawns to a pot of boiling water and boil until half cooked (i.e. still rare in the middle). Place in cooled stock to cool, peel, and cut in half. Steep in shuto base for about 10 minutes.

Sprinkle oil and salt on spring onion and grill until fragrant. Arrange prawns on dish, arrange grilled spring onion in front, sprinkle with a dash of shuto base. Top with grated yuzu zest.

Gion Matsuri no Hassun P. 156

Gion Festival *Hassun*

Hamo-zushi SERVES ABOUT 10

1 pike eel
360 g (12 oz.) sushi rice
¼ tsp. powdered *sansho* pepper
½ Tbsp. *sansho* peppercorns
1 Tbsp. sweet vinegar
Basting sauce
- Bones and heads from 2 pike eels
- 1.8 L (generous 7 cups) sake
- Scant 1 cup soy sauce
- 2 Tbsp. plus 2 tsp. *tamari* soy sauce
- 600 ml (2¼ cups) mirin

Chop bones into suitably-sized pieces and grill with heads until golden.

Make basting sauce. Place grilled bones and remaining ingredients in a pan, simmer over a low flame until reduced to ⅔ volume, then strain.

Cook sushi rice and allow to cool. Make sweet vinegar marinade for peppercorns: immerse peppercorns briefly in plenty of boiling water. Drain in a sieve and allow to cool, then marinate in sweet vinegar for 2 hours. Mix peppercorns into sushi rice.

Rinse pike eel in water, fillet, taking care to remove fine bones. Place on a skewer, grill skin side fairly close to a low flame until fragrant. When flesh starts to tighten, turn over and grill for a further 2 minutes or so. Pour basting sauce over top, grill both sides over a high flame, further away from the flame, drying sauce so that sauce does not drip off during grilling.

Shape half the sushi rice into a stick about 20 cm (7¾ in.) long. Place grilled pike eel on a piece of bleached cotton or plastic wrap, sprinkle with half of the powdered pepper, and top with sushi rice. Place on a sushi mat still in cloth or plastic wrap, and roll, forming into a stick shape. Repeat to make one more stick. Cut 10 pieces of equal size.

River Shrimp SERVES 10

20 river shrimp
Cooking liquid
- 450 ml (1⅔ cups) sake
- 2 Tbsp. plus 2 tsp. *usukuchi* soy sauce
- 2 Tbsp. plus 2 tsp. mirin

Remove legs and feelers from shrimp, cut tails into a V-shape.

Place all cooking liquid ingredients in a pan and bring to a boil. When the alcohol evaporates off, add shrimp. Once shrimp are heated through, transfer to a sieve and cool. Also allow liquid to cool. When both are cool, return to pan and marinate for 2 hours to allow flavors to absorb.

Saffron Ginger SERVES 10

50 g (1⅔ oz.) ginger
0.5 g saffron
80 g (2⅔ oz.) sugar
180 ml (⅔ cup plus 4 tsp.) water

Shave ginger and cut into 7 mm (⅓ in.) lengths. Boil water, add ginger, return to a boil, then remove from heat, drain in sieve. Season with salt (5% by weight).

Place sugar and water in a pan and add saffron. Bring to a boil, and when the suffron's color has been sufficiently released, allow to cool. When cool, steep ginger in this marinade for 2 hours.

Tokobushi Abalone SERVES 10

10 *tokobushi* (abalone, *Sulculus diversicolor supertexta*)
Cooking liquid
- 270 ml (1 cup plus 2 Tbsp.) sake
- 2 Tbsp. *usukuchi* soy sauce
- 10 g (⅓ oz.) sugar

Wash tokobushi clean. Plunge briefly into boiling water (blanching), and transfer to ice water. Remove from shells (sterilize shells and keep aside).

Place cooking liquid ingredients in a pan and bring to a boil. When alcohol evaporates off, add tokobushi flesh, cook over a medium flame for 2–3 minutes, transfer to sieve and allow to cool. Also allow liquid to cool. When both are cooled, return to pan, and steep for 2 hours to allow flavors to absorb. After marinating, put flesh back in sterilized shells.

Tilefish Cucumber Roll SERVES 10

120 g (4 oz.) tilefish (filleted, with any darker flesh near backbone removed)
90 g (3 oz.) cucumber
25 g (scant 1 oz.) ginger
3 Tbsp. plus 1 tsp. rice vinegar for ginger
3 Tbsp. plus 1 tsp. rice vinegar for tilefish
3 Tbsp. plus 1 tsp. Tosazu vinegar

Rinse tilefish in water, fillet, skin, sprinkle with salt (2% of fish by weight), and set aside for an hour. Pare cucmber *katsuramuki* ("roll paper") style and steep in 2% saltwater solution for 15 minutes. Julienne ginger. Boil water and add ginger. Return to a boil, then remove from heat. Transfer ginger to a sieve, drain, and marinate in rice vinegar for an hour.

Prepare Tosazu vinegar and cool. Dip cucumber in Tosazu, spread in a single layer. Marinate tilefish (salted to tighten flesh as described above) in rice vinegar for 5 minutes, then cut into 5 mm (¼ in.) slices. Arrange sliced tilefish on cucumber, wrap around ginger as core, and cut into 7 mm chunks.

Octopus Roe SERVES 10

200 g (7 oz.) octopus roe
Simmering liquid
  500 ml (generous 2 cups) ichiban dashi
  Scant 2 tsp. *usukuchi* soy sauce
  Scant 1 Tbsp. mirin
  100 ml (scant ½ cup) sake
  1 tsp. sugar
  ½ Tbsp.salt
  5 g *katsuobushi*

Tear roe sacs, turn inside out, and form into rounded shapes. Bring a generous pan of water to a boil, add octopus roe, reduce to very low heat (just enough so that roe moves around), and simmer until roe rises to the surface. When boiled, transfer to fresh water, and drain. Halve any large roe sacs.

Bring all simmering liquid ingredients except katsuobushi to a boil. Add roe. Place katsuobushi wrapped in gauze on top of boiling liquid in place of a drop lid (*oigatsuo*), and simmer at very low heat for about 20 minutes to allow flavors to absorb.

"Thunder-Drum Cut" Green Gourd with *Rikyu-fu* in Sesame Dressing SERVES 10

100 g (3⅓ oz.) green gourd
1 piece *Rikyu-fu* gluten cake (commercial product)
180 ml (⅔ cup plus 4 tsp.) ichiban dashi
Scant 2 tsp. *usukuchi* soy sauce
Scant 1 tsp. mirin
Sesame vinegar
  250 g (8⅓ oz.) sesame paste
  250 g (8⅓ oz.) cooked miso paste
  150 ml (⅔ cup)Tosazu vinegar
  Generous 2 Tbsp. rice vinegar
  Scant 1 Tbsp. soy sauce
  About ½ tsp. salt
  1 Tbsp. and 1 tsp. lemon juice

Cut top off gourd and scoop out seeds. Cut into a long spring ("thunder-drum") shape. Steep for about an hour in 3% saltwater solution, then hang to dry in a shaded, well-ventilated spot for half a day or so. Cut into pieces about 3 cm (1¼ in.) long. Cut Rikyu-fu into pieces 3 cm (1¼ in.) long, 7 mm (⅓ in.) wide.

Place all sesame vinegar ingredients in a food processor and process until smooth. Use to dress dried green gourd and Rikyu-fu gluten cake.

Oranda-ni P. 159

"Dutch-style" stew

SERVES 4

350 g (11⅔ oz.) tofu
50 g (1⅔ oz.) grated *nagaimo* mountain yam
10 g (⅓ oz.) *kikurage* wood ear mushrooms (dried)
20 g (⅔ oz.) lily bulb
20 g (⅔ oz.) carrot
20 g (⅔ oz.) kidney beans
Scant 2 tsp. mirin
Generous 1 Tbsp. *usukuchi* soy sauce
Scant 2 tsp. soy sauce
300 ml (1¼ cups) cooking base
  1.4 L (scant 6 cups) niban dashi
  300 g (10 oz.) dried tuna flakes (*maguro-bushi*)
  1 cup plus 4 Tbsp.mirin
  800 ml (3⅓ cups) sake

Place all ingredients for the cooking base in a pan, simmer for 15 minutes, then strain.

Wrap tofu in cloth, place a weight on top, and set aside for about an hour to drain off excess liquid. Rub through a sieve, then place in mortar, add the grated nagaimo and blend well. Add niban dashi (extra) as required to obtain about the right consistency to allow easy molding. Rehydrate kikurage. Peel one layer off of the lily bulb at a time and remove dark part. Chop carrot into matchsticks, blanch. Blanch beans and cut into 2 cm (1 in.) pieces.

Mix vegetables and kikurage into tofu/nagaimo mixture, empty out onto a board and form into a rod shape. Fry for 5 minutes in oil at 340°F (170°C). Drain. Pour boiling water over to remove oil.

Place in a pan with cooking base, bring to a boil, add sugar, mirin, usukuchi soy sauce and soy sauce to adjust flavor, and cook for about 10 minutes.

4 eggplants
Marinade
  2 tsp. sugar
  Scant 1 Tbsp. *usukuchi* soy sauce
  1 tsp. soy sauce
  Small amount salt
300 ml (1⅓ cups) cooking base
  1.4 L (scant 6 cups) niban dashi
  300 g (10 oz.) dried tuna flakes (*maguro-bushi*)
  1 cup plus 4 Tbsp.mirin
  800 ml (3⅓ cups) sake
12 snowpeas
2 *myoga*

Place all ingredients of cooking base in a pan, simmer for 15 minutes, and strain.

Cut tops off eggplants, and use a knife to gently score lines down length of each. Fry for about 2 minutes in oil at 325°F (160°C), turning during cooking, and allow to cool naturally.

Make the marinade: heat cooking base, add sugar, light and regular soy sauce, and bring to a boil. When boiling, remove from heat and allow to cool. Immerse fried eggplant in marinade and leave overnight. Blanch snowpeas in boiling water. Chop myoga ginger into thin strips.

Arrange "Dutch-style" stew and stewed fried eggplant on dish, with snowpeas on side. Top with strips of myoga. Serve with 2 Tbsp. of juices from stew.

Kikuna-hitashi P. 163

Boiled Chrysanthemum Greens

SERVES 4

4 large edible chrysanthemum flowers
1 bunch chrysanthemum leaves
150 g (5 oz.) *matsutake* mushroom
About ¼ tsp. salt
1 L (4 cups) water
1 Tbsp. vinegar
½ edible chrysanthemum flowers for garnish
Marinade
  360 ml (1½ cups) ichiban dashi
  Scant 2 tsp. *usukuchi* soy sauce
  About ½ tsp. salt

Combine marinade ingredients. Pluck the leaves (stalks are not used) from chrysanthemum greens and plunge briefly into boiling water to bring out vibrant green color. Transfer to cold water, then squeeze out moisture, and steep in marinade for 2 hours.

Pluck petals from chrysanthemums flowers, rinse and drain. Bring water and vinegar to a boil, add petals, and boil for 2 minutes over a high flame (to prevent any astringent taint). Cut marinated and drained leaves into 3.5 cm (1¼ in.) lengths.

Cut a cross into cap of matsutake mushroom (making it easier to tear apart after cooking). Sprinkle with about ¼ tsp. salt, grill quickly so that moisture is not lost, and tear into pieces by hand for easier consumption.

Combine chrysanthemum leaves, flowers, and matsutake. Sprinkle with chrysanthemum petals for garnish.

Shishigatani Kabocha Toji-jitate P. 165

Shishigatani Squash, Winter Solstice Style

SERVES 4

1 Shishigatani squash

Ebisu squash, cut into 3 × 3 × 3 cm (1¼ × 1¼ × 1¼ in.) cube

20 gingko nuts

Kintoki carrot, cut into 3 × 3 × 3 cm (1¼ × 1¼ × 1¼ in.) cube

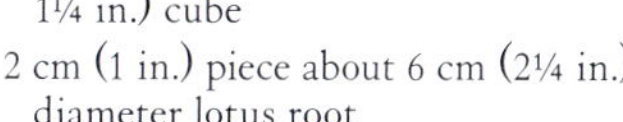

2 cm (1 in.) piece about 6 cm (2¼ in.) in diameter lotus root

8 g grated *yuzu* zest

Quail dumplings

100 g (3⅓ oz.) minced quail meat, minced twice *Mince with ribcage for added texture.

4 cm (2 in.) *naganegi* onion (white part) finely chopped and lightly crushed

½ tsp. grated ginger

½ tsp. grated *yamatoimo* mountain yam

Small amount powdered *sansho* pepper

½ egg yolk

Scant 1 Tbsp. sake

1 tsp. *usukuchi* soy sauce

1 tsp. mirin

Small amount salt

Chicken broth

- 300 g (10 oz.) boned chicken thighs, coated in ½ tsp. salt (1% by weight) and set aside for half a day
- 60 g (2 oz.) Kujo green onion
- 15 g (½ oz.) sliced ginger
- 1.3 L (5½ cups) water
- 3 Tbsp. plus 1 tsp. sake
- Scant 2 tsp. *usukuchi* soy sauce
- Scant 1 Tbsp. mirin

Place all ingredients in steamer and steam for 3 hours at 210°F (100°C). Strain, place liquid in a pan, and simmer over a medium flame until reduced to 800 ml (3⅓ cups). Add usukuchi soy sauce and mirin to adjust flavor.

Make the chicken broth. Mix quail dumpling ingredients thoroughly by hand until sticky (do not use a food processor as the spices will break down too much, altering the flavor). Roll into dumplings (12 g [about (⅓ oz.)] each). Simmer for 5 minutes at 185°F (85°C) in the chicken broth.

Take Ebisu squash chopped into 3 cm (1¼ in.) cubes, cut off corners and peel into balls. Steam for 10 minutes at 210°F (100°C). Chop Kintoki carrot into 3 cm (1¼ in.) cubes, cut off edges, and peel into balls as for squash. Boil for 3 minutes, then drain and allow to cool. To prevent drying, cover with a moist paper towel with all extra moisture wrung out.

Cut slice of lotus root in half crosswise, ensuring that each cut piece has three holes. Peel, rounding off edges and forming into a pine tree shape. Boil water, add lotus root, and cook for 5 minutes over a medium flame. Drain and allow to cool. To prevent drying, cover with a moist paper towel (as above).

Crack gingko nut shells, remove membrane, place in oil heated to 230°F (110°C) for 2½ minutes to cook throughly. After frying, place nuts in mortar. Crush and mix thoroughly, until glutinous. Then oil hands lightly (oil extra) and roll into balls.

Take the Shishigatani squash, cut off the rounded lower half, and remove seeds (i.e. hollow out) to form a pot shape. Place the Ebisu squash, Kintoki carrot, lotus root, gingko nut and quail dumplings in squash, pour in 600 ml (2½ cups) of boiled chicken broth (that used to simmer quail dumplings), and steam for 15 minutes at 210°F (100°C). Top with grated yuzu zest.

Toshikoshi-soba P. 166

Year-Crossing Soba Noodles

SERVES 1

80 g (2⅔ oz.) fresh soba

½ green onion

Broth

- 240 ml (1 cup) ichiban dashi
- Generous 1 Tbsp. *usukuchi* soy sauce
- Scant 2 tsp. mirin
- 5 g *katsuobushi*

Make the soba broth: bring all ingredients except katsuobushi to a boil, add katsuobushi and remove from heat. Cool and strain.

Finely chop green onion. Boil soba in a generous pan of water. Transfer soba to a bowl and pour in warmed broth. Top with green onion.

GLOSSARY

Aemono

Dressed foods. *Ae-ru* means "mix" or "combine." Shellfish, fish, and vegetables are mixed and seasoned with a dressing made of sesame, tofu, miso, and other ingredients.

Ainame/Aburame

Fat Greenling. A white-flesh coastal fish that is in season in the spring. Rich in both fat and umami, it is suitable for sashimi, soups, tempura, and other dishes.

Akamiso

"Red" miso, made from soybeans. Rice is used sparingly, if at all. The soybeans are steamed and fermented for a long period, resulting in a dark reddish-brown color. This type of miso is generally quite salty.

Amadai

Tilefish (horse-head fish). A high-quality fish often served in kaiseki meals. In Kyoto and vicinity it is called *guji*. The flesh is very soft, with a delicate flavor, and is used for **kobujime** rolls, steamed dishes, and as *misozuke* (marinated in miso and fried).

Amazu

Vinegar mixed with sugar. Depending on the intended use, it may be diluted with dashi or water.

Ashirai

Arrangement of food on serving dishes in a pleasing manner; handling and addition of garnishes to bring out flavor, aroma, and color of dishes.

Ayu

Sweetfish. A freshwater fish that feeds on river moss, giving it a distinctive fresh taste. In season in the summertime, it is usually salted and grilled over an open fire, then dipped in a special vinegar based sauce called *tadesu*. The entrails are salted to make a delicacy known as *uruka*.

Deaimono

Ingredients that come into season around the same time (*deai*) and are well matched, providing good combinations resulting from their mutual tastes, fragrance, color, or texture. Bamboo shoots with **wakame** seaweed and yellowtail (*buri*) with daikon radish are examples.

Ebi taro (ebi imo)

"Shrimp taro." A variety of taro (similar to the *satoimo taro*) originating in the Kyoto/Osaka area of western Japan that takes its name from its curved shape. The tuber is fine-grained and when cooked has a soft, paste-like texture and sweet flavor well suited to simmered dishes.

Enoki

Small mushrooms with long, thin stems and small caps, *enoki* have a faint aroma and a crunchy texture; well suited to stir-fried dishes and soups.

Eringi

Pleurotus eryngii (king trumpet mushroom). Similar to the oyster mushroom, the large *eringi* has a light brown cap and a thick white stem. A substantial, filling ingredient for simmered or grilled dishes.

Fu

A processed food made of wheat gluten. Often used in *shojin* cuisine.

Genmai

Unmilled rice, from which only the outer hull has been removed, leaving the bran covering, which is rich in vitamin B1 and other nutrients not present in refined white rice.

Ginnan

The fruit or nut of the gingko tree. The nuts are roasted in a pan. They may be eaten as is or used as ingredients in steamed or simmered dishes.

Gin-an

"Silver sauce" (*gin-an*) is made by seasoning dashi with salt and light soy sauce (**usukuchi shoyu**) and adding a thickener (**kudzu**) dissolved in room-temperature water. It is used to add gloss and flavor to dishes.

Gobo

Burdock root. This long root vegetable is rich in fiber with an aroma redolent of the earth. Pleasantly crunchy even after cooking, it is often used in simmered dishes, including **takiawase** combinations. It should be soaked after cutting or shaving to remove bitterness before cooking.

Hassun

The *hassun* was originally a flat plain cedar-wood tray (*oshiki*) eight *sun* (24 cm.) in length and width holding an assortment of tidbits served with sake in a *kaiseki* meal. It is usually served after the *sakizuke*.

Hijiki

A type of seaweed harvested in Japan, China, and Korea and sold in either dried or in fresh or blanched form. Dried *hijiki* is rehydrated before using.

Hone-kiri

Preparation process for fine-cutting the flesh and small bones of fish like *hamo* (conger eel) and **ainame** (fat greenling) for easier eating.

Honkarebushi

A type of katsuobushi cured by applying a specific mold several times to draw out moisture from the fish, harden it, and enhancing its umami flavor and characteristic aroma.

Ichiban dashi

Primary dashi. Of all the types of broth, ichiban dashi has the subtlest umami, clarity, and depth of flavor. It can be used in any type of dish, though its subtle and refined taste are most evident in soups and simmered dishes.

Irodashi

Bringing out the color of green vegetables or other ingredients by placing in boiling water (*yugaku*) until brilliant in color.

Irodome

Blanching to preserve the brilliant color of ingredients; greens or other vegetables are placed in boiling water (*yugaku*) until the color brightens and then plunged into cold water to halt further changes in color.

Ise ebi

Ise lobster. A large member of the lobster species with spines, it is considered a luxury food in Japan served on auspicious occasions, either raw or cooked.

Ji

Dashi seasoned with salt, soy sauce, and other ingredients. Varieties include *sui-ji*, which is used for thin soups, and *happo-ji* (versatile base), which contains dashi, sake, mirin, or other ingredients and is used in preparing a wide variety of dishes. Marinating ingredients in a seasoned liquid like this is called "ji-zuke."

Jomi

Choice parts of fish or fowl after bones and inedible parts have been removed. For fish, the flesh that remains after filleting (see **sanmai-oroshi**) and the removal of rib bones and other small bones.

Kabocha

Winter squash. A Japanese squash green on the outside and orange or yellow on the inside. The color is bright but the flavor is low in umami. It softens quickly with cooking and is well suited to soy sauce flavored dishes.

Kamo nasu

Traditional heirloom variety of eggplant from Kyoto that is nearly spherical. Larger and heavier than the usual Japanese eggplant. The flesh is dense and remains firm when cooked, so it is well-suited to boiled dishes and also used in fried/grilled or deep-fried dishes.

Kanoko-giri

Slitting the surface of an ingredient with grid-like cuts, straight or diagonal. When the slits are diagonal, the technique is called *matsukasa-giri* ("pine-cone cutting").

Kanten

Coagulating agent made from *tengusa* or other seaweed of the red-algae species. Tends to be cloudy and makes a firmer gel than agar powder, which is often used as a substitute.

Katsura-muki

A 6-7 cm (about 2¼ in.- 2½ in.) cylindrical section of a vegetable—usually a daikon—peeled while rotating into a thin continuous sheet. The sheet may then be cut into long threads.

Kinako

Made by grinding soybeans into a fine powder which is then toasted. Mixed with sugar and salt, it is used for various Japanese-style confections.

Kobujime

This is a technique of curing whereby the umami of kombu is transferred to other ingredients such as white fish by sandwiching or rolling up in strips of kombu.

Koikuchi shoyu

"Dark" soy sauce, the most widely used variety because of its balance of saltiness, sweetness, tartness, bitterness, and umami.

Koji

A malt made by growing *koji* mold spores on rice, wheat, soybeans, or other grains, it is an indispensable ingredient for making fermented foods like miso and sake.

Komesu

Vinegar made from rice. It has a strong flavor and a faint aroma. It is used for flavoring sushi rice, and for vinegared salads (**sunomono**) when a vinegar flavor is desirable.

Kudzu

A thickening starch made from the root of the kudzu vine, it is often used in Japanese cuisine because it does not change the taste or coloring of the food.

Kujo negi

An heirloom vegetable from Kyoto, Kujo long onions are distinctive for their larger green portion and tender texture.

Kuwai

An heirloom vegetable from Kyoto, *kuwai* is the arrowhead bulb, a water plant grown mainly in Japan and China. As a plant that sprouts easily and vigorously, *kuwai* is thought to encourage energy and fertility and is an auspicious ingredient included in traditional New Year's fare.

Kyuri

Japanese cucumber averaging about 20 cm (8 in.) in length. The skin is thin and edible and the flesh is crunchy and juicy.

Maitake

Grifola frondosa or hen-of-the-woods mushroom. Traditionally harvested in autumn, *maitake* mushrooms have a pleasant crunchy texture, a pungent aroma, and can be used in all sorts of dishes.

Matsutake

The *Tricholoma matsutake* mushroom, which grows in the wild on the floor of pine forests. It is the most highly prized and expensive of Japanese mushrooms. It has a distinctive woodsy aroma and a firm, crunchy texture.

Mirin

A sweet rice wine made by adding rice malt (**koji**) and distilled spirits to steamed glutinous rice and allowing the mixture to ferment. *Mirin* is often used in vegetable dishes to add sweetness and help the ingredients keep their shape.

Mukozuke

A side dish served in a kaiseki meal on a flat tray (*oshiki*) with rice and soup. It usually features seafood or **kobujime**.

Myoga

Buds of *Zingiber mioga*, a plant in the ginger family. Traditionally used as a garnish for summer dishes, it has a crispy texture and a lightly piquant aroma. It is also eaten as a sweet pickle.

Nagaimo

A long variety of yam, the *nagaimo* has a slimy, sticky texture. It may be grated or cut into strips and eaten raw. It has a pleasant starchy texture when included in simmered or fried dishes.

Naganegi

Allium fistolosum, a thick and long green onion similar to the leek that is native to China and other parts of Asia. The white part is generally diced for use as a garnish. The upper portions, which are tougher and green, are used in soups and other dishes.

Nasu

The Japanese eggplant is relatively small, averaging about 12 cm. (about 5 in.) The skins are thin and the taste neutral, making it well suited for a wide variety of dishes.

Niboshi

Small *iwashi* (sardines or pilchards) and other small fish that have been boiled and dried primarily for use in making **dashi**.

Nikiru

Boiling **sake** or **mirin** until the alcohol content has evaporated, leaving only its flavor.

Nori

Seaweed sheet made from edible algae that has been pressed and dried. The standard product is packaged in square sheets, but it is also sold in small bite-sized sheets, flakes, strips, and other forms depending on the intended use.

Nuka

The germ and bran covering left over when rice is milled to make white rice. Rich in oils and protein, *nuka* is very nutritious. It is used as an ingredient of the mash to make *nukazuke* pickles and in cooking fresh bamboo shoots to remove harshness.

Ohitashi

The name of this dish comes from the term *hitasu*, meaning "to soak" (*hitasu*). Greens, mushrooms, or other vegetables are first boiled and then soaked in dashi. After thoroughly draining and squeezing the water out of them, they are served with dashi or other seasonings.

Oigatsuo

Refers to the addition of more katsuobushi flakes to *katsuobushi*-based stock or **ji** stock in order to increase the umami. The flakes may be wrapped in a piece of gauze or other thin covering.

Oka-age

Removing ingredients from the pot to cool after boiling or simmering, not by immersing them in cold water, but rather by placing in a colander or other container.

Otoshi-buta

Drop lid slightly smaller than the diameter of the pot. The weight of the lid helps maintain the shape of fragile ingredients and promotes the even permeation of heat and seasonings.

Ponzu

A lightly seasoned sauce made of dashi, soy sauce, and vinegar and seasoned with **yuzu, sudachi**, or other citrus juice.

Saikyo miso

This sweet "white" miso is made in Kyoto. Two parts rice and one part soybeans are mixed together, steamed, and then fermented.

Sakekasu

Sake lees remaining from the making of sake—a solid, white-colored by-product. Rich in nutrients, they contain protein and edible fiber. *Sakekasu* is used as a marinade for fish and to make pickles.

Sakizuke

Appetizer (see called *tsukidashi*, *o-toshi*, *zensai*). A light dish served before the main courses, it is equivalent to the *amuse-bouche* of French cuisine.

Sanmai-oroshi

Literally, "three-piece cutting," *sanmai-oroshi* is the most basic of fish-dressing techniques. The head is removed and the body filleted, slicing off the "top fillet" (*uwami*) and the "lower fillet" (*shitami*), leaving the backbone and tail as the third piece.

Sansho

Japanese pepper, *Zanthoxylum piperitum*. The dried seeds have the sharpness of pepper and leave a tingling sensation that lingers on the tongue. The young leaves, called *kinome*, are used as an aromatic garnish.

Shimeji

Hypsizygus tessellatus, small mushrooms that grow in clumps. Pleasant in aroma and texture, they remain firm when cooked. They are used widely in Japanese cuisine.

Shimofuri

Blanching fish or meat by plunging briefly in boiling water, then immediately cooling in cold water, so that the surface turns white, leaving a pattern resembling frost (*shimo*). *Shimofuri* removes fishy or fatty smells and seals in the food's umami.

Shinjo

Dish made by grinding seafood, adding *yamaimo*, egg white, and dashi to form dumplings that are steamed, boiled, or deep-fried.

Shiokombu

Salt kombu. Cut into squares or strips, kombu is simmered with soy sauce and other seasonings and then dried. Used as a condiment with rice or as a seasoning for other dishes.

Shio-zuri

"Salt rubbing" is sprinkling ingredients with salt and rubbing it in, so as to remove the hairs from okra or the spines from cucumbers (**kyuri**). When the salt is rubbed in using the surface of a cutting board, it may be called *ita-zuri* (board rubbing).

Shiraganegi

"Silver hair onion" is a cutting technique for **naganegi** onions to be used as a garnish for soups and simmered dishes. A cylindrical section of *naganegi* is cut vertically into fine strips.

Shirako

Milt served as *sunomono*, grilled, or in soup. Cod *shirako* are also called *kumoko* ("cloud roe").

Shiroita kombu

"White sheet kombu," this is what remains when the front and back surfaces have been removed from strips of kombu kelp. Often used in varieties of **kobujime**.

Shiromiso

"White" miso is made from soybeans that are fermented for less time than **akamiso**. The color is light brown and the taste is rather sweet.

Shiso

Perilla frutescens, an herb belonging to the mint family sometimes known as Chinese or Japanese basil. Red and green varieties both have culinary uses. Known for its anti-bacterial properties, green *shiso* is often served with sashimi.

Shogoin daikon

An heirloom vegetable from Kyoto, this variety of daikon is large and spherical. The flesh is tender and sweet.

Shogoin kabura

The Shogoin turnip, an heirloom vegetable from Kyoto, is Japan's largest turnip variety, sometimes weighing as much as 4 kg. It is used in steamed and simmered dishes and also to make *senmaizuke*, a pickled specialty from Kyoto.

Soba

Noodles made from buckwheat, commonly eaten either hot in a seasoned broth or cold, flavored with a dipping sauce (*tsuyu*).

Soramame

Fava or broad bean. These bright green beans have a soft texture and a faint sweet flavor. Particularly large beans are called *issunmame* ("one *sun*" [3 cm] bean). The pods are slit, boiled in salted water, and the beans eaten as is.

Sudachi

A member of the citrus family, it is harvested while the skin is still green. Its tart juice goes well with grilled fish and sashimi.

Sunomono

A mixture of vegetables and sometimes seafood dressed with a vinegar-based sauce.

Takiawase

"Cooked and combined." A dish composed of various ingredients—vegetables, seafood, meat, etc.—that have been cooked separately to bring out their innate flavors and then combined.

Tamari shoyu

This "rich" soy sauce is high in umami and slightly thick. In cooking, it is used to add gloss and deep umami flavor to ingredients for *kanroni* simmered dishes (simmering of small fish or other ingredients in a sweet-salty sauce) and *teriyaki*.

Tororo kombu

Kombu soaked in vinegar to soften, then shaved into gauze-like sheets. May be eaten as is, used as an ingredient in various dishes, or as a topping for soups.

Tosazu

A vinegar mixture made by adding dashi, soy sauce, or other ingredients, heating and adding **oigatsuo** to deepen the umami. With this richer **umami**, it makes a suitable dressing for salads containing light-tasting seafood.

Udo

Aralia cordata. The stalk and young leaves of this indigenous mountain vegetable have a texture and a flavor resembling that of asparagus or celery.

Umeboshi

Pickled plums (*Prunus mume*) made by salting and sun-drying.

Unagi

Freshwater eel. The majority are farm-raised, with few caught in the wild, some collected in Japan, others imported. Generally dipped in a thick sauce (*tare*) made of soy sauce and **mirin**, and grilled. Rich in vitamin A, it is a dish customarily eaten in summer to ward off heat fatigue.

Usukuchi shoyu

"Light" soy sauce is mainly used in the Kansai area. It is light in color and is used when to bring out the color and flavor of ingredients. Its salt density is higher than that of dark soy sauce (**koikuchi shoyu**).

Wakame

A type of seaweed found in Japan and Korea, it is most commonly used in miso soup and **aemono** salads.

Yuan-yaki

Sake, soy sauce, and **mirin** are mixed to make a marinade (*Yuan*), in which fish, chicken, or other ingredients are soaked before grilling or frying. In some cases **yuzu** slices or citrus juice may be added to the marinade. *Miso Yuan-yaki* is a version in which miso is added to the marinade.

Yuba

When soy milk is heated, a skin forms on the surface. This skimmed skin, which is tasty when eaten raw and may be preserved by drying, is rich in vegetable protein.

Yurine

Lily bulb. Has a light, taro-potato-like starchy taste.

Yuzu

Japanese citrus. Is green in summer and turns bright yellow-orange in winter. The juice is quite sour but the skin has a pungent but delicate fragrance. Favored as a garnish for its aroma and tartness.

Zuiki

The stalks of the *sato imo* (taro) plant. The dried peels of the stalks, called *imogara*, have a pleasant, bracing texture and are used as **ohitashi** or in **aemono** salads.

INDEX

Page numbers in *italics* refer to a recipe.
Titles of a recipe are also in *italics*.

Measurements in this book are given in accordance with the metric system; conversions using standard U.S. measures are given in parentheses.

1 cup = 240 ml (rounded up from 236.59 ml)
1 ounce = 30 g (rounded up from 28.349 g)

Please use the conversion table below as a guide.

Volume

Metric	USA
5 ml	1 teaspoon
15 ml	1 tablespoon
50 ml	3 tablespoons + 1 teaspoon
60 ml	¼ U.S. cup
80 ml	⅓ U.S. cup
100 ml	⅓ U.S. cup + 4 teaspoons
240 ml	U.S. 1 cup
400 ml	U.S. 1⅔ cups
480 ml	U.S. 2 cups = 1 pint
1000 ml (1 L)	U.S. 4 cups = 2 pints = 1 quart

Weight

Grams	USA
10 g	⅓ ounce
15 g	½ ounce
20 g	⅔ ounce
30 g	1 ounce
50 g	1⅔ ounces
100 g	3½ ounces
150 g	5 ounces
200 g	7 ounces

Length

Metric	USA
3 mm	⅛ inch
6 mm	¼ inch
1.25 cm	½ inch
2.5 cm	1 inch
5 cm	2 inches
6.25 cm	2½ inches
7.5 cm	3 inches
10 cm	4 inches

Temperature

Celsius (°C)	Fahrenheit (°F)
100°C	210°F
120°C	250°F
130°C	275°F
150°C	300°F
160°C	325°F
170°C	340°F
180°C	350°F
190°C	375°F
200°C	390°F

Publication Committee Chairperson: Nakata Masahiro, Japanese Culinary Academy
Art Direction and Design: Miki Kazuhiko and Hayashi Miyoko, Ampersand Works
Editing: Kawakami Junko, Letras
Translation: Center for Intercultural Communication (text) and Kirsten McIvor (featured dish leads and recipes)
Copyediting and Proofreading: Greg de St. Maurice
Proofreading: Otaki Yoshiko and Center for Intercultural Communication

PHOTO CREDITS

Kuma Masashi: Jacket, pp. 10–13, 16–25, 27–29, 38–39, 44, 47, 48–51, 55, 66–67, 69–82, 87, 91, 96, 98–103, 105–109, 112–135, 138–153, 155, 156, 159–163, 165, 166, 168–173, 175, 176, 180–182
Yamagata Shuichi: Endpaper, pp. 14–15, 26, 42–43, 62–64, 88–89, 92, 93 (left), 110–111, 157, 158, 164, 178–179
Nakano Haruo: pp. 32–37, 40, 58–61
Saito Akira: p. 65

COOPERATION

The publisher would like to thank the following for their cooperation with the photography for this book:
p. 2: Mitsui Memorial Museum; pp. 4, 90: Tokyo National Museum (TNM Image Archives); p. 26: Tekisui Museum of Art; pp. 40, 58-61: Kibitsu Shrine; pp. 42–43: Matsunoo Grand Shrine; p. 44: Japan Food and Liquor Alliance, Inc.; pp. 52–54: Kagawa Museum and Matsudaira Koeki Kai; p. 69: Todaiji Temple; p. 86: Mokichi Okada Art and Culture Foundation; pp. 88–89: Udaka Michishige; p. 93 top right: National Museum of Japanese History; p. 93 bottom right: Cleveland Museum of Art; p. 138: Kyoto City Office; p. 154: Kōzan Bunko, Nogami Memorial Noh Theatre Research Institute, Hosei University; p. 157: Gion Festival Preservation Association; p. 167: Hirohito Hara / Sebun Photo / amanaimages; pp. 178–179: Fukui Doryoki (scales)

英文版 日本料理大全 プロローグ巻

2025年4月6日発行

監　　修　特定非営利活動法人 日本料理アカデミー
村田吉弘
執　　筆　熊倉功夫
伏木　亨
出版委員長　仲田雅博

発 行 者　栗栖正博
制作責任　築地　正
発 行 所　特定非営利活動法人 日本料理アカデミー
〒604-8187 京都府京都市中京区東洞院通御池下ル
笹屋町436番地
office@culinary-academy.jp
https://culinary-academy.jp/
Tel 075-241-4163／Fax 075-241-4168

印刷・製本　大日本印刷株式会社

ISBN 978-4-911188-00-2 C3077